REBEL MALES

REBEL MALES

Clift, Brando and Dean

Graham McCann

HAMISH HAMILTON · LONDON

To my students,
past and present

HAMISH HAMILTON LTD
Published by the Penguin Group
Penguin Books Ltd, 27 Wrights Lane, London W8 5TZ, England
Viking Penguin, a division of Penguin Books USA Inc.,
375 Hudson Street, New York, New York 10014, USA
Penguin Books Australia Ltd, Ringwood, Victoria, Australia
Penguin Books Canada Ltd, 2801 John Street, Markham, Ontario, Canada L3R 1B4
Penguin Books (NZ) Ltd, 182–190 Wairau Road, Auckland 10, New Zealand

Penguin Books Ltd, Registered Offices: Harmondsworth, Middlesex, England

First published 1991
1 3 5 7 9 10 8 6 4 2

Copyright © Graham McCann, 1991

The Acknowledgements on p. vi constitute an extension of this copyright page

The moral right of the author has been asserted

Printed in Great Britain by Richard Clay Ltd, St Ives plc

Filmset in Monophoto Palatino

A CIP catalogue record for this book is available from the British Library

ISBN 0–241–12884–6

Contents

List of Illustrations

(The author and publishers would like to thank the following film distribution and production companies whose film stills and publicity portraits appear in the book — Warner Brothers, Selznick, Paramount, Columbia, 20th Century Fox, Samuel Goldwyn, AA/PEA/UA — and which are reproduced by courtesy of the Kobal Collection. Any other photographs are accredited in the following list.

Grateful acknowledgement is also made to Riva Music Limited/Nineden Limited for permission to quote an extract from The Clash's 'The Right Profile'; and to Warner Chappell Music Ltd for permission to quote from 'With God on Our Side', by Bob Dylan © Warner Chappell Music Ltd.

The author and publishers have made every effort to make correct acknowledgements and would be pleased to amend acknowledgements in any future edition.)

Acknowledgements

In preparing this book, I received practical help, affectionate support and warm encouragement from many good people. My agent, Mic Cheetham, gave me the confidence to attempt the project in the first place; I will not forget her kindness. My editors at Hamish Hamilton, Peter Straus and Kate Jones, were splendid advisers; I am most grateful for their patience, understanding and tact.

For their various gifts of help and encouragement I would like to thank Angela Allen, Peter Aspden, Simon Callow, John Dunn, Bianca Fontana, Anna Grimshaw, Keith Hart, Lesley Levene, Karl Maton, David Reason and Bill Weatherby. More generally, I am pleased to acknowledge those colleagues who were sensitive enough to appreciate that the serious analysis of movies is not the uncomplicatedly pleasurable or relaxing activity others may imagine.

My thanks also go to the staff of the British Film Institute; the Performing Arts Library at the Lincoln Center, New York; New Hall, Cambridge; and the Kobal Collection. I am extremely grateful to the porters of King's College, Cambridge, for being so helpful. The support my parents gave me long predated this particular effort. The manuscript was prepared, copied and recopied by Silvana Dean, to whose intelligence, concern for detail and devotion to the enterprise I owe more than I can say. The book is dedicated to my students, who keep my hopes alive, and to the memory of another rebel, much closer to home: J. W. L. ('Nobody told me there'd be days like these').

Cambridge,
August 1990   G.K.M.

It is impossible to extricate oneself from the questions in which your age is involved. You can no more keep out of politics than you can keep out of the frost.

Ralph Waldo Emerson

Action from principle, the perception and the performance of right, changes things and relations; it is essentially revolutionary, and does not consist wholly with anything which was. It not only divides states and churches, it divides families; ay, it divides the individual, separating the diabolical in him from the divine.

H. D. Thoreau

What, then, is the American, this new man?

Jean de Crèvecoeur

1

Rebel Males

The modern hero is no hero; he acts heroes.

Walter Benjamin

Camp is the answer to the problem: how to be a dandy in an age of mass culture.

Susan Sontag

Montgomery Clift in *From Here to Eternity* (1953): a young soldier with a fine physique, a flawless face, yet tense and anxious, his eyes signalling some unspoken sadness, his actions prompted by a kind of desperate instinct for self-sufficiency (or else, if things become hopeless, self-destruction). 'A man don't go his own way,' he shouts, 'he's *nothin'*.' Marlon Brando in *The Wild One* (1953): dressed in a black leather jacket, black shades and blue jeans, his face sullen and strong, the hooded eyes that hide a hungry heart, the arrogant pose designed to unnerve his enemies. A young woman, astonished by his impudence, asks him, 'What are you rebelling against?', to which he replies, 'Whaddya got?' James Dean in *Rebel Without a Cause* (1955): a troubled teenage boy in a police station, almost overcome by his own fidgety moodiness, his hands clasping his head in tortured regret as the shrill sounds of his parents' bickering starts to break him. 'You're tearin' me apart!' he cries.

These three young men share similarly urgent concerns. How can one be sincere in an insincere society? How can one feel a 'real man' when real men are so different from that? How can one find one's 'true' self in a world obsessed with conformity? Their screams of confusion, anger, uncertainty and alienation continue to be heard

1

today: 'I can take *anything* you can dish out!'; 'Hey, Stella! *Hey,*
Stella! Stella!'; 'We are *all* involved!' Montgomery Clift, bloodied
and bruised in *From Here to Eternity*, hitting back at his tormentors;
Marlon Brando, muscles rippling under a torn T-shirt, crying out
like a wounded animal in *A Streetcar Named Desire* (1951); and James
Dean, hunched over in adolescent agony in *Rebel Without a Cause*.
Three great moments in the history not only of American acting
but also of American culture. With their quicksilver intensity and
unconventional eroticism, Clift, Brando and Dean seemed to herald
a revolution in acting style as well as in sensibility. Shredding
accepted notions of actorly behaviour, they caught their audiences
by surprise. They were self-consciously extraordinary: they were
considered neither innocent youths nor conventional adults; they
were strikingly handsome men yet they were unsure of their
masculinity; they were fascinated by American culture yet they
considered themselves 'indigenous émigrés'. Theirs was an existence
informed by the immediacy of modern life. Theirs was a performance
that had both unexpected scope and spontaneity, and the risks they
took required one to take some risks of one's own. The vernacular
American style, with its jolting emotional revelations that Clift,
Brando and Dean introduced, has inspired several generations of
actors and audiences.

Clift, Brando and Dean were, without doubt, the three most
influential (and probably the most gifted) male movie stars of the
1950s. They were highly aware of the sense in which they all
shared a set of basic values and concerns; indeed, in both their
private and their professional lives, the number of similarities
between them was remarkable. All three were products of the
American Midwest: Clift and Brando were born in Omaha, Nebraska
(in 1920 and 1924 respectively); Dean was born in Marion, Indiana
(in 1931). All three clashed with their fathers when it became
known that they were set on pursuing a career as 'effeminate' and
'frivolous' as acting. All three were, in very profound ways, obsessed
with their mothers: Clift's mother sought to enjoy success and high
status vicariously through her son, and she dominated him until his
premature death; Brando's mother encouraged him when he was a

boy, but died an alcoholic as he was being acclaimed a star; Dean's mother died of cancer when he was only nine years of age, and the bitterness and regret over her absence never left him. All three began their careers, learned their craft and became stars in the post-war years – the era of McCarthyism and the Cold War, television and the 'teenager', the Kinsey Reports and pop psychology (Brando entered analysis very early in his career and subsequently persuaded Clift and Dean to do the same). They all felt themselves to be bisexual and therefore well suited to roles which expressed an erotic quality bereft of rigid gender identity. As each man reached adulthood, he was confronted by a daunting array of social, sexual, cultural and political problems. It seemed as though society was unusually anxious (in the age of witch-hunts and 'juvenile deliquency') for its young citizens to conform to traditional values and familiar types. As did many others of their generation, Clift, Brando and Dean rebelled against this climate of conformity; the difference was that *they* rebelled in the most sharply self-conscious manner, in the most powerful medium, with the most memorable of images.

It seems significant that these young men, with all their defiant desire for difference and distinction, were products of the American Midwest. Out of the nation's heartland came its heroes: from the Prairie Table came Abraham Lincoln and Thomas Edison, as well as Gary Cooper and James Stewart, and now, with a new aggressiveness, Clift, Brando and Dean. 'The Midwest, the prairie country,' wrote John Dewey, 'has always been the center. It has formed the solid element in our diffuse national life and heterogeneous population. It has been the very middle in every sense of the word, and in every movement. Like every mean, it has held things together and given them unity and stability.'[1] The Mid-western hero embodies the contradictions at the centre of society: the same but different, the hero is torn between the traditional and the modern, the country and the city, the American Dream and the American reality. Clift, Brando and Dean left the Midwest, first for the East Coast and its culture, then for the West Coast and its power. In the east they nurtured their talent for self-invention; in the west they exploited this talent to its limit.

It is important to appreciate the significance of the fact that these rebels were actors. Their sense of personal insecurity and confusion (as 'young adults', as Americans, as heterosexuals) was made particularly intense – indeed, it was exacerbated – by their professional role-playing, the constant process of pulling on and peeling off a diverse set of selves. One of the consequences of acting is the heightened awareness of how arbitrary one's 'self', at any particular time, can seem, and how 'acting natural' is in many ways the hardest act of all. Critics have spoken of the artist's 'anxiety of influence', the 'horror of finding himself to be only a copy or a replica'.[2] As actors Clift, Brando and Dean were encouraged to discover what was distinctive and significant about themselves. It seemed likely that if one could get this recognition recorded on film, could summon up and show distinctive words or gestures or forms for one's own distinctiveness, then it would be apparent that one was *not* a mere copy or replica.

For young men who wished to rebel against the role models society had provided, acting also served as a potentially endless distraction. As actors they were obliged to remain receptive to new habits, mannerisms and moods; an index of their success was the extent to which they did *not* settle into a single, familiar, fixed personality. Acting offered a kind of redemption: their work involved a continual redescription whereby they made the best for themselves that they could. Their great imaginative gifts revealed the unnatural basis of gender identities, and this revelation invited audiences to recognize that their own identity was not as inevitable and inescapable as they had thought. The idea of 'masculinity' (and 'femininity') is provisional and precarious; it is dependent upon, and incessantly challenged by, social contingencies and psychic demands; and yet one constantly strives to fix it, stabilize it, say who one is by telling of one's sex. The professional role-player can rebel against this. Acting could be a release, a rebirth, a revision.

In the post-war years in America, ambitious young performers were drawn to New York – to the Actors' Studio – where such figures as Harold Clurman, Cheryl Crawford, Lee Strasberg and Elia Kazan taught the theories of Stanislavsky, later to become known (rather misleadingly) as Method acting. The Studio became an

4

intellectual and political barometer of the American theatre, a centre for anyone searching for new stars and styles. Bobby Lewis conducted the first class of aspiring actors. At that time his pupils included Marlon Brando, Montgomery Clift, Karl Malden, E. G. Marshall, Maureen Stapleton and Sidney Lumet. James Dean joined shortly afterwards.

The chief idea the Actors' Studio took from Stanislavsky was the belief that each dramatic role was a metaphor through which the deepest and most universal behavioural truths could be illuminated by the serious and striving actor. It seems obvious that the finest actors throughout human history must have devised ways of making this connection between self and fiction, but never before had these techniques been codified so that they were generally teachable; nor had the cultural ground ever been so fertile before. Technical advancements made possible a more intimate, subtle form of acting — it took good sound-recording equipment to pick up those mumbled lines. By the 1950s the movies, theatre and popular fiction were full of the metaphors of psychology, and an acting technique that, in a sense, did for the performer what psychoanalysis did for ordinary perplexed citizens (plunging them redemptively into the abyss of themselves, their buried past and hidden thoughts) was bound to be alluring. Although the Actors' Studio was based in the east and concentrated on the theatre, it achieved its greatest popular success in the west, on the movie screen. Its young actors seemed more fully and interestingly alive on screen than had any previous generation.

John Garfield (who had worked with the founders of the Actors' Studio during the previous decade) was a transitional figure between the traditional male and these post-war rebel males. Jewish, working class, a tough young man from the Bronx, Garfield brooded in character from the perspective of an angry individual who had just emerged from adolescence to find suppression and alienation in mid-1940s America. His debut movie, *Four Daughters* (1938), was extremely powerful and his promise seemed immense. However, rather like Frances Farmer, Garfield was even more uncompromising off screen than on, and his career was undermined by a succession of financial, political and emotional crises. Exploiting the vulnerability underlying his tough street-kid veneer, Hollywood typed Garfield a ghetto loser; in the 1940s he became Hollywood's token ethnic. This gnawed away at him, but his resentment was expressed in largely ineffectual ways: violence, heated arguments and absentee-ism, tactics the Hollywood bosses were experienced in dealing with. The occasional good movies he was given, such as *The Postman Always Rings Twice* (1946), only underlined how his talent was more often being wasted. When the FBI began investigating him for supposed communist sympathies, his career collapsed. He died in 1952, aged thirty-nine. Garfield was not a particularly versatile actor, but he was powerful, passionate, unpredictable and, at his best, unnervingly realistic.[3] Clift, Brando and Dean took his anger and frustration to new extremes, and brought richness and depth to his rebellion.

Clift, Brando and Dean brought a revolutionary intensity to the screen, their acting technique giving their work a kinetic charge. They were fascinating neurotics, exuding a primeval sexuality. Whereas the old Hollywood male stars, such as Clark Gable and John Wayne, regarded acting as a rather lucrative 'trick', an enjoy-able recreation, the new young rebel males were, ironically, far more serious in their approach. They were not afraid of roles which made them look weak, or foolish, or slow-witted, or sexually insecure. They sought out roles that led to suffering, both emotional and physical, and were frequently violent and always disturbing. Clift, Brando and Dean were in search more of 'authenticity' than of stardom. This caused them to clash with innumerable authority figures: screenwriters; directors and producers (because Method actors had to find the 'truth' of their roles from within and so the creativity and power of the performer needed to be reasserted); publicists (because these actors resented the focus on their private selves rather than on their screen incarnations); and the guardians of morality in society (because the new actors played 'realistic', contemporary characters who were often outlaw figures or aggres-sively iconoclastic). Clift, Brando and Dean became central figures in the 'generation gap' debates of the time. They were the first genuinely popular stars with whom young people could easily identify, and the fact that many parents regarded them as 'immoral' and 'indecent' revealed how fragmented the formerly 'mass' movie audience had become. These youthful male personalities came crackling with undirected energy, sexually alive precisely to the degree that they did not conform. From this moment on, one would no longer grant, or take it for granted, that a man who expressed no feelings had fires banked within him. The rebirth of unexpressed masculine depth required the rebound of culture that created the new possibility of the cool: the young Montgomery Clift, Marlon Brando and James Dean are prime instances of it.

Movie magazines and gossip columns struggled to understand the new breed of male sex symbols. Montgomery Clift (although he had a notably privileged upbringing in Europe) came to Hollywood only grudgingly, showing no interest in its glamorous image. He would deliberately break with convention, dressing down for important receptions, and sometimes he would distress his studio by publicly showing affection for his male lovers. Marlon Brando was, from the beginning, uncompromisingly independent. He wore his dirty blue jeans in Bel Air, frequently insulted Louella Parsons, rewrote his character's lines, picked his nose and scratched his crotch in public, and went out of his way to say critical things about powerful people. He was heroically the anti-hero. James Dean would be similarly rebellious (influenced, to some extent, by Clift and Brando). He was notoriously unpopular with many of his fellow actors because of his often selfish preparations for certain scenes (for example, before a scene with Elizabeth Taylor in *Giant*, 1956, he calmed his nerves by unzipping his jeans and urinating in front of the camera). Clift, Brando and Dean marked the end of the old Hollywood star system. Although they were intended as the new Hollywood heroes, they became the anti-heroes, rebelling against the old star images. The moment the young Robert Zimmerman (Bob Dylan) saw *Rebel Without a Cause*, he adopted James Dean's blue jeans and boots, his slouch and smirk; a black leather jacket was added in imitation of Marlon Brando in *The Wild One*. When Elvis Presley saw these young actors, he found his role models. Within a very short space of time, the new movie rebels had attracted a highly impressionable young audience.

The male sex symbols of the 1930s and 1940s, from Clark Gable to Errol Flynn, from Cary Grant to Humphrey Bogart, distracted out-of-work audiences from their troubles and the real emasculation caused by their inability to function as a result of the Depression. People did not go to the movies to see the boy next door, remarked Joan Crawford; they could go next door for that. These male stars were the strong, untrammelled figures ordinary men might be in their dreams. Anything in these actors' personalities which undermined the straightforwardly virile image (such as Cary Grant's bisexual inclinations or Clark Gable's false teeth) was repressed or 'corrected' by the studios. In this movie world one was always potent, always strong, always straight. Masculinity was to be of one type all the way through; and in order to achieve this, it had to control what threatened it both from inside and from outside.

However, the popular sexual icons that Hollywood offered its audiences in the 1950s were often strikingly different from those of any other period. The Second World War had absorbed national energies, distracting attention from domestic concerns – including matters relating to sexuality. With the war over, these concerns resurfaced. The all-male environment of the armed services had inadvertently exacerbated a confusion about the inherent sexuality between men who preferred each other's company but always chose women to prove their masculinity. The anxiety that these chaste male relationships might in any way be construed as homosexual was very real. The Kinsey Reports on male sexuality (1948) and female sexuality (1953) helped to undermine the old assumptions. According to Kinsey's best-known statistic, some 37 per cent of men had had homosexual experiences to orgasm. What was, upon reflection, an even more interesting statistic was the finding that less than 4 per cent were exclusively homosexual; and even they did not necessarily express a homosexual 'identity' – a concept of which, in any case, Kinsey disapproved.[4] Hollywood's old 'buddy' movies would never again seem so innocent, and the new movies of the 1950s reflected this fact. The most memorable and influential of these screen images are characterized, like that decade itself, by a curious ambiguity — products of what André Bazin called American cinema's 'long, rich, byzantine tradition of censorship' and precursors of the more permissive movies of the 1960s.

Throughout the classic Hollywood era of the 1930s and 1940s, the homogeneous audience had responded uniformly to the industry's products, with the consequence that there were no seriously underestimated movies or actors supported by coteries. The successful movies, the great stars, belonged to everyone in a way that was no longer true in the 1950s. In the post-war period, while John Wayne, Rock Hudson, Martin and Lewis, Marilyn Monroe and Doris Day ruled the box office, cults grew up around Montgomery Clift, Marlon Brando and James Dean, even though Brando made the Top Ten Box Office Attractions list only three times, and Clift and Dean never figured there at all. The cinema was no longer a simple mass medium. In the 1950s, more frightening for the movie industry than McCarthyism or the threat of atomic warfare was the apparently irreversible decline in movie attendance and the radical disruption of the industry's integrated and efficient institutional structure. Because the new television audience grew as the movie audience shrank, Hollywood made the obvious connection. Although changing patterns of suburban life and the multiplication of leisure options were probably equally responsible for the drop in attendance, these developments were esoteric and difficult for movie executives to focus on. Television was the most noticeable threat to Hollywood, and Hollywood responded with two strategies: first, by emphasizing its value as a spectacle (larger screens, colourful images, a communal theatre atmosphere) and, second, by exploiting its relative freedom to deal with 'adult' and 'controversial' topics (such as alcoholism, anti-Semitism, sex, racial inequality and so on). During a decade notorious for conservatism and conformity, the motion-picture industry, out of sheer desperation, became more technically innovative, economically adventuresome and aesthetically daring than at any other time in its history.

9

When Clift, Brando and Dean started their movie careers, this process was barely under way. What we see in their early appearances is a kind of uncertain eroticism, a partially repressed sexuality, which is complemented by the transitional nature of the American cinema (Janus-faced, not yet ready to break with tradition but realizing that radical changes were imperative). The sexual ambiguity and personal insecurity of these new rebel males were accentuated by a movie industry striving to undermine archaic censorship laws. Since 1930 the movies had operated under a strict Production Code, rigorously enforced from 1934 to 1954 by Joseph I. Breen. An upstanding Irish Catholic, Breen made sure that every Hollywood movie met the Code's exacting standards of morality. For example, the Code discouraged any movie-maker from featuring methods of crime, drug trafficking, alcoholism, 'excessive' kissing, sexual perversion, white slavery, miscegenation and subjects adversely reflecting on the integrity of the government and its officials. The Code's coy and unrealistic guidelines are justly notorious (some of its instructions could have been written by interior decorators: 'The treatment of bedrooms must be governed by good taste and delicacy.'), but no matter how impractical and hypocritical they may have been, there were a number of well-organized pressure groups keen to keep them enforced.

However, by the 1950s the economic vulnerability of the industry coincided with something of a revolution in public morality to produce significant changes in the world the movies depicted and upheld. In some cities, 'art houses' imported foreign movies to cater to those audiences eager for more daring movies. When the Supreme Court, in a case involving an Italian import, *The Miracle* (1952), appeared to grant movies the same First Amendment rights as print media, the conditions seemed propitious for an all-out challenge to the Production Code's authority. However, the studios remained cautious, preferring at first to release a modest number of 'daringly permissive' movies in order to gauge audience reactions. Otto Preminger's *The Moon Is Blue* (1953) represented a breakthrough: the director's refusal to delete the word 'virgin' from the movie and United Artists' decision to release it without

Production Code approval made it a meaningful challenge to the status quo. A number of similarly controversial movies followed: *The Man with the Golden Arm* (1955; dealing with addiction), *Tea and Sympathy* (1956; homosexuality), *Bachelor Party* (1957; abortion) and *Storm Center* (1956; censorship). However, during this same period the old stereotypes and the star vehicles continued, and the Hudson–Day heyday of safe sex-comedies was still to come. The decade was culturally schizophrenic: uniquely progressive at one moment, predictably conservative at other times.

The McCarthyite reign of terror during the first half of the 1950s fostered a social climate which facilitated the enforcement of conformity. Much American cinema, like the culture at large, devoted itself to the glorification and reinforcement of individual success and crass material gain, and to the most strait-laced adherence to puritan values. Prudery about erotic feelings fuelled the demeaning of women (for example, *film noir* and the amoral *femme fatale*) and their distorted representation on the Hollywood screen (for example, Jayne Mansfield, clutching two bottles of milk against her breasts, in *The Girl Can't Help It*, 1956). Heterosexuality in Hollywood came at a price: women were almost invariably stereotyped. Ever since the era of the American Revolution, the nation's political ideology has held a special place for women as the nurturers and educators of future citizens. In the anxious post-war years, women were pressured into reaffirming this idea. They were sent home from the wartime workplace, where they had acquired seniority, and were encouraged not to compete with but to serve men. In order to ensure that the message took hold, women were typically character-ized in popular culture purely as sex objects.[5] However, during the same period, one finds (for the first time since the 1920s) a cluster of movies offering a complex and nuanced examination of the male psyche. Previously, as far as movie-makers had been concerned, the sexual identity of men had been simple, solid and 'straight'. In the 1950s this changed.

Where men were concerned, the 1950s movie turned inwards. Indeed, in a society where dissent meant the loss of one's job and severe alienation, it seemed there was nowhere else to turn but the discrete self. Alone in the privacy of one's consciousness, individuality and integrity might, it was hoped, survive. The 1950s movies reveal the psychic price American culture paid for repression of the right to disagree with social and political policy. This repression led to an outpouring of frustration and rage, depression and confusion, which could not help but surface in popular cultural figures. America is a legalistic culture; it has always been obsessed with the individual's relationship to the law, even when its culture most seems to glamorize, glorify or even condone certain instances of lawlessness. The subject seems all-pervasive, from the beginning of the Revolution, through Emerson and Thoreau, Melville and Whitman, Frank Capra and James Stewart, to Mark Rothko, Lenny Bruce, Norman Mailer, Don DeLillo and beyond. In the post-war era, the theme was perhaps stronger than ever. Playwrights such as Arthur Miller and William Inge produced plays that caught the current mood: *The Crucible* (1953), ostensibly a study of the witch trials in Salem, actually offered, in allegorical form, an indictment of McCarthyism, while *Picnic* (1955) peeled away the romantic illusions about small-town America. Novels such as Norman Mailer's *The Naked and the Dead* (1948), Irwin Shaw's *The Young Lions* (1958) and James Jones's *From Here to Eternity* (1951) all contained indictments of that most formidable of American institutions, the Armed Services. Edmund Wilson's *Memoirs of Hecate County* (1946) provoked moral indignation for its supposed 'degeneracy'. The Beat movement, epitomized by the poetry of Allen Ginsberg and the 'road novels' of Jack Kerouac, reaffirmed the individualistic need for spiritual exploration, rebelling against the bourgeois conformity of the Eisenhower years.

America, as de Tocqueville remarked, was born in broad daylight; its inhabitants have always been unusually aware of what is *missing* from the social fabric. In movies, many screen males for whom politics held not the slightest interest nevertheless felt deeply alienated from their world, that society to which earlier heroes had had no trouble adjusting. Problems could no longer, it seemed, be solved through physical actions; the screen male was now obliged to respond on an emotional and intellectual level. The stress upon conformity thus only drew attention to the presence of the need to form individual judgements. Authority's one-sided words were now opposed by the rebel's inarticulate ambivalence. Whereas in wartime there seemed to be clearly defined heroes and villains, the post-war generation found that its enemies were not so easy to identify. The rebel now appeared as a particularly positive male role model in the American movie: the anti-hero as hero, the one 'guy' who refused to be 'one of the guys'. Whether he was tamed or chastised by the closing scenes, his presence provoked a positive result, a deepening of the image of men in movies.

This introspective turn of the screen male was in part encouraged by the new interest in psychology. Robert Lindner began his career as a prison psychologist, but moved on to general psychology, concentrating on the young and the new non-conformists of the 1950s. He wrote a book (largely for the academic market) called *Must You Conform?* (1956), offering a curious paradox: the very renewal of concern for the health of the inner self leads inevitably to the expression of social rebellion; the original need for repression produces a new concern for the imperatives of the self. Once it knows what it is, this self turns to experiences in the outside world in which it can be realized. Lindner argued that the 1950s demand for a 'mass man', a conforming, pliant male whose life was controlled by pressure from without, led to the development of a 'psychopathic' personality: 'Forced from without to conform, and from within to rebel, he makes a compromise: he rebels within the confines of conformity, he discharges his protest within the limits set by the social order he has by now permitted to be erected around him.' Such movies as *Rebel Without a Cause*, based loosely on one of Lindner's own studies by the same title, featured rebellious youth and the turmoil within the psyches of those who had been deprived of rebellion in any form other than an irrationally destructive one.

These were the 'teenager' and the 'juvenile delinquent'. What gave 1950s teenagers a sense of group identity both peculiarly intense and historically new was that their generational status, their social position as *teenagers*, was vigorously reinforced by the adult institutions around them. Sheer numbers and the group proximity caused by the population shift from rural to urban and suburban areas encouraged a collective and standardized response. The very nature of a complex bureaucratic society assured it. A soaring teenage crime rate put the 'problem of juvenile delinquency' high on the national agenda. J. Edgar Hoover rated 'the juvenile jungle' alongside communism as a threat to American freedom.[6] Throughout the decade, cultural guardians likened American teen-agers to barbaric hordes descending on a city under siege. At the same time, the business community was welcoming their arrival at the gates; a fortune was to be made selling trinkets to the invaders. Rock 'n' roll music became the youth culture's soundtrack. Holly-wood, with typically mixed feelings, started catering to the 'teenage' audience; Clift, Brando and Dean became the idols of the new 'youth-oriented' movies. Cinema audiences were getting younger, and the young were getting used to being young.

Heavily influenced by *film noir*, the 'youth rebellion' movies had protagonists who were extreme versions of the outlaw hero, with cars and motorcycles instead of horses. Inevitably, the young, with less invested in the traditional values and attitudes, were among the first to detect the damage done by the Second World War and the Cold War to the most basic American assumptions. It was no longer taken for granted that 'being an adult' meant something specific; and if it was taken to mean anything at all, then it was not necessarily something worthwhile. A piece of teenage fiction from the time, entitled 'Coke for Breakfast', illustrated the anxiety: a newly married couple rebel when their parents tell them they must abandon such adolescent habits as having Coke for breakfast. 'I know,' the young husband exclaims, 'married couples don't drink Coke for breakfast. They don't stay in bed till noon and they don't party till dawn . . . That is, *other* married couples don't. We do.'[7] In fact, the 'youth rebellion' movies reflected an actual spirit of disillusionment among the period's adolescents (one of Dean's characters cries out to the police: 'Please lock me up. I'm gonna hit somebody!').

The movies, however, sought to deny these intuitive protesters any reasons for revolt. Each of them demonstrated that the hero was a rebel *without* a cause, 'explaining' that the problem lay with a few troublemakers (for example, *The Wild One*, *The Blackboard Jungle*, 1955) or with psychological traumas of adjustment to adulthood (*A Place in the Sun*, 1951, *East of Eden*, 1955, *Rebel Without a Cause*). Typically, the teenage rebels were divided into two groups: thoroughly reprehensible 'bad' teenagers and the basically decent but misunderstood 'good' teenagers. The latter group ran foul of the law, rebelling against the restraints and hypocrisies placed on them by society (like Holden Caulfield in *Catcher in the Rye*, they found the adult world 'phoney' and 'crumby'), while members of the former group engaged in violence and mayhem simply because of their complete lack of conscience (like the motorcycle gang in *The Wild One*). The 'good' teenager was often redeemed by a 'nice' teenage girl or an understanding adult figure. The 'bad' teenager was either killed, exiled to reform school or, worse, humiliated and abandoned by his peer group.

The appeal of a life lived solely in terms of the self was never greater than in these movies, and their hold clearly lay entirely in the very acts of rebellion that the movies' endings usually sought to discredit as a passing stage. For example, despite the Production Code's interference (which included rewriting the more violent scenes and cutting out any reasons cited for rebellion, such as unemployment), *The Wild One* managed to preserve some of its intended sense of danger because of Marlon Brando's powerful performance as Johnny. Johnny's motorcycle gang (the 'Black Rebels') ride into the quaint Mid-western town of 'Wrightsville', commandeer the shops, break into buildings, terrorize a young female hostage and eventually, though accidentally, kill an old man. Because of censorship, the gang are made to seem inexplicably irresponsible; all possible social explanations are ignored and consequently the movie becomes a display of violence for its own sake. However, Brando plays Johnny with a subtle tenderness, a graceful resistance, that contradicts the movie's general tone. He is an intriguing character, physically tough but oddly insecure. He rarely instigates anything; usually he merely reacts. When, at the

15

end of the movie, he rides back into town alone, he takes his first step towards controlling his life. Brando is particularly impressive in the way he allows us to glimpse the sense in which Johnny's masculine bravado is an act, an aesthetic pose. The leather jacket is rather too self-consciously stylish; it even has the camp flourish of an embroidered 'Johnny' on the left side (this is not a jacket to get dirty or torn, this is something one shows). His cap is also the emblem of a dandy, playing on its 'officer' symbolism and its impractical material. His clean-shaven face is rather chubby and childlike, despite the well-practised grimace and glare. Brando also gives Johnny a mannered form of speech which simultaneously accentuates his 'rebel' image and throws into comic contrast the small-town ideals of the movie's 'nice girl', Cathy:

JOHNNY: On weekends, we just go out and have a ball.
CATHY: What do you do? I mean, do you just ride around or do you go on some sort of picnic or something?
JOHNNY: A *picnic*? Man, you are *too square*! I have to straighten you out. Now, listen. You don't go any one special place – that's cornball style. You just *go* (*snaps his fingers*). A bunch of us get together after all week and it builds up. The idea is to have a *ball*. Now, if you're gonna stay *cool*, you've got to *wail*. You gotta put something down. You gotta make some *jive*. Don't you know what I'm talkin' about?
CATHY: Yeah. Yeah. I know what you mean.
JOHNNY: Well, that's all I'm sayin'.
CATHY: My father was going to take me on a fishing trip to Canada once.
JOHNNY: Yeah?
CATHY: We didn't go.
JOHNNY: Crazy.

The movie is very much concerned with society's fear of the marginal man – the outsider, the figure at the fringes of polite society. The young rebel males never know what they want or where they are going, and even fairly plausible explanations of what they are after seem too rigid – a strait-jacket for longings whose very lack of clear contours is an aspect of their power. Anyone who thinks they know what is really the matter with these characters cannot, by definition, know what is the matter with them. In this context, it becomes clear why Clift's silent stare, Brando's mumbling and Dean's giggle were so much a part of what they had to say. Their inarticulacy, whether feigned or real, was a signal that words were inadequate to convey the tangle of inner feelings. Their war with words (the great authority figures) told us, in effect, that they had emotions that went beyond language. To instinctive characters like these, words were hard to come by and not to be trusted, because they often failed to honour the full complexity of feeling. Unlike the traditional Hollywood male heroes (Bogart, with his smart banter, Cooper, with his assured silences), these men are comfortable neither with words nor without them. Clift, Brando and Dean sometimes fulfil traditional expectations of the American masculine hero; usually, however, they defy them, insisting upon a more honest portrayal of the male and his feelings.

As personified by Montgomery Clift in *A Place in the Sun* and *From Here to Eternity*, the newly vulnerable 1950s male appeared to be in a state of constant inner conflict which alienated him from the rest of society. As George Eastman in *A Place in the Sun*, he seems almost unbearably ill-equipped to cope with other people's expectations of him, even though he tries as hard as he can. The movie ends with George (like so many of the rebel males of the 1950s) in a hopeless condition, being led away to the electric chair. What is so remarkable is Clift's rare ability for persuading the audience of his innocence and naïveté; despite his errors and his readiness to forsake his old loyalties, he remains a victim, a helpless young man. Clift portrayed characters with an introverted intensity which suggested a man unable (or perhaps unwilling) to comprehend the inner workings of his own mind, let alone the complexities of the outer world. Every gesture, inflection and expression conveys this vulnerable quality. His face is a cultured one, rather scholarly in its serious countenance, yet the eyes stare out with a mixture of wonder and fear. His shoulders are hunched, as though he expects to be attacked at any moment, and the voice sounds parched from spiritual drought. He is in fine physical condition, yet one suspects he rarely exercises; he has a languorous, melancholic look about him that contradicts his youthful energy.

17

From Here to Eternity (with Clift as Prewitt) captures one of the most memorable characterizations of the rebel male. It was a timely movie: the nation was preparing for the infamous Army/McCarthy hearings. It was also notable for its critical treatment of male power struggles, neatly delineating the bitterness in men's lust for power and its ultimately lethal results. The movie focuses upon two men's desire for women who are ostensibly unattainable (Prewitt's lover is first encountered in a thinly disguised brothel, where she is obliged to entertain all the men without forming attachments with anyone in particular; Prewitt's sergeant, Warden, has an affair with a married woman, the wife of his superior). When the women do become available, the men turn away from them. 'What do you want to go back to the Army for?' Prewitt's lover asks him after the bombing of Pearl Harbor. 'What did the Army ever do for you besides treat you like dirt and give you one awful going-over, and get your friend killed? What do you want to go back to the Army for?' Prewitt replies: 'A man loves a thing; that don't mean it's got to love him back.' In fact, Prewitt's response reveals his fear of that which loves him back: the last thing he wants is requited love. The Army, which he loves and which does not love him back, is thus a perverse kind of romantic ideal. Sergeant Warden, gazing down at Prewitt's dead body at the end of the movie, says: 'He was always a hardhead, sir, but he loved the Army.' Prewitt's death is a necessity for a narrative in which an explosive sexual desire is in need of constant repression. As Michael Wood has noted, Prewitt ends up 'a victim of the awkward question his character and presence seemed to raise'.[8] For men, the end of the movie is a perfect fantasy retreat into the 'good old days' of the Second World War, a celebration of the event which provided them with an honourable escape from domestic responsibilities. The end is also an escape for women, back to wartime, when they were free to idealize their past relationships and fantasize about the fulfilment of their romantic ideals in the future, without the disillusioning presence of men to douse their dreams in reality.

The movie allows both Prewitt and Warden to emerge as moral men in an amoral world, expressing their integrity in different ways: Prewitt by rebellion against society and the system; Warden by attempting to correct it from within. Lancaster's chesty machismo is darkly contrasted with Clift's angular glamour. Much of the movie's immense appeal at the time rested in the fact that these characters had already emerged as the most popular male hero 'types' of the 1950s, and while many movies centred around either one or the other, this was the single picture which maintained a delicate balance between the two. Montgomery Clift's performance in many ways captured both types in one: such was his talent for expressing a character's ambiguity and contradictions, one felt Prewitt was being torn apart by the desire for his lover and his duty to his company. The story forces him towards the latter, but Clift's portrayal is too powerfully resonant to allow such a specious conclusion.

Private Robert E. Lee Prewitt is the epitome of male sexual confusion in the 1950s. He seems a shock absorber for society's insensitivities; a *déclassé* loner with a streak of nobility. It is never entirely clear whether he is in rebellion against society or in flight from it. With his blazing eyes and boyish innocence, he seems ill at ease in his own body, as though trapped in an alien shell. Both Marlon Brando and James Dean would study Clift's performance, and their subsequent screen appearances were in many ways a response (or rather a succession of responses) to the ambivalent, courageous fragility of Montgomery Clift. Brando's first truly influential screen persona was Stanley Kowalski from Tennessee Williams's *A Streetcar Named Desire*. Kowalski is arguably the most overtly 'masculine' character of 1950s cinema, yet Brando somehow conspires to imply a lack and a repressed sensitivity which undermine Kowalski's aggressive, crude carapace. Brando's performance is an extraordinary *tour de force*. His eyes are hooded (he is not going to look at anyone – they must look at him); his bulk fills out his clothes and gives the impression of bursting physical force that his acting serves to supplement. In the words of one of his lovers, he has 'the face of a poet and the body of an animal'.

A Streetcar Named Desire brought blatant nymphomania to the screen, and the American cinema had also never before seen a marriage depicted with such sexual honesty. Brando captures Stanley's sexual power and latent torment in a particularly brilliant scene: he feels that Blanche is turning Stella away from him, so he erupts with anger, wrecking the room and then beating Stella with his bare fists. His poker-playing friends pull him away from his wife and she runs out to her neighbour's apartment. Stanley is dragged by the other men and pushed under a cold shower. He staggers into the street, T-shirt torn and his muscular frame bruised and wet. He looks up to where Stella is being sheltered. He is crying, his face twisted in sadness and pain, and he screams out, 'Stella! *Hey*, Stella! *Stella!*' It is an extraordinary cry, like the howl of a stricken animal, bleeding and fearful. Stella steps out on to a balcony and walks down towards him. He collapses at her feet, pressing his face against her thighs, burying his head in her breasts. Her hands slide down his back, exploring his body, and he carries her back to their bed. Kowalski is Williams's most potent version of his recurrent fantasy figure, the stallion who levels every woman (and most men) he meets. Yet with Brando playing Stanley, the character develops in ways Williams might not have intended.

In a curious way, Kowalski (like many of the rebel males) is a kind of 'dandy', dressing himself up (and sometimes down) in a certain type of 'manly' costume, employing his own form of stylish insensitivity. He is well aware of how he appears to others; he knows how to intimidate people with his body and bewilder them with his moody silences. 'The distinguishing characteristic of the dandy's beauty,' wrote Baudelaire, 'consists above all in an air of coldness which comes from an unshakeable determination not to be moved; you might call it a latent fire which hints at itself, and which could, but chooses not to, burst into flame.'[9] Stanley's outward, cocksure self-control belies his inner torment; he makes a shield out of his apparent transparency. Williams's studs were testaments to the almost magical power, for him, of the sexually potent male. At their most self-assured, though, his heroes satisfied, soothed and 'saved' women, and their obvious appeal to homosexuals (their creation, in fact, by a homosexual writer) was discreetly overlooked. The 1950s were not ready to consider what Marlon

Brando, stripped to the waist, his muscles rippling, might have been able (and even willing) to do for some of the frustrated men of that small, tight town in New Orleans.

Montgomery Clift and Marlon Brando were the two figures who set the tone for the representation of male sexuality in 1950s cinema. They were the two rebel males: Clift the aristocrat, Brando the proletarian. Dean became the bourgeois, the surly younger brother of the other two men. He followed them to the Actors' Studio. He started to copy their speech patterns, dress sense and life style. His movie career lasted less than two years and when he died in 1955, at the age of twenty-four, only one of his three movies had been seen by the public, yet his impact was immense. His audience was more specific than Clift's and Brando's, being composed predominantly of teenagers, but the effect was probably more concentrated and intense. He was the middle-class boy from the Midwest who dropped out (before there was any 'counter-culture' to drop into), the 'first American teenager'. Things happened faster than ever before: his success, his stardom, his changes of mood, his disenchantment and even his death.

Youthful rebellion in the 1950s, as in Dean's first movie, *East of Eden*, was depicted as a consequence of the absence of affection and meaningful contact between people. The central integrative structure of society, the family, was in trouble. Most movies in this era contained strong domestic elements, especially in comparison to the male groups of early 1940s war movies and the solitary males of late-1940s *film noir*. The problem posed was how to reconstruct the family unit. Nicholas Ray's *Rebel Without a Cause* was one of the most notable of these movies. Its promotional poster carried the banner: 'This is Jim Stark, teenager — from a "good" family.' In the opening sequence, Jim Stark (Dean) is picked up by the police and questioned at the precinct house by the youth officer, Ray (Edward Platt), as are two other teenagers, Judy (Natalie Wood) and Plato (Sal Mineo). The officer acts like a social worker — a common figure in 1950s movies, massaging the masses. Jim is dressed in a conventional 'smart' jacket, but he is drunk and mischievous, giggling and ignoring his inquisitors. Plato is being calmed by his guardian, and Jimmy and Judy are eventually collected by their respective parents. Judy's parents are cold and strict, and she seems terrified when they arrive to take her back home. Jim's parents are middle class and bland; his father is distressed and confused, his mother is outraged and embarrassed. All three teenagers seem thoroughly alienated and confused, unable even to communicate with each other in such a stressful situation. Jim is, in effect, a young outlaw, an outsider even when he is with people of his own age. Fascinated by Judy, he sees her walking to school in the morning and tries to befriend her: 'You wanna go with me?' She hardly looks at him: 'I go with the *kids*.' Before she joins the others, she glances at his puzzled face and says, 'You know, I bet you're a real loner.' Like Clift and Brando, Dean brings out the sense of total isolation felt by his character. The difference is primarily one of age – this character is younger, more entangled in his family's activities (they call him 'Jimbo', keeping him childlike), and even less certain of his own future.

Rebel Without a Cause is a movie that seems almost obsessively concerned with the dominant issues of American society in the early 1950s: the 'youth' problem, the erosion of traditional familial, sexual and social expectations, and the growing fascination with 'psychological' explanations of deviance. Judy's problem is, primarily, Oedipal: her father prefers his tousle-haired son to her and her increasingly erotic expressions of affection. Jim's problem is that his father is not strong enough: he is a permissive parent who refuses to discipline his son and evades the anguished questions. Watching his father wearing his mother's apron, scrubbing the kitchen floor, Jim senses the arbitrariness of conventional sex roles, and it scares him. Jim is an outsider; he lacks any role model and begins to panic. The domestic vision of the movie is so strong that all relationships are seen in family terms. Jim and Judy are potential threats to familial solidarity, and the story charts their gradual reconciliation with their parents. Plato *has* to die – not because his actions are in any way self-destructive, but rather because (as with *From Here to Eternity*) irreconcilable rebellion cannot be accommodated within the narrative: it is equated with insanity. From the perspective of social control, the problem is how to prevent Jim from assuming leadership of the teenage gang. As in *On the Waterfront* (1954), where Terry Malloy (Brando) must testify against the mob, Jim Stark is expected to betray the gang to the police.

The role of the informer (encouraged by McCarthyism) is an honourable one in American movies of the 1950s. Not only is informing construed as an act of courage; it is also the defining moral choice which separates Jim Stark from both the wall-eyed self-interest of his craven parents and the nihilism of the teenage delinquents. Jim and Plato have the same kind of latent homoerotic relationship as Prewitt and Maggio had in *From Here to Eternity*: both Plato and Maggio are small, weak and faintly retarded, and they look up to the man who can give them strength. When Maggio dies, Prewitt avenges his death and severs his links with society. When Plato dies, Jim makes peace with his killers. Jim betrays Plato. This is the 'positive' turning-point as far as the narrative is concerned. Jim abuses the ethic of trust and mutual responsibility that is the core of his moral position, because he tricks Plato into giving away his gun. 'Don't you trust me, Plato?' he says, as he furtively removes the bullets from the gun. 'You promised to give it back,' Plato remarks. 'Friends,' replies Jim, passing him the empty gun, 'always keep their promises.' The movie steadfastly refuses to see Jim's behaviour as a betrayal, and attempts to justify it as the only tactic available under the circumstances (after all, it is suggested, Plato is crazy). However, as the outcome of the subsequent events demonstrates, Jim's manipulative paternalism fails. Plato, castrated symbolically, holding a gun with no bullets (the rebellious form deprived of its dangerous content), is shot dead. Jim's behaviour can be explained only by concluding that, once his own alienation has ended (he has found Judy), he adopts society's view of the rebel and therefore is no longer certain that the people outside the planetarium are not his natural allies. Jim perceives himself as a free moral agent making voluntary choices, but the movie reveals, despite itself, that this is an illusion. On the level at which these choices are carried out, Jim remains, like Plato, an object of forces he barely understands.

Jim Stark is someone whose problems are relative; it is everyone else who has problems (the quintessential teenage conceit). This is a reverie of adolescence. James Dean, an actor with fewer colours and less technical imagination than either Clift or Brando, was fortunate to be offered the kind of roles which mirrored his own anxious, sexually ambiguous, catatonic personality – a personality that seemed on the verge of disintegration, perpetually challenging its own authority. *Rebel Without a Cause* was (and still is) the touchstone for generational strife in the 1950s. From Dean's opening cry of anguish to his friend's sacrificial death, the movie is shot through with soon-to-be archetypal images of teenage angst. In the film, inarticulateness was a virtue; it said much about the confusions, doubts and fears of modern adolescents. Significantly, it was not so much Dean's sexuality that made him Hollywood's most popular cult hero since Valentino; rather, it was his stance, his representative power as a teenager. An image frozen by death, Dean can be the eternal teenager. He enshrined what Pauline Kael has termed 'the glamour of delinquency', a self-hugging loneliness that society cannot entirely resolve.

Clift, Brando and Dean, despite their individual differences, combined to form the new sexual trinity, subverting the traditional masculine solidity of their predecessors. Montgomery Clift's rebel male is a Rousseau-like wanderer, incapable of full integration into society (as Clift himself remarked of his characters, they 'have a skin missing' – a tragic fragility about them). He eschews competitiveness and power because they imply limitations on the individual's freedom and on the applicability of equality. The ideal is self-reliance, the virtue born from the union of revolution and independence and christened in the temple of democracy. He was an ethereal kind of sex symbol: he often seemed passive and naïve, and he rarely allowed his body to be seen in any state of undress. Caryl Rivers recalls the nature of her teenage 'crush' on Clift:

At the same time as I was in love with Montgomery Clift, I found the growing awareness of how people 'did it' pretty revolting: all that touching and pinching and groping about . . . With me and Montgomery, it wasn't that way at all. Love with him would be long, languorous sighs, pressing close against his manly chest and telling each other those secrets we had never told anybody, gazing eyeball to eyeball, and he wouldn't think of putting his hand on my thigh.[10]

His sexual appeal was promissory; it was epicene, elusive, intriguingly understated. He so completely identified with the image of the rebel hero that he was naturally offered the role of Terry Malloy in *On the Waterfront* and that of Cal Trask in *East of Eden*, but he turned them both down and the roles went to the (then) lesser-known Marlon Brando and the newcomer James Dean.

In the spring of 1978 the Regency Theater in New York City ran a series called 'Three Rebels', seventeen movies starring Clift, Brando and Dean. The programme, which lasted twenty-eight days, provided the theatre with its highest-grossing three days: those in which it played two of Clift's movies, *The Search* (1948) and *A Place in the Sun*. The week of 11–17 June, during which the Regency screened *Raintree County* and *Judgement at Nuremberg*, was the best week in the history of the theatre. It was a reminder of how gifted an actor Clift was, and it highlighted his originality as the first, and probably the most complex, of the 1950s rebel males. Clift developed the new sexual vocabulary, the novel means of expressing conflicting desires. The others followed his example.

Brando's behavioural style exaggerated such elements as competitiveness, aloneness, misogyny, dominance and control. Men such as Stanley Kowalski do not have many personal or institutionally based ties with other men. Conventional political activity has no appeal for them. Their desire for complete freedom and self-determination makes them suspicious of involvement, for they see the world as filled with threats to the self. Only unlimited personal power (or else an outlaw existence) can prevent their losing control over their lives. The rebellion against the power and authority of others is an aspect of their passionate quest for personal independence. Not surprisingly, they regard relationships with women as fraught with danger. On the one hand, they feel constantly frustrated in their desire for total supportiveness; on the other, they regard women as adversaries in the struggle for mastery within relationships.

These rebel males represent an extreme version of individualism which rejects even sexual categories: men must deal with other men and with women directly and alone. Thus the quest for power in all aspects of life is inherently self-defeating, for such males lack the social resources to obtain and exercise it effectively ('I coulda been a *contender*,' complains one of Brando's characters, '. . . instead of a bum . . . which is what I am.'). Whereas Brando's Kowalski wants to acquire and wield as much personal power as possible, Clift's Prewitt has little interest in such power. Power is a social phenomenon, and Prewitt is simply not sufficiently immersed in the formal processes of society to make it a significant factor in his life (he is a Thoreau figure, rebelling by withdrawing). Both male types place a high premium on freedom, and both dramatize the importance attached to the individual in America and the closely related scepticism about fulfilment through organized social structures and majoritarian systems. The Brando male regards these with little confidence and feels that only in conscious opposition are freedom and individuality realizable goals. The Clift male is actually more removed from the ordinary pressures of society, for he simply goes his own way without really adhering to the conventions against which most men struggle.

James Dean's rebel feeds off the former two images. Dennis Hopper remembers Dean telling him: 'I've got Marlon Brando in one hand screaming, "Screw you! Screw you!" and Montgomery Clift in the other saying, "Help me! Help me!" And somewhere in between is James Dean.' Lee Strasberg said that Dean 'belonged in the nut-house', and Elia Kazan found him 'revolting', 'a pudding of hatred'; he lived the 'rebel' image. Sal Mineo, who played alongside Dean in *Rebel Without a Cause*, remarked: 'Before James Dean you were either a baby or a man. There was nothing in between.' His image appealed romantically to the 'hurt' children of post-war upheaval. His callow face had the flickering mobile uncertainties of adolescence continually passing over it; his speech was a secret mumble; his myopia gave him a naturally withdrawn, wincing look; his dress was self-consciously sloppy, purposefully unkempt. He seemed, more so than Clift or Brando, to merge with his screen image of the hyperactive, androgynous, impatient teenager. He took to fast cars: 'It's the only time I feel whole.' He also loved bullfighting, kept a Colt .45 on the movie lot, was known as 'the human ashtray' for his sexual proclivities and enjoyed repeating a line from Nicholas Ray's *Knock on Any Door*: 'Live fast, die young, and leave a good-looking corpse.'

All three rebel males were torn between traditional and novel images of masculinity. Montgomery Clift was, according to Elia Kazan, 'sexually ambivalent. At the same time he was a young man with honor and uprightness. When he was in his late teens he found the sympathy he wanted in my wife ... He used to come to my house and sit at her feet and seek a replacement for – I had to suppose – his mother.'[11] Indeed, Clift had long-standing relationships with women considerably older than himself, and also lived with male lovers for prolonged periods of time. His elder brother, Brooks Clift, describes him as 'bisexual ... I think he just liked a good lay.' Marlon Brando, for all his body-building, bongo-playing, blue-collar machismo, was similarly insecure. He would repeatedly telephone Clift to solicit opinions of his screen image ('I just see a guy with a fat ass' was one of Clift's typical responses), and he felt hopelessly ill-suited to the strutting masculinity of Stanley Kowalski. 'Marlon,' said Elia Kazan, 'is fully sexed but unisexed.' In 1975 Brando told an interviewer from *Ciné-Revue*: 'Like the vast majority of men I've had several homosexual experiences and I'm not remotely ashamed of it.' The actor Cameron Mitchell recalls that Brando once described himself as 'trisexual'. When James Dean was asked by someone if he was gay, he coyly replied: 'Well, I'm certainly not going through life with one hand tied behind my back.' Dean felt that he was both prey to and attracted by his latent homosexuality. Androgyny is the traditional sexuality of the classic performer; the rebel males' interest in their own bodies has the autoerotic quality of all good actors. The rebel males, through questioning their sexual identity (its 'feel', its objects of desire, its modes of appearance), underlined the arbitrariness of all images of 'manhood'. More lasting than any of their own personifications of masculinity was their critique of the constraining aspects of the conventional, contrived sex roles in modern society. They were eminently prepared for 'playing at being masculine'; they had been doing so for many years.

Clift, Brando and Dean are the great promissory icons of 1950s male sexuality. Conviction in their depth depends upon their being young and upon the natural accuracy of their physical movements, suggesting unknown regions of physical articulateness and endurance. In this figure, the body is not unhinged from the mind, as in the brute; it is the expression of selfhood, of the ability to originate one's actions. The T-shirt and the blue denim jeans, the uniform of the manual worker, become a costume with its own aesthetic and moral symbolism (a kind of blue-collar chic). D'Aurevilly recognized that the social and aesthetic rebel is not content with elegance alone; elegance has its mirror-image in inelegance: 'to have their clothes torn, before wearing them . . . so that they become a sort of lace – a cloud. They wanted to walk like gods in their clouds!'[12] The vanity in the young man's careless slouch is not the vanity of personal freedom: it is a vanity of *distinctiveness*, not of distinction.

It is the democratic equivalent of Baudelaire's dandy. Its guiding myth is the myth of youth itself: that life has not yet begun irretrievably, that the time is still for preparation, and that when the time comes to declare oneself, one will be recognized. Its motivation, as Baudelaire noted, is

the burning need to create for oneself a personal originality, bounded only by the limits of the proprieties. It is a kind of cult of the self which can nevertheless survive the pursuit of a happiness to be found in someone else – in woman, for example, which can even survive all that goes by the name of illusions. It is the joy of astonishing others, and the proud satisfaction of never oneself being astonished. A dandy may be blasé, he may even suffer; but in this case, he will smile like the Spartan boy under the fox's tooth.[13]

When society demands greater uniformity, consensus crowding out of the claims of consent, then the strategy of individuality and distinctiveness is to become identifiable within the uniform – not by it, adopting its identity, but despite it, accepting no privilege or privation accruing from it. Method acting facilitated this stance of the rebel male. In Method acting the most important element is the inner subtext which emerges, often in silences between the lines, from the character's struggle with the group and with the character's own fissile nature. Clift, Brando and Dean are at their best in schismatic parts based on the unresolved tension between an outer, social mask and an inner, private reality of frustration and confusion which usually has a sexual basis.

Camus observed that 'the rebel ... from his very first step, refuses to allow anyone to touch what he is. He is fighting for the integrity of one part of his being. At first he does not try to conquer, but simply to impose.' [14] Americans are, perhaps, especially vulnerable to glamorous pleas for the self; society, in the sense of the dense, demanding medium in which European lives are embroiled, does not seem to exist in America. The dandy emphasizes the double nature of the self in society, dressing up (or dressing down) in order to step back from involvement in society. What American rebels represent is not merely a certain heroism of self, but a very slender grasp of the arguments *against* selfishness (especially slender in the case of social arguments), which tend to crumble in the face of such charisma. The rebel male addresses an issue that has fascinated Americans since at least 1835, when de Tocqueville suggested that being American technically meant unlimited power. The challenge is, 'How come I am not as powerful as God's programme of self-reliance claims for me?' The question is asked at a price. On the individual level it invites a potentially destructive self-absorption. The rebel's search for sensation is in psychological fact parasitic on the restraint and fragility of everyone else; without the dependable dullness of ordinary people, the rebel's search would cease to be an adventure. The rebel male's search is even more problematic: in the process of humanizing the male image, 1950s movies, seemingly unaware of the direct relation between male rigidity and female passivity, continued to insist upon the virginal purity of the woman (*Baby Doll*, in 1956, signalled the slow, somewhat prurient change in this view). She must never have had a man other than her husband, and certainly must never have become pregnant or allowed herself to fall into the hands of an abortionist. If men looked inwards during the 1950s, women in the movies continued to have *tabula rasa* minds, waiting to be imprinted with male values. In order to loosen their own sexual identities, men increased their hold over women's identities. One gender was held still while the other explored itself. The success of the rebel males' image was thus to some extent a reflection of the continuing role of patriarchy in Hollywood. None the less, in their honest approach to their lives and their unprecedented emotional openness, the rebel males helped to indict the men who profited from them.

Clift, Brando and Dean offered in their personal magnetism, erotic ambiguity and introspection Hollywood's inventive obeisance to those frightened by political pressure and the frantic orthodoxy engendered by the witch-hunt. These men played characters so intriguing that they beguiled people into forgetting the nature of the times, suggesting that the grey oppressiveness was but an external, surface condition. Movies offered images of men capable of forging exciting lives, personalities far grander than the audience male could ever be. In an era of nationally orchestrated paranoia, Hollywood turned with unprecedented openness and intensity to the exploration of what it meant to be a man. In the knowledge that advocacy of dissent would induce a summons before an investigating committee, Hollywood replaced social dissent with an exploration of sexual politics. Identity is not a destiny but a choice; sexual identities are not so much about who we really are as about what we want to be and could be. The rebel males reminded people that they were all responsible for their sexuality. The assumed definitions of the male sex role were challenged as movies discovered the male capable of sensitivity and an open expression of tenderness – feelings previously ridiculed as effeminate. In such an overwhelming atmosphere of insecurity, the vulnerability of the ideal screen male became the experience of all, and on the screen it was now not merely acceptable but desirable – an indispensable aspect of male sexuality.

2

Montgomery Clift

Is there not a sort of blood shed when the conscience is wounded?

H. D. Thoreau

'Monty was *the* actor,' said Marlon Brando. 'He was the one you measured yourself against.' Montgomery Clift, who appeared in a mere seventeen movies, was one of the most important movie stars of his time. Not aggressively sexual, not forcibly chauvinist, Clift can plausibly be regarded as the first 'rebel male' of 1950s cinema: he displayed coolness without callousness, youthfulness without callowness, independence without conceit. He was equally appealing to women and men. Fan magazines often described him as 'the most beautiful man in the movies', and many actors, including Marlon Brando, concurred. Part of his attraction, paradoxically, was his apparent lack of concern about having any kind of effect. He chose not to work unless he felt the project was worthwhile; he eschewed the long-term contracts the studios were only too keen to offer him; he stayed away from the major movie premières and the prestigious Hollywood parties; he refused to indulge in fake romances to please his publicists; he never married. He said of himself: 'I am neither a young rebel nor an old rebel, nor a tired rebel, but quite simply an actor who tries to do his job with the maximum of conviction and sincerity.' Yet there was nothing 'simple' about Montgomery Clift. On the contrary, he was among the most complex personalities of the 1950s – as well as being one of the finest actors in the history of motion pictures. As Spencer Tracy said of him: 'He makes most of today's young players look like bums.'

Clift's movie image is, in the context of Hollywood iconography, an exquisite mistake. It breaks all the old rules concerning what a male sexual symbol should look like and, in so doing, embodies all the new anxieties about sex and gender that dominated American society in the 1950s. His arched, dark eyebrows, long eyelashes, delicate nose and slender body seemed erotically alive while being almost sexually undefined. He looked as though he was someone who had seen in daylight the kind of nightmares that other people see only when asleep. He wore his masculinity at an angle; it nearly fitted, but not quite. Many men identified with his evident discomfort. Even his acting career was, for the period, rather unconventional in that before he even visited Hollywood he had appeared in thirteen Broadway plays. His movie career started with a success; he was, as the phrase has it, 'an overnight sensation'. Bobby-soxers screamed when his face appeared on the screen, and fan clubs were formed all over the country. Yet by the end of the 1950s his appearances were infrequent and his classical good looks had been damaged in a serious accident. Unlike Brando, he could not bring himself to accept roles he did not believe in; unlike Dean, he did not die at the height of his popularity. Although he was the role model for all the later rebel males, he is not the most famous. His whole career, his entire life, seems fraught with painful ironies.

Clift was as much a symptom as a symbol of his time. More so than most actors, he was profoundly influenced (some would say imprisoned) by his upbringing. His childhood experiences, as he liked to remark, 'never stopped haunting me'. Edward Montgomery Clift (known to his family and friends as 'Monty') was born on 17 October 1920 in Omaha, Nebraska, several hours after his twin sister, Roberta. 'I was always the gentleman,' he was later to joke. 'I let Sister see the moon before I did.' The twins had an elder brother, Brooks, born the previous year. The Clift family was now complete. After the long and painful delivery, the twins were held by their mother, who vowed, 'never again . . . never again'.

Ethel 'Sunny' Clift was a diminutive yet feisty woman of regal bearing. When she was eight years old she discovered that she was really an orphan and that her natural parents had been 'aristocrats'. She became obsessed with finding her true family and gaining their acceptance. When she was eighteen and on the verge of leaving for Cornell on a scholarship, she learned that her mother was Maria Anderson (the daughter of Colonel Robert Anderson, the Union commander of Fort Sumter) and her father was Woodbury Blair (the son of Montgomery Blair, postmaster general in Lincoln's cabinet). Studying her genealogy became Sunny's lifelong preoccupation – almost a kind of existential necessity – earning her the right to share her families' lives (at least vicariously). While at Cornell she met and married Bill Clift, a rather shy man from a Southern family. When she found herself pregnant in 1919, she told Bill she intended to raise the child and any others they might have 'like Anderson-Blairs' – in the elegant, princely manner which she felt that they deserved.

At the time of the twins' birth, the Clifts were living in a comfortable three-storey house. Bill Clift had recently become first vice-president of Omaha National Bank, so he could afford a maid and a nurse for his burgeoning family. When the children were still very young, Sunny took them to New England, where she rented a series of large summer homes. Bill Clift stayed behind in Omaha at the bank. He tried to accept his wife's restless need to be on the move, realizing that she was determined that her children should absorb the American history she felt was part of their heritage. In 1924, when the twins were four years old, Bill Clift obtained a more lucrative position as sales manager of Ames Emerich Investment Company in Chicago. Sunny and the children were able to move from Omaha to Highland Park, a wealthy Chicago suburb. The family lived in a capacious Tudor-style house filled with exquisite antiques and the finest of silverware. However, although Highland Park was the family home, for the next four years the children were continually uprooted, travelling with their mother from New England to Bermuda and Europe and then back to America. Bill Clift, as usual, stayed behind, making money to keep his family in the lavish style to which Sunny wished them to become accustomed. When he did manage to spend some time with his family, he was usually exhausted and invariably preoccupied with business worries. Privately, it seems, he did not approve of the manner in which his children were being raised, but, partly because he genuinely adored Sunny and partly because he was by nature a reserved man, he said nothing.

The children were treated as though they were triplets, being given identical haircuts (Dutchboy bobs), matching clothes and the same lessons and responsibilities, regardless of age or sex. If Sunny could never quite reinvent herself, she reasoned, she could certainly invent the identities of her children. She taught them how to read and write and spell phonetically. They would never go to school, she told her husband, until they were ready for college. It had been hinted by a relative that if Sunny's children grew up to be eminently cultured individuals, they might be 'recognized' by her 'real' family. No promises were made, but the challenge was there. Tutoring became part of her grand scheme to raise her children as she believed the Andersons and Blairs had been raised – in an isolated but classical tradition. They would be beautifully educated, supremely elegant, but they would have to associate only with each other, 'with their own kind'. They began to learn Latin. In the evenings Sunny would read to them from Shakespeare, Goethe, Proust or Dickens. Brooks Clift recalls: 'I thought Ma was more interested in us being successful than happy. The word happy wasn't in our vocabulary.'

In May 1928 Sunny left with the children on the SS *Ile de France* for a tour of Europe. It proved a traumatic voyage for Monty. One day, swimming in the ship's pool, he was held under the water by another boy and was very nearly drowned as he struggled to break free. Trying to catch his breath, he burst a gland in his neck and developed a temperature of 104° and an abscessed ear. His mother, learning of a gland specialist who was said to have treated the Kaiser, rushed her children to Munich. Monty underwent a lengthy operation which, although successful, left a long scar down the right side of his neck which would be visible in his future screen appearances. He spent a lengthy period in convalescence. The incident marked the beginning of an extraordinary series of accidents and illnesses for Monty which, perversely, contributed to his distinctive image. Although outwardly healthy and handsome in appearance, Clift would be plagued by several major physical and emotional ailments which gnawed away at the surface beauty. After the swimming-pool accident he grew more reserved and nervous.

The tour of Europe was an immensely privileged, ambitious affair. They stayed at the finest hotels, visited the grandest sights and the greatest museums, and received excellent tuition in French and German until they were fluent in both languages. The children were always dutifully kept apart from other young people, and Sunny was forever insisting upon their 'difference', their 'aristocratic heritage'. There were also nightly visits to the opera, the ballet or the theatre, and on one occasion in Paris they saw the Comédie Française (an experience which was especially memorable for Monty). After such an extraordinary spell away from their Midwestern homeland, the children started to feel very unsettled and disoriented. When they returned to Highland Park in February 1929, after nine months abroad, they were behaving, according to their father, as if 'they'd forgotten America'. Sunny was at the centre of their lives. She decided on what games they should play, what tastes they should cultivate and what interests they should pursue. They never had other children to play with and they never grew accustomed to any single neighbourhood. Sunny's obsession with giving her children the privileged life-style that had been denied to her made them unnaturally dependent upon her. She came to lose sight of their needs as individuals and, when another of her estranged relatives decided the Clift children were still unworthy of the Anderson-Blairs, she had no hesitation in taking them away for yet another period in Europe. They left in the autumn of 1929 and, once settled, intensified their cultural and academic schedule. The children received personal tuition in history, languages and science; they were given regular violin and piano lessons; they were taught to ski and to play tennis and croquet. It was actually a very 'American' approach to culture: enthusiastic, ambitious, impatient and rather desperate. The 'experiment' was interrupted in October 1929 by the Wall Street Crash, which seriously undermined Bill Clift's financial stability. By January of 1930 Sunny and the children had returned to the family home in Chicago.

Although funds were now low, Sunny (by this stage oblivious to the surrounding chaos) was adamant that her children should complete their unique education, and so, in June of 1930, despite her husband's increasingly impassioned protests, she took the children back to Europe, spending periods in Berlin, Salzburg and Vienna. The typically rigorous, unfeeling regime continued, this time having a particularly upsetting effect upon Monty. Someone recalls seeing him at this stage in his life, looking 'strikingly handsome', his manners 'like those of a little prince', yet with a personality that seemed 'oddly aloof and rather melancholic for one so young'. He would often appear rather docile, clinging to his twin sister for comfort and protection. Brooks, the oldest of the three, was more self-assertive and outgoing, whereas Monty remained withdrawn, developing his own 'private language' with Roberta.

Late in 1931 Bill Clift became bankrupt. Sunny and the children were forced to return, rather shamefaced, to America. The family home was sold and most of its antique furniture and silverware auctioned. By December the family had moved into a small, furnished room in Greenwich Village, New York. 'Everything happened so fast to us,' Brooks Clift recalls. 'One minute we were travelling first class on the SS *Leviathan* and spooning up caviar at the captain's table. The next minute we were crowded together in one room above an Italian restaurant on West 9th Street, and Pa was sitting in a chair staring into space.' Sunny, with that indomitable mixture of optimism and single-mindedness, simply refused to acknowledge that anything of significance had changed. She made up all the beds with silk sheets, continued to lay the dinner table with some of her highly prized, expensive silverware and, somehow, found ways of continuing her children's tuition. 'How she managed *that* I don't know,' said Brooks Clift.

In the autumn of 1932, while Bill Clift worked in New York, Sunny took the children to Florida, where it was cheaper to live. She rented a relatively large house in Sarasota. It was at this stage that all three children (now in their teens) started to rebel. Monty, aged twelve, was a gifted mimic and started to mock his elders; Roberta would question her mother's decisions and conduct; and Brooks was increasingly keen to meet other people from outside the suffocatingly small family unit. The harder Sunny tried to cast everyone in their assigned roles, denying their individual needs and personal aspirations, the more fiercely each was forced to fight for freedom and self-definition. Now, although their whereabouts were still relentlessly monitored by their mother, they began escaping from the dull confines of their Sarasota home as frequently as possible. Sunny, still determined to achieve her objectives, managed finally to persuade each of her children to accept her career guidance. Brooks was sent away to Friends' School in Germantown in order to prepare for Harvard and Roberta enrolled at Dalton and then Bryn Mawr. Monty convinced his parents that he wanted to enter the theatre. When he was fourteen years old they had got him a job in summer stock in Stockbridge, Massachusetts, in *Fly Away Home*; it transferred to Broadway on 15 January 1935 for a seven-month run. 'I had found my calling,' he said.

Now based in New York, Sunny effectively 'managed' Monty's day for him. In the mornings he would continue to be tutored, while in the afternoons she would accompany him to Broadway, where they would try to find auditions. She decided that the John Robert Powers Model Agency might provide Monty with an entrée into the theatre, so he grudgingly accepted a series of modelling jobs. It was at this time that Monty began to argue with his mother over her attitude towards him. He would try and provoke her by behaving in vulgar ways and peppering his conversations with expletives, but she refused to rise to the bait (which infuriated him further). He was almost eighteen years of age and his relationship with Sunny was turning increasingly combative as he fought to gain his independence. She alternately indulged him and reproached him bitterly whenever he tried to break free. 'When I was a little boy,' recalled Clift at this time, 'I never knew the joy of being right.' He felt he could never please her, yet he always needed to win her critical approbation. Whatever friends he brought home from the theatre, they were, according to Sunny, 'not good enough' for him. She had been at his side, instructing him, guiding him, all of his life; he was unsure whether he could cope without her. Certainly, her presence at auditions and rehearsals was a humiliating experience for Monty. A fellow actor recalled: 'When she was not there he seemed to blossom and be himself, and the moment she appeared he would withdraw.'

A series of good performances in Broadway productions ensured that Clift began to attract the critics' attention. He was a fast learner and his ability to take a minor, underwritten role and make it memorably intense or colourful impressed his early directors. Yet his progress was threatened by an insecurity exacerbated by such a stifling relationship with his mother. He encouraged his elder brother to elope and he tried to help his sister establish her independence, yet, paradoxically, their successes only served to heighten his own anxiety. He complained that his upbringing had contributed to his sense of alienation: 'I call all that travelling a hobgoblin existence for children. Why weren't roots established?' He worried that his succession of tutors had helped only to confuse him: 'My formal education was a mess ... If I want to know something, I've got to ask my brother, who was a Harvard man, or my sister, who went to Bryn Mawr.' His mother's fixation on her 'aristocratic' lineage, which seemed at once both farcical and tragic, was too painful a memory for Clift ever to erase. He once told his brother, 'I don't give a damn about my bloodlines', yet the older he became the more he behaved like a dispossessed aristocrat. Although he would mingle with both lowlifes and celebrated achievers, he would regard them all – depending on what mood he was in – with respect or contempt, and always with amusement.

When he became an actor he refused to discuss his childhood with anyone. 'His family – where he came from – was shrouded in mystery,' said his actor friend Kevin McCarthy. When journalist Eleanor Harris tried to question Clift about his background for a profile in *McCall's* magazine, he would not respond. 'It was as if he had amnesia,' she said. 'Psychologically,' remarked Brooks Clift, 'we couldn't seem to take the memories, so we forgot.' Yet Montgomery Clift always yearned to understand his past. He would discuss his mother's coldness and obsessive haughtiness with his closest friends; there would be occasional, unsuccessful, attempts at reconciliation with his parents; and he would often go for nostalgic visits to

Europe. After he started analysis this desire to come to terms with his past became more acute.

Clift's loathing of his mother's conceitedness caused him to be almost as obsessively self-deprecating in public. He would make a point of not dominating conversations and he was a very good listener. Actor Bill Le Massena recalls:

In those early days on Broadway . . . he didn't drink or smoke and it is no exaggeration to say that he had the innate, organic morality of a saint at that time. Very early on, I learned that any kind of transgression that violated his friendship would hurt him tremendously and leave him helpless with emotion; cruelty, any kind, whether to animals or children, just injured him. He couldn't cope with it.[1]

One of the positive effects of Clift's peripatetic childhood was his unusual sensitivity to the differences between cultures, nations, races and individuals. His years of travel had precluded the growth of lazy notions of what is 'natural' or 'eccentric'. He was an open-minded young man with a fine capacity for wonder and this obviously assisted him in his work as an actor. 'He was so childlike in the way he related,' recalls Ned Smith, one of Clift's earliest friends. 'He would sit across from me, and watch me like an amazed child. He'd absorb everything I did, every facial expression I made, every word I said. Monty never grew out of that; he never learned to see people in an adult way.' This sense of wonder became part of Clift's distinctive image. Another element was an odd kind of physical fragility which contradicted his conventional masculine beauty. The scar on his neck was a permanent reminder of the traumatic accident he had suffered as a child. In 1939 he visited Mexico City and contracted amoebic dysentery, a disease from which he never fully recovered (he would later be rejected by the draft board as 4F). While he worked on Broadway he would pride himself on having a lean, hard body, visiting a gym each day in order to keep in excellent shape. Yet at the same time he would be suffering from serious stomach pains and internal bleeding, and was obliged to eat only raw steak and drink milk by the quart. His dysentery and colitis required powerful opiate painkillers like codeine. Clift (as rigorous as his mother in many respects) became an expert on the nature and types of drugs available, and in later years he would start using mild mood elevators like Ritalin and, eventually, hard drugs. He was given to binges, periods of drinking or drug-taking or party-going, partly as a reaction to his years of intense discipline. An actor friend recalls how Clift's mother even continued to ban him from eating chocolate when he was over eighteen years of age; 'She stifled and repressed Monty ... If she forbade him to do something, he obeyed.'[2]

If part of Clift's ambition during these years in New York was to free himself of his mother's authority, he achieved this somewhat ironically only by finding another authority figure: Alfred Lunt. Lynn Fontanne and Alfred Lunt had for over twenty years been the most glamorous husband and wife in legitimate theatre. At the end of 1939 the Lunts signed up Clift to appear with them the following year at the Alvin Theater on Broadway in Robert Sherwood's Pulitzer Prize play *There Shall be No Night*. He was to play their son, and as with so many of their relationships, the Lunts continued to treat Clift as their son when the play had ended. Clift had always admired the couple, and he was particularly keen to learn from Lunt's approach to acting. The essence of his art was what went on behind the lines, the thought processes and specific character needs; subtexts were always meticulously worked out, colouring each performance, making them original and provocative. In many ways he was not the ideal teacher for Clift: there was often something rather 'camp' about Lunt's stage manner (both Jack Benny and Bob Hope had adapted his 'stylish' gait and his somewhat prissy hand gestures) and, by this stage in his career, he sometimes indulged himself in a kind of celebratory form of self-parody. None the less, he certainly liberated Clift from an overly reverential reading of the text, and taught him how to develop an 'inner life' for each character by using elements of himself. Like Lunt, Clift was a natural actor, a born mimic, and he found it impossible to avoid copying Lunt's speech mannerisms (some of his words would run together quickly in mid-sentence, while between others there would be extraneous pauses). Although he eventually developed his own unique style, Clift retained traces of Lunt's technique. It was a powerful influence at a formative period in his career.

The Lunts became a surrogate family for Clift. One of Clift's most prized possessions was a photograph of them inscribed: 'From your *real* mother and father'. They took personal pride in his development as an actor and encouraged him to read more plays to broaden his range. They came to regard him as their disciple and even encouraged him to marry so that another acting team might carry on their tradition. Although Clift drifted away from them after he started his movie career, he invariably credited the Lunts for his development as an actor. 'Acting is an accumulation of subtle details,' he was to say. 'And the details of Alfred Lunt's performances were like the observations of a great novelist – like Samuel Butler or Marcel Proust.'

For the rest of the 1940s, Clift continued to act in several Broadway plays, establishing himself as one of America's most talented young performers. He grew in self-confidence and started to relax and explore his sexuality – having affairs with both men and women. He developed two of the most important – as well as ambiguous – relationships of his career at this time: first with Mira Rostova, who was five years his senior and was to become his acting coach, and, second, with Libby Holman (a former torch singer and Broadway singing star of the 1920s who had been married to an heir of the R. J. Reynolds tobacco fortune and had accidentally shot and killed him). These two women – part mother figures, part lovers – became Clift's closest companions for the next few years. Rostova (much to the chagrin of Clift's directors) would accompany him on set and help him work on his performances; Holman would take Clift to parties and join him in drunken binges (Billy Wilder was to base the central characters in *Sunset Boulevard* on Clift and Holman, with Clift cast as the leading man until Holman threatened to kill herself unless he withdrew). His mother found them both to be 'perverse' – a judgement that served merely to encourage his ebullience. Her once-pampered son had worked up so much resentment against what she had done to him that he made it impossible for her to visit him.

In 1947 the Actors' Studio was starting its classes in New York, and Clift attended its first sessions – along with Marlon Brando. Clift had first met Brando on a train to New York earlier that year, and they had recognized each other as potential rivals. At the Actors' Studio they had an early opportunity to study each other's techniques. Clift felt that Brando was erratic and impetuous, lacking the necessary patience to think things through; Brando announced that Clift acted 'like he's got a Mixmaster up his ass and doesn't want anyone to know it'. Despite their often critical comments and occasional arguments, both men came to respect and admire each other. They were both from Omaha, were both preoccupied with their relationship with their mothers and were both unsure of their sexuality, but there the resemblance ended. Brando would take several more years before he allowed his real feelings of inadequacy and pain to surface, while Clift was already quite openly confused and anxious. Edward Dmytryk, who directed both men in *The Young Lions* (1958), said that Clift 'was an exceptionally bright man who liked to pretend he wasn't, unlike Marlon Brando, who likes to pretend he's bright, whereas in fact he isn't . . .'

Clift was certainly less enthusiastic about the Actors' Studio than most of his contemporaries. He felt that many of the standard 'exercises', such as 'private moments' (when one acts out an activity not normally seen by anyone else, and which may well be highly intimate and sensitive in nature), were sometimes allowed to degenerate into mere exhibitionism and, according to Arthur Miller, he considered Lee Strasberg 'a charlatan'.[3] However, Elia Kazan's classes made a significant impact on both Clift and Brando, particularly because Kazan seemed to be encouraging men to undermine the simple, conventional readings of 'masculine' roles. Indeed, Kazan expressed a desire to work with men who did not have a traditional masculine image: 'Men have to be constantly proving something that is often not worth proving – their muscles, their fearlessness, their affluence, the strength of their erections . . . Many of the men I've liked best have had strong "feminine" characteristics . . .'[4] Clift was an actor Kazan found it easy to admire.

Hollywood studios had been sending offers to Clift's agent for several years, yet he took his time before considering any screen acting and was never especially enthusiastic about a career based exclusively in movies. For a considerable period, stretching from the late 1940s to the early 1950s, Clift felt that he should devote most of his energies to stage acting, and throughout his career he retained a nagging feeling that he was wasting his talent in movies. Clift, in spite of complaints about his mother's 'aristocratic' pretensions, retained the patrician mien. 'He was,' said Bill Le Massena, 'conceited as hell because he was such a great beauty.' He was also unusually well read, and critically acute, causing him to reject a whole series of potential movie roles because, he felt, they were 'substandard'. Eventually, in February 1946, Howard Hawks persuaded Clift to sign for a major role in a Western he was preparing called *Red River* (1948), dramatizing how a group of cowboys organized the first cattle drive from Laredo, Texas, to Kansas. Clift's decision was, for once, not entirely motivated by aesthetic concerns: he was $1,300 in debt and had been collecting unemployment insurance, so Hawks's offer of a $60,000 fee was most attractive.[5] Clift was intrigued by the idea of portraying a kind of elegant collegiate cowboy; it appealed to the iconoclast in him, feeding off his ambivalence about Hollywood conventions and sexual archetypes. When it became known that John Wayne, the polar opposite of Clift, both in his 'acting' and in his masculine image, was to play Clift's foster father, the prospect seemed too exciting to miss.

The movie was shot in Rain Valley, sixty miles east of Tucson, Arizona, from June to November 1946. It became evident almost immediately that Wayne and Clift found each other repugnant. Clift hated Wayne's mannered machismo, 'because it seemed so forced and so unnecessary'. Wayne (for whom book reading was dangerously effete) regarded Clift as 'an arrogant little bastard'. Hawks, who revelled in this kind of tension among his cast, deliberately exacerbated the conflict, charging his fight scenes with an intensity born of genuine hatred. For instance, Hawks rehearsed a fight between Wayne and Clift in such a way as to make Clift look hopelessly weak and clumsy, causing Wayne to burst into mocking laughter. When the fight was actually filmed, Clift was (according to Hawks) really out to hurt his opponent. The tension between the two leading men fits admirably into the symbolic conflict in the movie, where the moral righteousness of Tom Dunson (Wayne), the dynasty founder, becomes an inefficient and tyrannic weight on the next generation. Hawks was fascinated by the theme of male bonding, the special relationship that friendship between members of the same sex creates. This has always tempered the physicality of his protagonists, marking the point at which the strength of the flesh must yield to more humane powers, those of emotion, loyalty and need. Garth (Clift), Dunson's adopted son (he had no need of a woman in order to have a son – he just 'found' this boy), faces down Dunson when the tyranny threatens to destroy the community of Dunson's cowhands by forcing the trail drive to take a slow, clearly dangerous route to Missouri instead of trying a new, much faster way to a rumoured railhead at Abiline. 'Remember,' says Dunson, 'every man who signs on for this drive agrees to finish it. They'll be no quitting along the way, not by me and not by you.'

Both Dunson and Garth are western individualists who hate being pushed around. The difference is that Garth has an empathy with the weakness of others, whereas Dunson considers everyone lacking by the standard of his own brute strength. Dunson recalls the masculine ideal of bygone times, when the land was taken and held by muscle and rifle power. Dunson has the ruthless determination of the masculine ego; at one point he declares, 'I am the law.' Blind self-righteousness (Dunson) has to give way to circumspect self-righteousness (Garth), and, at the end of the movie, in the final fight between the two men, there is no conclusion. When challenged, Garth will not draw his gun and Dunson is not prepared to shoot. They are still father and son but they realize their separateness. They fight savagely, with fists and feet, with physical fierceness. Dunson is angered by his son's initial unwillingness to fight back: 'Won't *anything* make a man out of you?' Then (as so many of Clift's later characters would do) Garth starts to respond. The woman who loves them both stops the fight by firing a gun at them. 'You two love each other,' she shouts. 'Don't you realize that, you two crazy fools?' The two men, looking up from their brutal fist-fight, must finally gaze at each other and acknowledge the truth of their interdependence. It is one of the rare unambiguous statements in American cinema about male friendship. Like little boys puzzled by the ways of women, they make up and Dunson gives his blessing to Garth's marriage: 'You'd better marry that girl, Matt!' (although the son cannot resist one final retort: 'When are you going to stop telling people what to do?'). All Dunson needs, it is implied, is a good beating to show him that his brand of individualism no longer works. His old-time aggressiveness, perhaps useful for winning the West (and the Second World War), can be made to slot into the new society.

Hawks's definition of the interplay between the social and sexual values represented by Wayne and Clift relies in great part on their different acting styles – Wayne's bluster and Clift's fumbling. In terms of American history, the new, 'softer' individualism of Matthew Garth (finely articulated in Clift's subtle performance) must defeat the old, aggressive individualism of Tom Dunson because after the Second World War the economy itself changed from production to consumption, and the hard-shelled entrepreneur had to turn into the organization man. It is also Clift's most aggressively sexual screen performance. He is angular and tense and audacious, cocksure and cunningly ambitious. The symbolism was almost too neat: Wayne's grudgingly middle-aged conservative giving way to Clift's youthful rebel male. Few people failed to spot the significance of the transition. After he completed *Red River*, Clift was introduced to Fred Zinnemann, who was planning to direct a movie about the fate of concentration camp survivors called *The Search*. The project appealed to Clift (who was ashamed of his parents' anti-Semitism) and he signed for the movie in March 1947.

The Search was filmed in a semi-documentary style, and Clift improvised a substantial amount of his dialogue. The story concerns Steve (Clift), an Army engineer, who finds a young boy, hungry and ragged, wandering in a German ruin. He brings him home and, despite the boy's hostility, makes him feel cared for. A parallel plot concerns the boy's mother, who roams Europe looking for her lost son, working for a time in a UNRRA camp. There, mother and son are reunited when Steve has to bring the boy to the camp to stay before he can get him to America. The movie is rather basic in structure: there are no villains, except the vanquished Nazis, so everyone is a hero. Clift's performance is perfect for the movie's 'realistic' style: when the movie was released, Fred Zinnemann was asked, 'Where did you find a soldier who could act?' – an ideal tribute to the authenticity of Clift's portrayal. He looks relaxed, very thin and, at twenty-seven, already stooped – yet notably handsome. His best scenes are with the young boy. At one stage he has to tell him that his mother may well be dead; the boy struggles not to cry, breaks down and embraces him. Clift ruffles the boy's hair, holds him tight and says, 'Don't say anything . . . I know.' He shows how his character appreciates the uselessness of words in moments of extreme stress and their inability to convey the profound, incoherent emotions the boy is experiencing. The performance won him his first Academy Award nomination and received unqualified praise from the important movie critics of the day.

Clift's first two movies had been successful, admirable works which made him the most sought-after young actor in Hollywood. He went on to consolidate his position with roles in *The Heiress* (1949) and *The Big Lift* (1950), gently extending his range and improving his screen technique. As Morris Townsend in *The Heiress* (William Wyler's treatment of Henry James's novel *Washington Square*) Clift saw straight through to the ambiguity at the heart of the role and allowed one to glimpse the moral corruption beneath the surface respectability. In *The Big Lift* (a much less engaging movie, burdened with clumsy Cold War propaganda) Clift is a charming American abroad whose innocence is his undoing. In both movies Clift's acting attracted critical praise for its maturity and restraint. He became a new, radically unconventional hero to post-war audiences: a man with a conscience and a graceful dignity, a man whose vulnerability and disillusionment with society he was not too embarrassed to reveal. It was as though one of Kinsey's interviewees had wandered on to the movie screen; he stared out at the audience, somewhat puzzled as to how he had arrived there and what he was supposed to be doing. He was skilful enough to seem natural; his good looks were never allowed to appear contrived or exaggerated. Kevin McCarthy described Clift as 'the personification of the actor's art, masculine beauty, photogenic personality'. There was something intriguingly enigmatic about Clift's screen image: profiles in *Time, Life, Look, Collier's* and *Variety* struggled to pinpoint his appeal. Obviously he was not another Gable or Tracy – a traditional, tough, taciturn leading man; he was rather remote, displaced, a loner, and somewhat androgynous in his appeal. Without being aware of it, audiences were witnessing a new kind of eroticism on film – an eroticism and a vulnerability which sprang from the contradictions in Clift's personality: he seemed open yet private, strong yet gentle, young yet mature. He represented the 'new' kind of man for the 1950s; a man who refused to make judgements on sexual preference. He was perhaps the most Jamesian actor of the era. Inwardness, calculation, coolness and warmth combined in a single character, a calmness about enduring anguish – these were the qualities Clift embodied. He reflected the loneliness, the emotional dislocation, the smouldering hostility and the quicksilver charm that soon became characteristic of an entire generation of actors. As actor Bill Gunn put it: 'Monty was the first movie star to seem obsessed – slightly nuts.'

Jane Fonda recalled the impression Clift made on her when she first saw his movies: 'No one had ever seen an attractive man who was so ... *vulnerable*. He was like a wound.'[6] His unique appeal caused him to suffer the pressures that accompanied the label 'Hollywood's latest sex symbol'. Where he once drank only milk, he now drank Martinis and vodka – a somewhat impetuous reaction to the increasingly inaccurate images that were being imposed on him. Everything he did and said was news and he struggled to keep control of his public identity. He rewrote his past and his personality for the fan magazines and the gossip columnists. In part to obscure his bisexuality and in part to offend his parents, Clift indulged in a fanciful portrayal of himself as a 'rough and ready' boy from Middle America. In February 1950 *Modern Screen* carried a story on him entitled 'Barefoot boy with shows [sic] on', describing how he was seen 'wearing a pair of tattered blue jeans, a T-shirt and a jacket full of holes. He looked like a bum.' The young 'aristocrat' who had spent time in all the major European cities by the time he was twelve, who had been taught several languages, who had a weakness for Pouilly Fumé and the finest caviar, and who was a master of etiquette, now shuffled in, shrugged his shoulders and explained to reporters how he owned only one suit ('which I intend to keep as long as the good moth spares it to me') and confessed that he felt overawed by the 'glamour' of Hollywood society. He enjoyed irritating his mother with this farcical rusticity, and the 'small-town boy' (with the 'healthy' appetite) tales helped placate Hedda Hopper and Louella Parsons (both of whom had let him know of the 'rumours' they had heard about his sexual tastes), but the pose also served a rather more urgent purpose: it made him even more marketable than before, sending out discreet suggestions as to the potential leading roles he could play. Clift, for all his misgivings about Hollywood, was very ambitious – and very confident of his own ability. He did not hesitate to promote himself in the first few years of his movie career. He succeeded. Paramount signed him, acknowledging his value by granting him director approval and the option to appear in movies for rival studios or on the stage – an exceptional contract for a young newcomer.

The studio intensified the media interest in Clift, depicting him as 'Paramount's next great sex symbol – the most eligible bachelor on the screen!' Although he had worked to establish himself in movies, Clift soon realized that his success was largely at the cost of his personal happiness; he was obliged to play out the role of an uncomplicatedly heterosexual celebrity. 'Becoming a public figure – a celebrity – tore Monty up,' said Bill Le Massena. He 'hated, loathed, and despised deception, and here he was having to hide. In the theater he could have swung both ways and it wouldn't have mattered. But as a Hollywood star he had to be the all-American male 100 percent or else.'[7] Yet Clift's profound disenchantment with the 'masculine' image he was given caused him to subvert it through his acting; he was a sexual rebel, undermining all the old clichés concerning how men should behave. His eroticism is more subtle than that of other male stars: one has to look out for it. His appeal was such that when the camera moved in close on him, something intangible occurred: what appeared on the screen was not merely a splendid watchful face or a finely expressive style, but a complex mysterious presence, full of depth, indisputably alive, undeniably alert. There is a certain fine-drawn tremulousness, a flickering glimpse of frailty, which gives the image an unsettling aura. It was a bitter irony that Clift's self-censorship off-screen probably contributed to his on-screen self-exposure.

A Place in the Sun, Clift's next movie, was arguably the first really to capture the ambiguity of his image. It placed his character in a variety of social settings, with a number of sharp changes in emotional intensity, and Clift was able to bring out more of the conflicting desires and values that lurked beneath the surface persona. The movie was also memorable for its casting: Clift played opposite Elizabeth Taylor, and they worked together with an erotic intensity that was missing in Clift's earlier movies. Hailed by Charles Chaplin as 'the greatest movie ever made about America', it was certainly one of the emblematic films of the 1950s, and a new generation of soul searchers responded keenly to the tormented youth portrayed by Clift. With his portrait of the young outsider George Eastman, one sees the beginnings of the obsessions with inwardness and with privacy that will come with the best roles of Marlon Brando and James Dean. Director George Stevens had intended to remain faithful to the original plot of Theodore Dreiser's *An American Tragedy* (which was based upon a 1906 murder trial in Herkimer, New York). However, his studio was extremely keen for a 'reworked' plot which toned down the 'un-American' themes in Dreiser's story, and Stevens accepted the shift from social comment to modern melodrama. Stevens's narrative is a romance and its attention is on two conflicting desires: one born of loneliness and need, the other of ambition and fascination. These desires are embodied in the figure of George Eastman.

George Eastman, a young man without formal education or independent means, hitches a ride to 'the city' (an unnamed Mid-western city), where his uncle finds him a job in the family bathing-suit factory. At first he seems profoundly ill at ease: as we see him waiting to meet his uncle and then visiting the luxurious family home, George is constantly at a loss for something to say, somewhere to look, someone to meet. He wears a cheap tweed suit which hangs on him like a hastily contrived accent, false and ill-fitting; he never manages to blend in, either sartorially or socially. As the family relax in their elegant home, George is sinking down deep into his chair, folding in upon himself in fear, his head leaning forward, his knees pointing up towards his chin, his hands wrapped tightly around his shins. He looks like a child in its father's chair, dwarfed by the size. His voice, constrained by his bent-over body, is dry, almost strangled by his feelings of inadequacy. In the factory he is able, in time, to relax; he strips off his jacket, puts on a plain white T-shirt and shows a shy, boyish pleasure as the female workers gaze at his youthful, lithe physique. Despite a ban on fraternization, George becomes the lover of Alice Tripp (Shelley Winters), an ordinary, rather humdrum, assembly-line worker. Eventually, she is made pregnant by George.

During the same period, George is introduced to the glamorous milieu of his wealthy relations. He starts to enjoy their grand parties and fine clothes, and comes to entertain dreams of being accepted in this high-class world. He labours to make himself suitable for the Eastmans: by night he studies 'Teach Yourself' business texts and writes suggestions on potential improvements in factory organization, and by day he observes the gestures and mannerisms of his 'superiors'. A beautiful young socialite, Angela Vickers (Elizabeth Taylor), becomes the principal object of George's hopes and desires. She embodies all that he yearns for: she is capricious where George is methodical, she is relaxed where George is uneasy, and she belongs where George feels lost. 'You seem so strange,' she says, gazing at his face, 'so deep and far away.' Angela and George fall in love, but Alice refuses to be abandoned and insists that George marries her. He hears a radio report of a man losing his wife in an accident at sea and a partially formulated plan to kill Alice starts to take root in his mind. Finding (with some relief) that they cannot marry over the Labor Day weekend, George takes Alice rowing. Although he cannot bring himself to murder her, fate intervenes, the boat overturns and Alice is drowned. George returns to Angela, but eventually the police track him down and arrest him. He is charged with murder and found guilty. Although he truly believes he is guilty only in thought, not in deed, he faces death with equanimity.

The movie is centred upon the leading man's anxious search for himself. Clift's characterization is of a likeably innocent, confused victim of circumstances − and, as such, it is the first full-blown appearance of the definitive 1950s hero. His glance and stance, his expression and unblinking gaze, convey the character's vague restlessness. He is hunger personified; he is attracted to those things that can feed him. From the very first scene on the highway, George is drawn, almost hypnotically, to the dual images representing luxury: first, he sees Angela Vickers speeding by in her convertible (symbolic of all that is unattainable and attractive); and second, he sees a billboard bathing beauty reclining in her Eastman bathing-suit. He is the outsider looking in, the poor western boy wanting to become the prosperous 'East-man'. He is basically a decent young man who, coming from a humble background marked by poverty and piety (his mother runs a religious mission), is fascinated by wealth and position. He knows, however, that such a comfortable, cultured life is beyond his grasp so, pragmatically, he applies himself to carving out his own modest career. His relationship with Alice Tripp is, at first, both tender and stable; they are stoical about their lowly class position, yet hopeful of a secure future together. The divisions between workers and management are disturbed when George's uncle takes him in hand, promoting him and introducing him to Angela Vickers. It is at this point that George, alienated suddenly from his own class and still not accepted by this other class, is forced into an outlaw position, a rebellious role. He cannot keep his morality intact as he moves from one class to the next; he has to start deceiving Alice in order to see more of Angela, and he cannot bring himself to tell Angela about Alice. Nothing can ever seem 'natural' again for George. If he stays with Alice, the thought of Angela, the angel, will haunt him, reminding him of how grey and impoverished his life is; if he goes with Angela, Alice will follow him and reveal their past relationship and ruin his new-found social status.

George Stevens misses no opportunity to counterpose the drives at work within George. We see him in a T-shirt and jeans, working next to Alice on the assembly line; next we see him in a new dark suit, dancing with Angela in the Eastman mansion. It is not just Angela's magnetic dark beauty (which is everywhere contrasted with Alice's mousy, washed-out pallidity) that entrances him; rather, it is the whole complex upper-class life-style she represents – the world of fashion and success, of celebrity and sex, easy living and big business. At a glamorous party, Angela starts to flirt and tease George while he speaks on the telephone to his mother. He is embarrassed when Angela's giggling is heard by his pious mother. The audience is always made aware of the past from which George is struggling to escape and the future he is trying to make for himself. Particular stress is given to the sense in which George's masculinity has never been allowed to develop very far; his early years were dominated by his censorious mother, and his life as a young man is marked by his weakness for two women. He makes Alice pregnant, yet he seems mystified as to how he did it; when she tells him the news he is stunned, and she has to explain the events which led to the conception. Whenever Alice, Angela or his mother speaks to him, George is as attentive and as impression-able as a child. His world is dominated by women and their demands on him. In his old childhood home, a poster on the wall announces, 'Mother knows best.' Angela, warming to this unusually shy, nervous young man, says to him, 'Tell Mama all.' He is given little opportunity to discover an identity that is not defined by the conflicting urgencies of the women who constrain his life: his mother, who wants him to be good, Angela, who desires him, and Alice, who depends on him.

George never had the opportunity to act on his own initiative when he was a child, and for most of his life he remains someone who simply responds to the ideas, needs and suggestions of other people: the Eastmans, Alice Tripp, Angela Vickers. His single act of defiance is revealed in court during cross-examination, when he denies the allegation that he murdered Alice; he is, by that time, an experienced interviewee. George's pacific nature contributes to his epicene personality. What was hinted at only occasionally in previous appearances is a constant aspect of George's appearance: namely, Clift's cruising sexual swagger (which Brando and Dean picked up on). Few audiences at the time were aware of the significance of that androgynous swagger – it was very subtle – but it was as though Clift was telling his female admirers, 'I'm as beautiful as you are – so who needs you?' George's relationship with Angela brings him comfort, but his sexual needs remain unfulfilled; as he rests his head on her shoulder and she strokes his face, he wears a look of puzzlement, as though something, somehow, is missing. At such moments he seems to be a lost child again. Clift's vulnerability serves him well in this movie. He aches with unvoiced longings; his introversion and ambivalence are as appealing as other actors' expressiveness. The hints of neurosis and ambiguity he brings to the role only add to the character's attractiveness.

George is drawn into society by his class aspirations and driven back out by his sexual desires. This is very revealing about an important theme in this cultural perspective: the basic literary–philosophical tradition of America began not with Emerson's idealism or Thoreau's optimism, but with Jonathan Edwards, Edward Taylor and a whole board of Puritan trustees in the seventeenth century who warned against the demonic potential within each citizen, always ready to strike out if one relaxes one's self-control. *A Place in the Sun* reflects some of this anxiety about the absence of repression and self-restraint. Sex, in this movie, is portrayed as disruptive, explosive and profoundly dangerous. George's career is held back because he becomes the lover of an assembly-line worker, and his life is cut short because of his hopeless love for the wealthy young socialite. An early remark made by Alice Tripp – 'If you're an Eastman, you're not in the same boat as anybody' – becomes a central motif: George Eastman is forced to be an outsider, an outlaw, a rebel, not in the same boat (symbolically) as his upper-class relatives, not in the same boat (literally) as the pathetic, doomed Alice Tripp.

Clift's acting in *A Place in the Sun* is peerless in its subtlety and its quiet assurance. One watches him more attentively than the people around him, as though he has more to do and more time to do it in, like an hour hand in a world of second hands. The quality he possessed of appearing removed from others around him – as though he is both a participant in the action and an outsider looking in – helps him convey equally George's growing torment and his consuming infatuation. He demonstrates D. W. Griffith's boast that film 'photographs thought' when he faces the camera and listens to the radio report that first suggests to him the possibility of murdering Alice: he is silent and still, the camera moves in close to his face, and all we see are his eyes moving as the thoughts come into his mind. For the crucial scene in which George sits opposite Alice in the boat and contemplates murdering her, Clift conveys his character's complex thoughts with the barest resources: his eyes slide from side to side, the semi-mobile mouth refuses to do more than half form his words, the smile (never wholehearted) has never seemed more forced. Clift shows that George is afraid of his own demonic potential: the brow wrinkles, the eyes turn in on some previously unacknowledged murderous impulses. It is brilliant screen acting, precise, intense and beautifully understated. He is both introverted and exploding out of himself, the ex-mission boy who wants so much he can even contemplate murder to achieve it. Clift rehearsed all of his scenes with Taylor without any dialogue being spoken, the meanings being communicated through their eyes; the technique served to heighten the intensity of the on-screen relationship. 'I guess maybe I loved you before I saw you,' he tells Angela in a confession of abstract longing made concrete in the person of this fascinating creature.

MGM exploited the obvious appeal of the Clift–Taylor roles, even going so far as to consider changing the title of the movie to *The Lovers*. The fact that the two stars (it seems) had an affair during the making of the movie was something no publicist refrained from alluding to. Taylor told reporters: 'I thought he was

Brando's rebel, and the pose that inspired a generation: the white T-shirt, the insolent slouch, and the hooded eyes hiding the hungry heart.

The cultured outsider: Montgomery Clift, the young American back from Europe.

The Dean Look: a mixture of moodiness and myopia, it suggests a
private joke shared only by a privileged community. He is pointing to
the left but looking to the right, the symbol of misunderstood youth.

Male bonding in process: Dean in *Rebel Without a Cause*, the
centre of attraction.

The Wild One: the blandness of the others is as studied as Brando's
self-conscious non-conformity. 'At first he does not try to conquer,
but simply to impose.' (Camus)

'One of the most beautiful couples in movie history': Clift and Elizabeth Taylor in a publicity still for *A Place in the Sun*.

Dean's most enduring relationships, perhaps, were with machines –
especially fast cars, 'the ultimate fix'.

Full leather jacket: Brando in *The Wild One*, shielded by leather and metal. He conveyed how the old emblems of masculinity were actually defence mechanisms, hiding the vulnerable self.

Clift in *From Here to Eternity* as the 'hardhead' Prewitt: 'A man don't
go his own way, he's nothin'!'

the most beautiful thing in the world.' It was suggested that she wanted to get a divorce from her then husband, Nicky Hilton, so that she could marry Clift, and there is evidence that he was, for a time, quite serious about the possibility of marriage.[8] When the movie was released, a critic declared: 'Clift and Taylor are the most beautiful couple in the history of the cinema' (a claim later repeated by critic Andrew Sarris). Certainly, the scenes featuring George and Angela are particularly memorable. They may not be the most erotic of Clift's career (*Red River* contains more aggressive moments, and *From Here to Eternity* shows Clift at a more intense level), but one is left in no doubt as to the sexual nature of the desires on display. Various factors combine to frustrate the lovers, but one remembers their needs and their unfulfilled ambitions.

Pauline Kael described Clift's performance in *A Place in the Sun* as being 'almost too good, too sensitive'. It was certainly strikingly original and authentic for a Hollywood movie, transcending the plot's creaky predictability. Clift remarked that 'the best acting is an accumulation of subtleties — like shaking ash from a cigarette when the character is supposed to be completely absorbed in a conversation'. Perhaps Clift's most felicitous quality was his capacity for stillness, sensing the appropriate moment in a scene to rely entirely upon his silent presence to dominate the scene, forcing one to study his face, his eyes, for signs of his inner feelings. He controls his audience by skill rather than strength. His sheer gift of poignant physical presence is an essence of movie acting, for the weight that a movie accords to sensuous detail is one of its great potencies, distinguishing it sharply from the theatre. There is evidence that Clift was aware of this fact at the very start of his movie career. In *Red River* he nearly throws away some of his lines and allows the camera to study his physical gestures: hiding his mouth with his hand, speaking into a cup while drinking his coffee or running a finger alongside his nose in a mannerism imitative of his 'father', John Wayne. Burt Lancaster recalled working with Clift on *From Here to Eternity*: 'The only time I was ever afraid as an actor was that first scene with Clift ... I thought they might have to stop because my trembling would show. But I'd never worked with an actor with Clift's power before; I was afraid he was going to blow me right off the screen.'[9] Myrna Loy, who co-starred with Clift in *Lonelyhearts* (1959), observed:

He had extraordinary instincts. I had a scene with Bob Ryan that didn't work – it was beautifully written; there was just too much of it. I brought it to Monty's dressing room, where we often lunched together ... He took a pencil and just started striking out words, like a surgeon removing his hundredth appendix. His cutting saved that scene and strengthened my impact.[10]

Throughout his career, he would often decide, on set, to eliminate pages of dialogue, saying simply, 'Just move in close on my eyes.'

In close-ups one is drawn to these eyes. Large, grey, infinitely expressive in his handsome but rather impassive face, they could register yearning, compassion, intelligence and despair in rapid succession. They articulate the ineffable, making Clift something of an *auteur* as he goes far beyond the screenplay. Indeed, the close-up of the eyes became a kind of signature. In *A Place in the Sun* one sees George Eastman change from a naïve young man into a potential murderer in a scene free from any dialogue, with Clift's expressive eyes reflecting his thoughts. In *I Confess* (1953), when Clift, playing a priest faced with imminent arrest, is walking the streets deep in thought, the audience understands his extreme tension and the insolubility of his problem purely from the anguished expression in his eyes. Later on in the same movie, interrogated by a police inspector, Clift delineates the priest's conflicting emotions with the subtlest nuances of expression – his face, vulnerable but enlivened by discerning yet benign eyes, reveals his suffering with the most eloquent intensity (as Truffaut observed, 'It's only through his eyes that we see his bewilderment at all the things that are happening to him'). Even John Huston, who had a poor relationship with Clift when filming *Freud* (1962), admitted: 'It was impossible not to marvel at and admire his talent. Monty's eyes would light up, and you could actually "see" an idea being born in "Freud's" mind.'[11] The examples seem endless, and each one is remarkable for its role in the narrative, compressing an extraordinary amount of information and emotional energy into a relatively brief and memorable moment. The technique was part of Clift's thoughtful approach to all his acting. He was meticulous in his preparation for each part (a discipline he said he learned from Alfred Lunt). Before he played the priest in *I Confess*, he flew up to Canada to stay in a monastery for a week (discussing the plot with the monks to discover whether or not the basic premise seemed plausible) and then he memorized the entire Latin mass. He spent weeks with a boxing coach, fighting in the ring, as he prepared to portray ex-boxer Prewitt in *From Here to Eternity*. For the same movie, he learned how to play the bugle in order to look convincing in a scene where he mimes a tune with it, and he almost broke his back learning how to ride a bronco in Reno when he was preparing to play the eccentric cowboy in *The Misfits* (1960).

Clift took what he needed from several schools of acting. He was a tremendous admirer of Olivier (at least for his stage work), and spent a great deal of time studying his performances. Although Clift attended classes at the Actors' Studio, he was uncomfortable with Method acting because he felt that many of its exponents merely played variations of themselves. Clift's own range, on the contrary, was extraordinary: his characters were by turn extroverted, ductile, withdrawn, manic or serene, articulate or monosyllabic, assertive or passive. Among his most consistent qualities is a diffidence towards the events of his movies which gives one the immediate impression of a real intelligence meeting those events not in a predetermined way but with a flexible novelty of experience. As the attitude attracts one's interest, so the completeness of one's involvement in the wide potential of his decisions reflects on one's interest and thus on what, in similar circumstances, one's own decision might be. He was a great believer in the psychological gesture: the physical manifestation of an emotion. It could be expressed in the way he enters or leaves a room (a defiant slouch in *From Here to Eternity*, a dazed lurch in *The Misfits*), in a nervous mannerism (the absent-minded fidgeting in *The Big Lift*) or in a striking gaze (*A Place in the Sun*'s scene where George looks at Alice and is ready to kill her, or a scene from *The Misfits* where

Perce ends a telephone conversation with a dazed expression as though he has just been punched). His voice is similarly expressive, extracting the most passionate meaning from each line, skipping along each phrase, shaving off pathos in great flakes. It is a highly risk-laden technique, a filigree enchantment, forever on the edge of self-parody, but it produced some extraordinary performances. Clift once said:

When I play a role I put all my energy and emotion into it . . . Your body doesn't know you're kidding when you become angry, tearful or violent for a part. It takes a tremendous toll of the performer emotionally and physically . . . I can't pace myself the way some other actors can. I either go all out or I don't accept the picture. I have to dredge it out of me. I'm exhausted at the end of a picture.[12]

From the beginning, audiences and critics alike were impressed with the dialectical tensions in Clift's image, the way in which he seems to regard his considerable strength as redundant and the way in which his strong face is, in a curious sense, feminine. There is an element of narcissism in Clift's acting; he, as much as anyone else, was fascinated by his physical appearance. Loretta Young recalls that 'his face was so gorgeous and so romantic, and everything he did, if you just looked at him, oh, you just died!'[13] His friends Kevin McCarthy and Roddy McDowall would take dozens of photographs of him whenever he stayed with them; he enjoyed being photo-graphed and would analyse each facial expression – how his mouth looked when open, shut, relaxed or tensed-up, the various moods his eyes could evoke. Sometimes he would stop and gaze at his reflection in the mirror, coming to see himself 'from outside', monitoring his surface behaviour. His face was his screenplay; he wrote his own stories with it. Clift in repose is the recurring figure: sitting or reclining, meditating on some complex moral dilemma. Typically in Hollywood movies one saw men *acting* on their sexual desires; with Clift, one sees him *feeling* his desires, sensing them intensifying within him. It is often a very private, sometimes almost masturbatory, experience for him. Sex is usually only suggested in Clift's movies. He is a romantic rebel. There is something unnerving in his hesitant reaction to his own felt desires. In *The Heiress* he accompanies himself on a parlour piano as he croons to Olivia de Havilland: *'Plaisir d'amour ne dure qu'un moment, chagrin d'amour dure toute la vie'* (The pleasures of love last but a moment; the pain of love lasts a lifetime). His first screen love scenes, in *Red River*, display the tender sensibility and intensity which would become his hallmark throughout his career. He meets the young woman (Joanne Dru) in the fog. He fondles her hair and strokes her neck. As rain envelops them, she leans against his chest while he explains his step-father's behaviour. She embraces him and he flirts with her, saying, 'I've always been kinda slow making up my mind.' He gazes at her as though she is an intriguing puzzle, her presence a question that is being asked of him. This attitude of appearing to consume his leading woman with his eyes (recapitulated in later movies with stars as diverse as Cornell Borchers, Shelley Winters, Elizabeth Taylor, Jennifer Jones, Marilyn Monroe and Lee Remick) is one of Clift's most potent instruments as an actor and is largely responsible for his reputation as one of the screen's most ardent and compulsive romantic figures.

It seemed that Clift did not have one sexual centre; he was too mercurial, too diffuse a personality. He was nothing if not complicated. His self-doubt led to a splendid tension in his work, but also to great misery for himself and those who surrounded him in his private life. As his image as a 'sex symbol' became more pronounced, Clift started to show his feelings of desperate ambivalence in various eccentric gestures and actions. He would behave as though he was a child trying to embarrass his parents: he would get drunk at parties and pass out on the floor, eat exclusively off other people's plates at dinner, drive his car at reckless speeds and wander through movie executives' offices shouting expletives at no one in particular. It was a directionless rebellion, irrational but intensely urgent. Sometimes he would invite his friends to his room and they would arrive to find him hanging from the window ledge by his fingertips, thirteen floors above street level; on one occasion he climbed down from the roof of a friend's house and appeared, head downwards, outside the window. It was a bewildering mixture of self-inflicted masochism, spoilt-child, attention-seeking self-centredness and outrageous experimentation. He once said: 'The problem is how to remain thin-skinned and yet survive. One can uncallous one's self, you know ... The problem is to remain sensitive to all kinds of things without letting them pull you down.'[14]

Clift started having daily psychoanalysis sessions with a distinguished analyst, William V. Silverberg. He wanted to curb his drinking and come to terms with his background and his sexuality. He continued the analysis for over fourteen years. Silverberg was co-founder, along with Karen Horney, of the Association for the Advancement of Psychiatry. A well-known neo-Freudian, he introduced the extremely controversial concept of 'effective aggression', which he once described as 'the ability to achieve what one wishes regardless of obstacles'. Clift was impressed with Silverberg's approach, although the majority of his friends maintain that the sessions had an extremely damaging effect: Silverberg was a homosexual and, it is alleged, was not sympathetic to Clift's bisexual nature; he always insisted that Clift did not have a drinking problem, even after Clift admitted he feared he was an alcoholic. Silverberg once presented Clift with a copy of his book *Childhood Experience and Destiny*; the inscription on the flyleaf reads: 'To Monty, my hero, Billy'. Clift remarked to Mira Rostova: 'You know? Billy Silverberg is becoming my Mephisto!' Clift's secretary, Marge Stengel, remarks: 'People around Monty had different theories. Some people thought what was happening to Monty was Silverberg's fault, but others felt that Monty might not have stayed afloat without him. I was with those who thought he was a bad doctor.'[15] It certainly seems that, on several occasions, Silverberg allowed Clift to drink during sessions and once invited him to stay at his home. For a man who needed objective, dispassionate advice, Silverberg was surely a very poor choice. Mira Rostova said: 'Monty was totally split sexually ... That was the core of his tragedy, because he never stopped feeling guilty about being conflicted.'[16] Clift's vulnerability – which made his performances so poignant – threatened to overwhelm him. He once scribbled in a notebook, 'The sadness of our existence should not leave us blunted, on the contrary – how to remain thin-skinned, vulnerable and stay alive?' This was the question he took to Silverberg; this was the problem he sometimes tried to forget through alcohol and drug abuse.

If Clift had felt himself to be uncomplicatedly homosexual, he would probably have been considerably more secure: the identity settled, the public deception is straightforward (consider the case of Rock Hudson). Yet Clift's identity was *unsettled*. Most of his homosexual relationships were short-lived, tempestuous and, in his final few years, quite violent. One of his female friends claims that he was a passive lover and often impotent.[17] He needed constant sexual reassurance, and he was able to get that from men more easily than women. Ben Bagley, one of Clift's confidants, recalls that Clift was extremely embarrassed about his small penis (in the unexpurgated version of Kenneth Anger's *Hollywood Babylon*, Clift was called 'Princess Tiny Meat' by several Hollywood male prostitutes). He was a man who felt unhappy with any single sexual category: 'I don't want to be labelled as either a pansy or a heterosexual. Labelling is so self-limiting. We are what we do – not what we say we are.' His elder brother, Brooks, insisted:

Monty was a bisexual . . . I met two girls he got pregnant. He was never exclusively one thing or the other; he swung back and forth. Because we'd been raised in Europe, where homosexuality was more or less accepted, he never felt ashamed – until much later when he grew up. Once a secretary of Monty's asked me, 'What do you think about Monty being a fag?' and I said, 'My brother isn't a *fag*.' Monty disliked effeminacy, and he used to talk wonderingly about how some heterosexual men are so effete and gay men so masculine.[18]

Clift's deep emotional involvements were always with women: Elizabeth Taylor, Libby Holman, Augusta Dabney and, later, Myrna Loy and Marilyn Monroe. Bill Le Massena recalls: 'He'd pick up guys and bring them back to the duplex. He'd sleep with them and that would be that. He'd get bored. Once he said to me, "I don't understand it. I love men in bed but I really love women."' Myrna

Loy, in her memoirs, made the same observation: 'He wanted men but loved women, a contradiction that tormented him. He couldn't accept it. It was a tragedy.'[19] Some of Clift's screen characters, because of his own contradictions and those of the role, appear almost presexual, their desires kept latent. It was as though he was poised on the edge of a gender image, like a lost and bewildered child.

The childlike or childish rebel was a major figure of the 1950s because the actor had been identified as a child in the eyes of society. The search for a true father was naturally a major theme, going back to *Red River*. 'Monty's sexuality,' said Elia Kazan, 'was that of a child waiting for his mother to put her arms around him.'[20] His somewhat skittish insecurity and shyness seem to stem from an excess of sensitivity. The drama in his movies lies generally in the manner in which he is forced out of his shell to attain adult status. His characters seem exasperated by the rituals and rules of adult society, and they rebel against its bland and burdensome conformity. Sometimes they try to destroy that conformity; sometimes they try to escape from it. It is hard not to think of Clift's performances when one reads Emerson's description of contemporary Transcendentalists[21] in 1842:

Their quarrel with every man they meet is not with his kind, but with his degree. There is not enough of him — that is the only fault. They prolong their privilege of childhood in this way; of doing nothing, but making immense demands on all the gladiators in the lists of action and fame. They make us feel the strange disappointment which overcasts every human youth ... With this passion for what is great and extraordinary, it cannot be wondered at that they are repelled by vulgarity and frivolity in people. They say to themselves, it is better to be alone than in bad company. And it is really a wish to be met — the wish to find society for their hope and religion — which prompts them to shun what is called society.[22]

Out of the seventeen movies Clift appeared in, seven featured him in some form of conflagration (such as the American Civil War in *Raintree County*, 1958, the Cold War in *The Defector*, 1966, the Second World War in *From Here to Eternity*, and the aftermath of that war in *Judgement at Nuremberg*, 1961). His rebel stands out in the lonely crowd, forced into action at a time of great anxiety and uncertainty. Clift plays characters who come up against authority in some shape or form: the Jew in *The Young Lions*, *Judgement at Nuremberg* and (of course) *Freud*; the step-son in *Red River*; the rebel cowboy in *The Misfits*; the compromised priest in *I Confess*; and, probably most memorably of all, the 'hard-headed' Private Prewitt in *From Here to Eternity*.

In the days immediately preceding the Japanese sneak attack, Private Robert E. Lee Prewitt is transferred into the Pearl Harbor-based company of Captain Dana Holmes (Philip Ober), an insecure commanding officer desperately in need of asserting his masculinity by having his team win the forthcoming army boxing matches. Learning that Prewitt is both an excellent bugler and a prize-winning lightweight, he offers the young soldier the position of company bugler provided he will fight on the team. Though he yearns for the position, Prewitt refuses; he once blinded a friend in the ring and is determined not to break his vow never to box again. Prewitt shows himself to be a loner, a 'hard-head'. He insists upon his individuality even though the Army tries to mould all men into an amorphous mass that acts only for the good of the unit. Someone tells him: 'In the days of the pioneers, a man could go his own way. But today ya gotta play ball!' When he hears someone saying that all men have to be treated alike, he rejoins: 'We may *look* all alike. We *ain't* all alike.' Captain Holmes decides that he must be seen to break Prewitt's spirit, so he orders his underlings to administer 'the treatment' – a brutalizing process intended to shatter a man's resistance. Prewitt finds some temporary relief during his visits to Lorene (Donna Reed), a 'hostess' at a club, a B-girl who loves him but cannot bring herself to marry a common serviceman (she wants a 'proper' reputation, 'because when you're proper, you're safe'). The one male friend he has is Angelo Maggio (Frank Sinatra), a wisecracking young Italian buck-private, who lacks Prewitt's physical strength and thus comes to admire him. Prewitt's dogged refusal to submit to his torturers is watched by Sergeant Milton A. Warden (Burt Lancaster) with a mixture of irritation and envy; although Warden is a strong, powerful man, he lacks the moral courage of Prewitt and has to take orders from his incompetent superior, Captain Holmes (whose wife he falls in love with).

Both Prewitt and Warden feel pressured by the women they love to compromise their integrity and seek career advancement — Prewitt so that he can give Lorene 'respectability', Warden so that he can safely marry his captain's ex-wife. Since both men love the Army as a kind of American ideal which power (exemplified by Captain Holmes) has corrupted, neither wants to advance to a position of power. The Army, for all its problems, is the only real 'family' either man has known. Warden has been a soldier for years, and Prewitt left home when he was seventeen: 'I'm a thirty-year man,' he tells Lorene. 'I'm in for the whole ride.' Although both men, intoxicated by love, 'weaken' and agree to acquiesce, fate intervenes to preserve the masculine solidarity: Maggio dies as a result of injuries inflicted by an Army thug who runs the stockade, and, in revenge, Prewitt goes off in search of the killer. Although he succeeds in stabbing the man to death, he too is badly wounded in the process and is forced to hide in Lorene's apartment. Captain Holmes is made to resign when his misconduct is brought to light, but Warden cannot bring himself to make a commitment to his lover. 'You're already married,' she says, 'to the Army.' The Japanese attack Pearl Harbor. Prewitt ignores Lorene's pleas and tries to return to help his company; in the darkness, he is mistaken for an invader and is killed by one of his own men. In the final scene the two women leave Hawaii on a boat for the mainland, both, in different ways, mourning their former lovers.

Private Prewitt's rebellion, it seems, can lead him only to a tragic end unless society changes the way it treats individuality. Clift described the character as 'a limited guy with an unlimited spirit'. He is forced to suffer the most irrational and nugatory aspects of his fellow men's machismo (such as their decision to make him first dig a huge hole, so that they can toss down a newspaper, and then fill it up again). In an all-male organization Prewitt assumes the onerous role traditionally accorded to women; he seems alienated from patriarchy *per se*. That knowing-rebel quality of Clift's comes through here in spite of his having to punctuate his remarks with 'ain't', which grates on the ear. The corrupt Army, even in the movie's muted portrayal, is seen as an implacably brutalizing organization, pushing the gentle Prewitt towards murder, court martial and death. A 'smarter' man, like Burt Lancaster's tough sergeant, makes his accommodation with the system and emerges a conventional hero when war brings the Army to life. A lesser figure, like Frank Sinatra's Maggio, is simply crushed trying to escape (but where to?). Prewitt's way is to return to his unit precisely when danger, both personal and corporate, threatens most. When his lover asks him for a reason for his decision, his reply has the simple dignity of tragedy: 'I'm a soldier.'

The major thematic point of the movie seems to be that the winner is the strong, selfish man (Lancaster) who can fool anybody. At the end Maggio, the company thug and Prewitt are all dead, the negligent captain is discharged in disgrace, but Lancaster's Sergeant Warden remains on the dangerous shores of Pearl Harbor. There is little doubt that he will survive the war, just as he survived the local army strife: his kind always wins; his tight fists and bright teeth and cool nerve will always see him through (who knows, one day he might even run for President . . .). Prewitt seems supremely isolated in such an environment. He gives the impression of being uncommunicative not because he is inarticulate or uneducated but because he is quietly determined to overcome the obstacles that face him. The most famous scene in the movie features Prewitt standing alone in the shallow grey light of dusk, playing his 'Taps' (the last-post elegy) in memory of his murdered friend. The tears stream down his cheeks, but his eyes stare out into the distance, at the emptiness and the hopelessness. It conveys perfectly the mixture of pain, sensitivity, isolation and bravery which was the trademark of the rebel male's image and which reflected Clift's own solitary, relatively unhappy personality.

Clift's performances are depictions of marginal figures − social outsiders, outlaws or *émigrés* − whose narrative predicaments emphatically mirror their psychological states of marginality and of verbal and social alienation as they are expressed in the acting performances themselves. Clift's technique is able, at certain moments of tension and drama, to leave behind language and social interaction in all of its rhetorically nuanced manifestations, and to offer in its place the concept of the primordial cave of the mouth and a sense of the body as an animal reality, beneath or outside of all social forms, understandings and arrangements of experience. Silences, gutturals, gasps or gestures replace poised or controlled verbal and social interactions. This rebel male offers private intensities of feeling and imagination in place of the codes of interactions legitimized by society, business, politics or the family. Romanticism has left the lyric poem and found its way on to the performative stage of the modern world. Arthur Miller observed: 'Monty had a culture behind him. He could read; he could think. It doesn't hurt for an actor, who wants to attempt more and more things, to have a brain in his head. He could have done the great roles.'[23]

What caused Clift's disenchantment with his movies was the feeling that his characters were consistently being compromised by 'unrealistic' plots. *Red River* is notorious for its thoroughly contradictory and unconvincingly 'upbeat' ending, and Clift believed that many of his rebellious figures were similarly undermined by Hollywood's eagerness to give its audiences a 'positive' resolution. Consequently, he started to reject an extraordinary series of starring roles in movies such as *On the Waterfront* and *Désirée* (1954) (both of which passed on to Marlon Brando), *East of Eden* (which was eventually made with James Dean), *A Star is Born* (1954) and *Cat on a Hot Tin Roof* (1958) (which finally appeared with Paul Newman, who was then hailed as 'the new Montgomery Clift'). Between 1953 and 1958 Clift turned down 143 movie projects. He tried another stage play – *The Seagull* (a *New York Times* critic praised his 'lonely, brooding Constantin . . . beautifully expressed without any foolish pathology') – but he was now a movie star, and movie stars of his stature were not allowed to turn their backs on their screen 'image'.

He did not have serious financial worries that necessitated any rash ventures, although he had entirely overlooked the need to pay tax and would eventually require additional funds. His old drive slowed down and his self-abuse speeded up (Clift's thorough knowledge of drugs seems to rule out theories of accidental misuse). He agreed to appear in *Raintree County* mainly out of loyalty to his old friend Elizabeth Taylor. He did not like the story, and felt disenchanted and irritable with everyone except Taylor. Half-way through shooting, she gave a small dinner party in his honour on the evening of 12 May 1956. As far as his admirers were concerned, he was probably at the peak of his career. The producers had warned him that his drinking was sometimes affecting his perform-ance, and he had promised them he would try to be sober for the remainder of the movie. Taylor's party was intended as an oppor-tunity for Clift's friends to coax him out of his current depression. Clift was withdrawn and dishevelled, complaining of exhaustion, and at 11.30 he excused himself politely and left. He muttered a complaint about having to drive back down the twisting road in the dark (it was his chauffeur's night off). Kevin McCarthy, a fellow guest, went ahead of Clift in order to guide him down the steep canyon into Sunset Boulevard. In McCarthy's rear-view mirror it was soon evident that Clift was losing control of his vehicle. Twenty minutes later, he was pounding on Taylor's front door, yelling for help: 'Monty's been in an accident! I think he's dead.' Taylor and the other guests arrived at the scene of the crash to find Clift's car crushed against a telephone pole; it had smashed through the guard rail at the foot of the twisting mountain road. The engine was still running and there was a strong smell of petrol. McCarthy feared an explosion. Taylor crawled over the front seat to try to free Clift from the wreckage. His body was jammed under the dashboard and his face was a bloody, unrecognizable pulp. Taylor somehow managed to comfort him while waiting for an ambulance to arrive, but he seemed completely helpless. She managed to remove a tooth he was beginning to choke on. His face was severely swollen; he had numerous cuts, especially under the eyes; his lips had been lacerated badly, and a hole gouged right through the middle of his upper lip; two front teeth had been knocked down his throat; his jaw was broken in four separate places; his nose was broken in two; and one whole upper cheekbone was broken, with cracks running into the sinus area. Incredibly, the rest of his body had escaped serious injury – only his face, his famous face, the face of 'the most beautiful man in Hollywood', had been wrecked. The principal damage was underneath the skin, to the bones (and to the psyche); only limited plastic surgery was necessary. Eventually, he was able, with the help of painkilling drugs (from now on a life-long necessity), to complete *Raintree County* and allow the audience to indulge in ghoulish attempts to spot those scenes that were completed after the tragic accident.

Although Clift had made what in the circumstances represented a remarkable and courageous recovery, nothing was ever the same for him again. Rock Hudson, who was one of the guests at Taylor's party, said that the accident 'was the beginning of the end for him, a long-drawn-out hell-on-earth time for the poor guy'. A typical ectomorph, Clift had always been more prone to physical ailments than most. Not surprisingly, his health now started to deteriorate. His blood pressure would rise to dangerously high levels at one moment, then sink to relatively normal levels the next; he developed sebaceous cysts; his intestines (already damaged by his amoebic dysentery and colitis) were soon wrecked by alcohol; he developed a thyroid condition, intensifying his nervousness and causing a bulging of the eyes; his left cheek was paralysed, and he later suffered from cataracts; and the crash left him with frequent sharp pains in the head, which he numbed through drugs and drink. His final decade was described by one of his old teachers, Bobby Lewis, as 'the slowest suicide in show business'.

The main change in Clift's appearance on screen in the scenes from *Raintree County* concerned his eyes. A cameraman said, 'They had a dead quality ... They were always slightly bloodshot and veiny. We had a hell of a time trying to compensate. All we could do was give him a little softness and photograph him so that the camera never saw two eyes at the same time.'[24] Actor Jack Larson felt that Clift's eyes 'were still brilliant and glittering and they stared right through you, but they were now brim-full of pain'.[25] His old colleagues were shocked by the manner in which the youthful appearance had aged and altered so suddenly. Elia Kazan wrote, 'He was no longer handsome, and there was strain everywhere in him – even, it seemed, in his effort to stand erect.'[26] However, after a while Clift came to the conclusion that he still had a career in movies. A friend claims that Clift was one day found looking into a mirror, weeping and saying, 'I still have a *face* . . .'[27] Certainly, his face, though it now had its bad angles, was still striking and expressive; it was now the face of a very experienced middle-aged man. He had to find new ways of using his appearance, different methods of communicating his inner thoughts and sensations. As he said to W. J. Weatherby, 'I had to try to master myself, find the real me outside my looks which people were hung up on and so was I.'[28]

Clift was still receiving plenty of movie offers, but their quality began to deteriorate. Male actor friends were warned by studio bosses that it was becoming bad for their image to be seen as a close friend of that 'queer' Monty Clift. For stars like Clift, the question of insurability was a serious problem. Starting in the mid-1950s, no major movie company would use a star who could not be insured against sudden inability to work (Marilyn Monroe was a special case; her 'bankability' as a box-office draw was simply undeniable). Clift knew he was in danger of being ostracized by the studios, and he sometimes felt destined to fail. Inge Morath (who later married Arthur Miller) remembers Clift telephoning her late one night, reciting German poetry to her: 'He spoke beautiful German – and his knowledge of German poets was quite marvellous, but they were all young, tragic, beautiful poets who'd died before they were thirty.'[29] His personality seemed to fragment into a cluster of competing selves. To some he was a miserable, fatalistic figure, while to others he was full of hope and determination. In 1957 he emerged from his cocoon to sign for another movie. No one was quite sure how he would cope.

The Young Lions featured Clift as Noah Ackerman, a lonely Jew (a racial counterpart to Clift's sexual outcast), alongside Dean Martin as Marco Whiteacre, a Broadway entertainer – two US soldiers during the Second World War. The story of their friendship runs parallel to the growing confusion of a young Nazi officer, Christian Diestl (Marlon Brando). Eventually, by accident, the two Americans come across Diestl, mistake his attempt to surrender as an attack and shoot him. Early on Ackerman says, 'I don't think I have a single opinion in the whole world.' As the story develops, he is forced to change his mind. Years before, Clift had torn a picture of Franz Kafka from a magazine. He studied it almost daily and now, with its narrow, skeletal face and prominent ears, the portrait became the inspiration for the character of Noah Ackerman. Clift starved himself down from 150 to 139 pounds, distended his ears with putty and slightly altered the shape of his nose. He plays Ackerman as a Jewish version of Prewitt: both are 'hard-heads', determined to be true to their own principles. They both have a self-destructive resolve to go against the prevailing system. The chief difference is that Ackerman, unlike Prewitt, is accompanied by a loyal friend and he survives to marry the woman he loves. Hope Plowman (Hope Lange), a young Christian woman from Vermont, is attracted to the dark, urban Ackerman because his delicate vulnerability and decent honesty strike her as preferable to the glittering, superficial sincerity she finds in most of her non-Jewish men friends. The way in which her conservative father comes eventually to accept this 'exotic' outsider is unsatisfyingly fanciful – a forced resolution of Ackerman's rebel status. Further evidence of the movie's inexorable conformity is the conventional process whereby Ackerman 'proves' his manhood to his anti-Semitic fellow soldiers. As in *From Here to Eternity*, the young rebel is subjected to a number of harsh lessons (they confiscate his copy of Joyce's *Ulysses*, they insult him verbally and physically, and they punish him with naked violence). He is pushed to the limit and, like Prewitt, challenges the platoon's strongest men to a fight. His valiant counter-attack wins their respect and he is welcomed back by his former enemies (he even gets his book back). The movie encourages one to see Ackerman as an 'honorary Gentile' (his father-in-law sees he is not just an ordinary Jew) and a man who, beneath the sensitive exterior, is as tough and as combative as the thugs who harass him (so all is well after all . . .). Even his sexual inadequacy is eventually resolved. Early on, when he fails to notice an attractive woman walk past, Whiteacre remarks, 'Hey, your antenna's switched off!' At the end of the movie, he has a wife and child. This is the conservatism of *From Here to Eternity* without its tragic ending. Noah Ackerman is a rebel male who is welcomed back into society through a thoroughly implausible denouement. Clift now lacks the formerly prodigious range of techniques necessary to undermine this sense of predestination, although his efforts, in context, are none the less quite captivating. His performance, coming after such a traumatic accident, is certainly remarkable. Many of his familiar mannerisms remain: the habit of putting a cigarette in his mouth by folding his hand over it and placing it on his lower lip; the way he bounces on his toes when he walks; the way his eyes search his lover's face in that distinctive expression of yearning. He uses these gestures in place of words. The prison sequence, especially, is almost wordless; the emotional urgency of the young couple is communicated through fleeting looks and small gestures. It seems that the prospect of acting with his greatest rival, Marlon Brando (although they do not really 'share' any scenes), gave Clift the competitive edge he needed. Indeed, the two men struggled to out-perform each other. The breaking-point came when Brando tried to turn his death scene into a bizarre form of crucifixion, the Nazi rolling down a hill with barbed wire tangled up in his hair. 'Look at Marlon!' exclaimed Clift. 'He can't stand not being sympathetic. He's turning that bastard Nazi into a martyr!' On Clift's insistence, the scene was rejected, and he preserved his authority over Brando.

From the late 1950s onwards, Clift was obliged to husband his energy in a fairly ruthless way. It was too late in his career for him to alter his passionate, committed approach to performing, yet he no longer possessed the stamina to cope with long, demanding roles. He tried to concentrate on the cameo performance, the series of short scenes, the emotion-charged fragment. *Suddenly Last Summer* (1959) featured a pacific Clift, his character little more than a receptacle for the neuroses of the female characters. 'I'm afraid I'd make a miserable jester,' he says. 'You see, I get concerned when people stop wanting to cry.' His voice sounds on the verge of breaking, his face looks immobile and he is somewhat glassy-eyed. Mercedes McCambridge, who acted with Clift in the movie, recalls: 'Monty was in torment. I can see him now, with his shoulder blades hunched and pinched in that way of his . . . there was always that terrible tension.' The pain was often unbearable for Clift, and the painkilling drugs put him in a trance-like state; his performances were consequently withdrawn and passive in nature, which served to emphasize the 'feminine' aspects of his later screen characters. For example, in Kazan's *Wild River* (1960) Lee Remick's woman is dominant and decisive to Clift's fragile, indecisive man. Remick said Clift arrived on set looking 'like a wounded bird – so vulnerable'. Kazan felt that Clift's acting had 'a sensitivity so complete that it rather unmanned him. He quivered with emotion and this was not generally useful.'[30] Remick, in the love scenes, instinctively drew him to her rather than the reverse – an accident of personality which Kazan exploited. His brief role in *Judgement at Nuremberg*, playing a castrated Jew called Rudolf Petersen, was a tremendous strain, with his hands shaking throughout the shooting. *Freud* practically destroyed him; he could no longer move his body with ease and was forced to concentrate on expressing emotions through his hand gestures. His director, John Huston, appalled at what he saw as Clift's 'weakness' and 'unmanly conduct', tried to scare him into performing by threatening to beat him up if he continued to forget his lines.

Huston, a self-styled disciple of 'Papa' Hemingway, could not understand why any man could not solve any of his neuroses by playing a good game of poker, or drinking a few glasses of Jack Daniel's, or maybe wrestling with a wild horse. He believed Clift was weak because he 'allowed' himself to be a 'pervert'. Angela Allen (Huston's assistant) told me of the increasingly hysterical campaign against Clift and his friends: 'A doctor was sent over from London to view outtakes to certify that Monty was brain-damaged – this was done behind our backs – and our phones were tapped, and we were sometimes followed.'[31] The more Clift suffered, the more unforgiving Huston became. The cast and crew could only look on as the tension grew (Angela Allen remembers her response when, years later, Huston told her he was writing his memoirs: 'I can't *wait* to see how you explain *Freud*!'). The movie's publicists tried to spice the publicity with some sly innuendo on the posters: 'Alone he fought against his own dark passions . . . knowing that the shocking truth could ruin his career.' After this harrowing experience, Clift was in need of almost constant professional care. It was becoming almost impossible for any studio to insure him, and each performance began to look like his last. Arthur Miller, with an odd mixture of compassion and cruelty, wrote a part for him so clearly based on his own personality (one of his lines was to be, 'No, my face is all healed up, good as new . . .') that it was impossible for anyone else to take on the role.

The Misfits appealed to Clift because the part of Perce Howland involved only fairly short, intense scenes, allowing him to concentrate all his energy on them. 'Everyone says it's *me*,' he said. The plot focused upon three misfit cowboys (Clift, Clark Gable and Eli Wallach) who drive wild horses out of the mountains in order to trap them and sell them for dog food. Roslyn (Marilyn Monroe) is a recent divorcée who comes to confront the pointless machismo of these anachronistic figures. Perce, who is younger than the other two men, is the only one open to Roslyn's argument for compassion. His first appearance comes as Roslyn and the two cowboys are driving to a rodeo. We see him in a glass-enclosed telephone booth beside the highway. He is speaking to his mother, telling her about a silver buckle he won ('Ain't you *proud*?') and arguing about his step-father. The two-minute scene is one of Clift's finest pieces of acting. He seems to be merely shrugging and uttering a few half-swallowed words, but his behaviour has so much weight and urgency and conviction that it enlarges the meaning of the scene. As in *Red River*, the rebel is still in conflict with his parents: 'Ma? Say hello to Frieda and Victoria, will you? . . . OK, say hello to him, too. No, Ma, it just slipped my mind, that's all . . . *OK!* I'm sayin' it *now*! . . . Well, *you* married him, I didn't! Tell him hello from me. Maybe I'll call you Christmas . . . Hello? Hello?' He chews his lip, the connection cut, looks down with great sadness and (with his anxiety giving way to a grave sense of disappointment) mumbles into the dead receiver: 'God bless you, too.'

The other memorable scene with Perce takes place when he becomes dizzy after dancing in the saloon. Roslyn takes him outside to get some air. She sits on a broken car seat with her back against the wrecked body of an old Chevrolet, while Perce is stretched out with his head resting in her lap. He looks up at her and grieves for his lost past: his mother's defection, the insult when his step-father offered him wages on the range *he* was supposed to inherit (more than a hint of an Oedipal motif here) and the girl he lost to his 'friends' when he was out cold after the last rodeo. He is reaching out to Roslyn, hoping that she will respond but knowing that she is involved with an older man. As she strokes his head, he gazes up at her. Their despairing directness with each other becomes a metaphor for acute sensitivity that is often poetically touching. Off screen, Monroe and Clift were drawn to each other: 'I look at him and see the brother I never had and feel braver and get protective,' said Monroe. It was certainly an important relationship for both of them and, although it remained a largely platonic affair, Clift confessed, 'We fooled around a lot.' He later admitted that they had one abortive attempt at love-making but they were both too drunk. 'Maybe Marilyn and I would have gotten together one day if we weren't so much alike. As it is, it's too much like brother and sister getting together.'[32] Brooks Clift recalls his brother remarking of Monroe: 'She's the most, for me, rewarding actress I've ever worked with. I could look into her eyes and whatever way I read what I read, she heard it all, so we were both listening.'[33]

Perce Howland, like so many of Clift's rebel males, is painfully frail in appearance, wire-drawn, thin-spun and fugitive, essentially unanchored to the earth. Sometimes his masculinity just evaporates, leaving nothing but ambiguity. Angela Allen told me that she once 'had to stop a scene because Monty's walk was too camp, and John [Huston] hadn't noticed. Monty hadn't done it deliberately. That's how Monty walked!' It was only around women that he seemed at ease. There was little suggestion of anything sexual, but in several movies, including *A Place in the Sun* and *The Misfits*, one sees a symbolic shift of allegiance from the mother to the mother substitute: George Eastman and Perce Howland both speak to their mothers on the telephone as their young female friends watch, and later they are seen with their heads resting in the laps of the young women, seeking comfort. Arthur Miller, when he advised Clift on how to play *The Seagull* on stage, elicited a reaction which revealed how profoundly Clift's relationship with his mother still plagued him:

I talked to the actors a couple of afternoons, searching out some consistent metaphoric line they might follow, but nothing took except one remark that Monty repeated for years to come, even into the shooting of *The Misfits* some seven years on. As Treplev, he was not quite sure why he commits suicide, and I suggested that he thinks of Treplev aiming the revolver through his own head at Arkadina, his mother. This idea absolutely delighted him and made him wish his suicide occurred on-stage instead of off-stage.[34]

Clift remained, even into his thirties and forties, a painfully vulnerable person who seemed, in some odd way, abandoned. He became a kind of mothering symbol. Maureen Stapleton recalled an incident during the making of *Lonelyhearts* that underlined Clift's fragility :

Once, we were sitting in my dressing-room waiting for our call and he was laying with his head in my lap. He had always suffered from insomnia, now it was worse. I looked down, and found he had fallen asleep, and I began to cry as I looked at this childlike figure before me and I just held him there until he woke up.[35]

Myrna Loy recalls: 'Monty inspired the maternal instincts of the women around him. You wanted to protect him. He was really terribly timid beneath it all. Yet, if he was sure of you, he could be a bit of a rascal. He used his keen intuition and sensitivity to his advantage. He knew how to get to you.'[36] Angela Allen observed that Clift always responded to women's advice: 'He sometimes behaved outrageously in public. I'd say, "For God's sake *behave*, Monty!" You see he would accept it from women. Men would *never* speak so directly to Monty. I think he liked that directness.' Both Elizabeth Taylor and Marilyn Monroe felt that Clift was one of the few people to take them seriously as sentient, feeling human beings. 'He was the kindest, gentlest, most understanding man I have ever known,' Taylor told journalist Eleanor Harris. 'He was like my brother. He was my dearest, most devoted friend.' Both women were fiercely protective: Taylor (in an extraordinary gesture of loyalty) arranged to guarantee Clift's insurance in order for him to appear with her in *Reflections in a Golden Eye* (he died before the movie was made – Brando took over the part); Monroe defended him against the movie bosses and the *Hollywood Confidential* gossip columnists (she exclaimed, 'People who aren't fit to open the door for him sneer at his homosexuality. What do they know about it ?').

Strangely enough, in spite of four Oscar nominations and a string of excellent performances, no single movie ever gave Clift 'mythic' status. It was, ultimately, a disappointing career. It promised so much more than it actually realized, and too often the fine performances were undermined by unworthy vehicles. He was a more generous actor than Brando, helping his fellow performers and eschewing the opportunities for scene-stealing. Apart from Prewitt (and that role is in a movie with two or three other leading men), Clift did not play the obvious eye-catching roles: there is no Stanley Kowalski or Terry Malloy, no Jim Stark. He turned them all down, and nothing else came to replace them. His subtlety allowed him to play each character without becoming typecast but, although he preferred this approach, he did start to feel rather abandoned by the critics and fans. In the last of his Academy Award nominated performances, as the sterilized mental incompetent Rudolf Petersen, Clift turns a modest cameo appearance into an unforgettable personal drama, drawing on his anxieties about his relationship with his mother and his masculinity. In court, Petersen takes the stand. He fumbles and falters during his testimony, and his eyes wander. One can hear his breathing as he struggles to deal with the questions. He frowns, scratches his eyebrow, twitches, shifts in his seat, drops then raises his voice. He makes a fist, tightly clenched, then splays his fingers along the edge of the witness box, as though motion will help him think. Clift's carefully nuanced performance is agonizingly credible and poignant. He breaks down in tears as he acknowledges how he was castrated. When it is suggested that his mother was feeble-minded, he takes an old picture of her from his pocket and shows it to the judge, several feet away, and implores: 'I want that you tell me – was she feeble-minded – my mother? Was she?' It is probably the most deeply affecting moment in the movie, and it is Clift's last great performance.

Clift's attempts at recovering his strength and self-confidence took place in relative isolation. Nearly all of his friends had deserted him. His final movie, *The Defector* (released, posthumously, in 1966), was a poor spy story and he agreed to do it only to prove he could get through a role without delays due to ill-health. His scenes show for the most part a demoralized, weary actor with a gaunt face and a body so emaciated that the insides seem boneless. A glazed, pained look of mute misery never leaves his eyes. He was very much aware he had destroyed himself physically. It was an unworthy ending to an illustrious œuvre. On 23 July 1966 Clift died of an occlusive coronary artery disease; he was forty-five years old. Against his own expressed wishes and those of his brother and sister, his mother arranged for him to have a Quaker burial. His grave was identified by a simple granite marker.

In the 1950s movie audiences were looking for new heroes – unconventional ones. Montgomery Clift fulfilled that need, and inspired an entire generation of young actors. As Brando said: 'In some ways Monty's success made possible my success.' The loners, the stubborn idealists he played, the self-absorbed young men alienated from their culture, made him more than just a visual icon and fantasy figure. 'You dreamt about him,' said a fan, 'but you related to him too.' He dispelled the cosy notion that handsome young men could sail through the difficult, paranoiac post-war years unscathed. The screenwriter William Goldman has remarked, 'Clift, for me, is the most overlooked of the great stars. His was a talent that ranked right up with Brando's.'[37] 'He was the exception to my theory that a movie star has to be ignored to be good,' said

Truman Capote. 'He knew exactly what he was doing. I once asked him why he wanted to act in movies and why he didn't want to do something more interesting and he looked at me and said, "You don't understand. It's my life. It's all I know." He was an artist and had all of an artist's sensibilities and flaws.'[38] W. J. Weatherby observed that Clift 'always gave me the impression of someone who wanted to cry but had decided to try to laugh it off'.[39] The indeterminacy of the image was part of its appeal. He was as much the poet of anxiety as he was the victim of society. Clift's rebellion was not consciously political or social, nor did he pretend to be Bohemian. He was a sensitive, sensual, anguished young man seeking to discover and define his identity. None the less, in doing so he did raise some doubts about the nature of American culture and, in an indirect way, expressed some of the dark uneasiness that existed in the 1950s. He liked to quote the line from Emerson, 'Heroes usually become bores'. Clift was never boring. As he once told his brother:

If one is not a troubled man, problems can be solved easily in one day, but life is too complicated for such glibness, particularly if you're an actor. You cannot play out your life as a middle-of-the-roader or you'll never learn anything about yourself or other people. Whatever hurt may happen, you've got to force yourself to keep on being able to be deeply involved and open to whatever happens – an innocent.[40]

3

Marlon Brando

It is difficult to know something and to act as if you did not know it.
Ludwig Wittgenstein

'When one stops seeking to find out who one is,' said Marlon
Brando, 'one has reached the end of the rope.'[1] When Charles
Chaplin first saw Brando act, he exclaimed, 'He's *dangerous!*' Audiences agreed: Brando was unsettling. Critics described him as 'the
Valentino of the bop generation', 'the male Garbo', or 'the walking
hormone factory'. He was the most celebrated American actor of
the 1950s and one of its most powerful sex symbols. The contradictions were fascinating: he was the star who despised the idea of
stardom, the powerful man who doubted his own masculinity, the
movie idol who showed contempt for the movies. Montgomery
Clift brought realism to the rebel male; Marlon Brando brought
danger. Brando's rebel is anti-bourgeois, anti-adult, ready to take on
the world. There is no law, no convention, no teacher, no preacher,
no power that can turn him back. He pulled no punches; he offered
no solutions and was responsible for nobody but himself. The
adolescents who thrilled to Brando's unflinching portrayal of their
world had parents who were appalled by his 'pernicious' influence;
the students who admired his commitment to radical causes often
came from towns where his movies were banned. From America's
heartland came its anti-hero.

Brando was a challenge. His selection of roles, his approach to
performances, his off-screen activities – these had symbolic implications, even cultural consequences, that no performing career had
previously had in the minds of a substantial portion of his audience.

He was capable of exhibiting strong masculine bravado while through the same character displaying the inarticulate, mumbling insecurities of the awkward post-adolescent male who feels trapped by the repressive society that was America in the 1950s. His tendency to avoid learning his lines, his insolent distaste for the profession of acting itself and his outright hatred of studio executives have added to his mass popular appeal and enhanced his image as an eternal rebel. He possessed the physique of a fighter and the broken nose which, in the words of his make-up man, 'dripped down his face like melted ice-cream'. Brando was a lonely boy who grew into a solitary man, withdrawn and brooding, seemingly unfriendly and yet forever campaigning against social and political injustices.

He was born in Omaha, Nebraska, on 3 April 1924, the third and youngest child of Marlon and Dorothy Brando. Both parents came from old American prairie stock, originally French on the father's side (the family name was once spelled 'Brandeau'). The Brandos were comfortably middle-class, Mid-western people, prosperous enough to employ several servants. Marlon Senior was regarded as a minor pillar of Omaha society; he was a manufacturer of chemical feed products and insecticides, and made a good living from the trade. However, behind the immaculate Episcopalian front was an aggressive, temperamental man who stole away for sexual excitement in the brothels of Chicago; a teetotaller at home but a drinker out of town. Dorothy Pennebaker Brando ('Dodie' to her friends) was a cultivated, sensitive woman (a Mid-western Madame Bovary) with ideas that were regarded as 'liberal and advanced' for a rural community of Bible readers. She was, in stark contrast to her solemn husband, an outgoing, gregarious individual. She wrote, painted, sculpted and acted. Acting was her great passion. She was an important figure in the highly respected Omaha Community Playhouse, a semi-professional theatre group which served as a training school for young actors such as Henry Fonda (a family friend) and Dorothy McGuire.

Marlon (nicknamed 'Bud' by his parents to distinguish him from his father) had two older sisters, Jocelyn and Frances. Dodie raised her children in what used to be termed the 'progressive method' of upbringing: she stressed self-expression and underplayed discipline. Her two daughters were exemplary pupils; her son, however, was a mischievous little boy with a disdain for 'correct' behaviour. It seems likely that his family's frequent relocations contributed to his distaste for formal education. Shortly after Marlon's sixth birthday, his father's business concerns obliged the family to move: first to Evanston, Illinois, then California, Minnesota and, finally, Illinois once again. In 1936, when 'Bud' was twelve, the family settled in Libertyville, Illinois, a prosperous town on Lake Michigan. The Brandos moved into a three-storey house with ample grounds and a wide assortment of livestock. It is said that Brando drew on his memories of this time when he improvised a monologue in *Last Tango in Paris* (1972):

My father was a drunk, a screwed-up bar fighter. My mother was also a drunk. My memories as a kid are of her being arrested. We lived in a small town, a farming community. I used to have to milk a cow every morning and every night, and I liked that. But I remember one time I was all dressed up to take this girl to a basketball game. My father said, 'You have to milk the cow', and I said, 'Would you please milk it for me?' He said, 'No, get your ass out of there.' I was in a hurry, and I didn't have time to change my shoes, and I had cowshit all over my shoes. Later on, it smelled in the car . . . I can't remember many good things.

Interviewed by Truman Capote, Brando described his childhood as a fairly traumatic period, with a 'relentlessly masculine' father and an affectionate mother. 'My father was indifferent to me,' he recalled. 'Nothing I could do interested him, or pleased him.'[2] As a young boy he had been very frightened by his father's party trick, which involved taking lemon peel, slicing it into a zig-zag pattern and placing it in his mouth, growling like a beast (Brando introduced this old trick into his final scene in *The Godfather*, 1972 – an ironic tribute to Marlon Senior). His mother, he said, 'was everything to me'. Dodie's growing awareness of her husband's crass affairs drove her into periodic alcoholic binges. Marlon learned about the seriousness of her condition when he was in his early teens. Returning home from school one day, he found the house empty and the telephone ringing. He was informed that his mother was at a bar, drunk, and needed to be collected. All three children were, by this stage, well aware of their parents' troubled relationship. Marlon came to side with his mother, yet in a way he continued to strive to emulate his father – who remained unresponsive to his efforts.

School remained a tiresome obligation for Marlon. He sought relief from the boredom in exhibitionism: he pestered his fellow students, aggravated their parents and overtaxed the most patient of teachers. He was the kind of pupil who sat at the back of the class, furtively planning irreverent gestures and pranks. He discovered a blend of wool which, when set alight, would blaze menacingly before harmlessly extinguishing itself. He used this for his favourite 'shock effect', which involved running into crowded rooms with his sweater on fire. He also liked to interrupt adult conversations and deliver lengthy, unorthodox opinions on a variety of subjects – fascism, communism, FDR, the latest plays and movies – with a glib authority that belied his total ignorance of what he was discussing (the form was what mattered). Some of his teachers recall him as an unruly pupil, obsessed with disrupting the class with calculated clowning (such as his request to be excused in order to get his spectacles, with the teacher unaware that they were at a distance of four miles from the school). Other teachers remember him as a rather remote, dreamy child: 'I'd ask him a question and he wouldn't even hear me call his name. He'd be staring out of the window, lost in thought.'

Marlon was actually a fairly ungainly-looking adolescent. His eyesight was poor and he was forced to wear a pair of thick glasses (which he removed whenever his parents were elsewhere). He wore dental braces and consequently felt acutely self-conscious about smiling and revealing his teeth. He also suffered from a tendency to put on weight and, when a teenager, he voluntarily embarked upon a physical fitness programme. It was probably the only decision that pleased his father, who encouraged him to develop a more 'manly' physique and to excel at sports. He became a good, fast runner, and did well at football and track events. However, one day he injured himself during a game, fracturing a leg and kneecap, and his sporting activities came to an end. Shortly after this accident, he was expelled from Libertyville High School, apparently for smoking in the gymnasium. It was his junior year. Dodie wanted her son to finish his education at an experimental school where problematic but gifted children were guided towards constructive forms of creativity. Marlon Senior, however, insisted that what his son really needed was discipline. In 1942 Marlon was enrolled at Shattuck Military Academy in Faribault, Minnesota.

Brando detested Shattuck. He spent much time feigning illness and for a long period affected a limp. One teacher recalled that Brando would do 'anything to duck out of assignments, classes, duties'. The daily schedule was extremely rigid. The students were woken up at 5.45 each morning. They showered, then prepared their uniforms for inspection. After early-morning drill, everyone went off for classes, which started at 8.30. In the afternoon there were military hikes and exercises, and then compulsory athletics. After a full hour of military formation drill, classroom study lasted from 7.30 to 9.00, with lights out at 9.30. Brando was fairly popular with his classmates, who enjoyed his irreverence and good humour. He developed a magnificent physique, and took advantage of the rigorous exercise programmes. He even found time to read Shakespeare – usually when he was supposed to be on duty outside. The school tolerated him until May 1943, when he was expelled for smoking – done not from enjoyment or conviction but simply because it was forbidden. He did not join the millions of his fellow Americans fighting in Africa and the Pacific; he failed his draft medical exam. The appropriate records are inaccessible, but Brando claims he pretended to be psychologically disturbed. A more plausible explanation is that his earlier injury on the football field had left him with permanent cartilage damage.

Brando was nineteen years of age, without any notable talents or any qualifications. The future must have seemed dismal. He later claimed that an acting career was something he 'just drifted into'. His mother's enduring love of the theatre must have had some influence on his decision (and his sister Jocelyn was beginning her own acting career). His father, predictably, was horrified by his son's acting ambitions. Acting, he informed his family, was a profession reserved for 'faggots and fairies'. After much debate, Marlon Senior agreed to finance a trial period at an acting school. If, after six months, 'Bud' had made no impression on his teachers, he agreed to return to Libertyville and a job in the insecticide business.

Jocelyn Brando was studying at Erwin Piscator's Dramatic Workshop at the New School for Social Research in New York. In 1943 Marlon joined her, and was assigned Stella Adler as his teacher. Like other Mid-westerners arriving in New York City for the first time, Brando was captivated by its urgency and diversity. It seemed a unique kind of living theatre for a young actor, with its myriad sights, smells, styles and accents — a modern world in microcosm. Brando would spend hours in Greenwich Village, wandering the streets, browsing in bookshops, going to nightclubs and sitting in cafés. He would study everyone he encountered and he could mimic their gestures and almost any accent — French, Italian, Spanish, Yiddish, German or Russian. He wore T-shirt, jeans and a leather jacket long before they became popular with the teenage rebels. He lived on hot dogs and hamburgers, Cokes and beers, and slept (he boasted) with woman after woman. To many of his contemporaries, he appeared aloof, suspicious and perhaps rather dangerous. He was certainly very competitive and extremely keen to 'improve' himself. He supplemented his acting classes with New School courses in French, fine arts and philosophy, and took lessons in dance, fencing and yoga.[3]

Stella Adler was a disciple of Stanislavsky, and the daughter of Jacob Adler, one of the great stars of the American Yiddish theatre. She had worked with the cooperative Group Theater during the 1930s, collaborating with Clifford Odets, John Garfield, Harold Clurman (her husband) and Elia Kazan. 'Stella had the deepest influence upon me,' Brando later recalled. She insisted that the actor become the instrument of the playwright's vision. Such a thesis was in contrast to Lee Strasberg's approach, which relied on actors drawing everything from within their own entrails, as a silkworm draws silk. While Strasberg emphasized Stanislavsky's notion of 'emotional recall' (finding suitable feelings and motivations for a performance in one's own private repository of experiences), Adler stressed his 'method of physical actions' (concentrating on the behaviour and actions of the character). In Adler's class, Brando was taught that acting was more than a set of technical tricks; it was a creative process in which one used every fibre of oneself to create a form for the playwright's ideas.

It was not long before Brando impressed his teacher. 'I taught him nothing,' Adler recalled. 'I opened up possibilities of thinking, feeling, experience, and I opened the doors, he walked right through. He never needed me after that . . . He lives the life of an actor twenty-four hours a day. If he is talking to you, he will absorb everything about you, your smile, the way your teeth grow. His style is the perfect marriage of intuition and intelligence.'[4] Brando certainly learned a great deal from his teachers, but it was *how* he used this knowledge that made his acting come alive. One can be taught technique, correct breathing, pace and rhythms, but there is no trustworthy way of showing an actor how to *believe* in a character, entering its reality – that is necessarily a personal, indirect process which in many ways says the most about the actor's own personality. Brando, said Adler, recognized this from the beginning and reacted with a burning desire to explore his own self. Acting offered self-analysis.

In October 1944 Brando (assisted by Adler's patronage) made his professional acting debut on Broadway in *I Remember Mama*, a series of sentimental sketches strung together by John Van Druten. There was a large cast and Brando was not especially noticeable, but the play was a great success and enjoyed a long run. In 1946 he acted in Maxwell Anderson's explosive *Truckline Café*, a roadhouse tragedy about two waitresses who stray while their husbands are serving overseas. Brando played a GI who murders his unfaithful wife and then publicly confesses his crime. Although the play closed after only thirteen performances, it was a significant experience for Brando. Harold Clurman and Elia Kazan were the producers, and they worked hard on Brando's technique during rehearsals.

At first he slouched and mumbled his lines, making his key speeches practically incomprehensible. Clurman dismissed the rest of the company and asked Brando to repeat his opening speech. 'Scream! Louder!' cried Clurman. Brando began to shout (in part out of irritation at his director's hectoring manner). 'Now roll on the floor and scream,' Clurman ordered. He then rushed up on stage and started insulting and kicking Brando, who was by this time almost hysterical. For the duration of the production, Brando never mumbled any of his lines (although his voice grew more hoarse each night). He also started to experiment with 'Stanislavskian' techniques for preparing certain dramatic moods and gestures. For one scene he had to arrive on-stage drenched, exhausted and shivering; to achieve this effect he would run up and down the lighting stairs backstage, have two buckets of cold water thrown at him and then stagger out into the spotlight. His performance, although ignored by many critics, led to Katharine Cornell casting him opposite her as Marchbanks in a Broadway revival of Shaw's *Candida*. In the same year he played a leading role in *A Flag is Born*, a pageant about Israel written by Ben Hecht to Kurt Weill music. His powerful performances started attracting the critics, who were fascinated by the unpredictable nature of his acting.

In 1947 Brando was offered the role of Stanley Kowalski in Tennessee Williams's *A Streetcar Named Desire*. John Garfield had been everybody's first choice for Stanley, but he felt the role was 'too slight' to make an impact, fearing the character would be overshadowed by Blanche DuBois. Brando made the part his own. The image was undeniably memorable. His slow blinks simultaneously betokened boredom and muted sensuality; his laconic raising and lowering of the eyebrows gave him the look of a man who could never be surprised by anything this side of the grave. Stanley may have a heart that can be touched, but he lives essentially by his muscles. Blanche DuBois is astonished when she first sets eyes on him: 'He eats like an animal, has an animal's habits! Eats like one, moves like one, talks like one! Thousands and thousands of years have passed him right by, and there he is – Stanley Kowalski – survivor of the Stone Age!' Tennessee Williams spoke of the

Clift's androgynous swagger: the suggestion of sexual ambiguity is a
quality one often perceives in his performances.

'How did you get such trust in your eyes?': Montgomery Clift and
Marilyn Monroe in *The Misfits*. 'I could look into her eyes,' said Clift,
'and whatever way I read what I read, she heard it all, so we were
both listening.'

'If I had one day when I didn't feel confused, didn't have to feel
ashamed of anything': Dean with Natalie Wood in *Rebel Without a
Cause*, putting the woman on a pedestal.

The sensual self: Brando in *A Streetcar Named Desire*.

Even when women are physically close to Clift, his thoughts seem elsewhere: pictured with Donna Reed in *From Here To Eternity*.

While the rebel male is allowed to seem more flawed and fragile, the woman is obliged to appear as a nurse–mother figure, nurturing the tortured male psyche.

'Ma, I just met her!' The cork is about to pop, and mother is set to be usurped. In *A Place in the Sun*, sex is presented as a threat, a siren's song, drawing the male into danger.

Masculinity as make-up: the surly expression is supplemented with
the distinctly unrealistic pumped-up muscles.

One of Clift's most distinctive qualities was his capacity for stillness, sensing the appropriate moment in a scene to rely entirely upon his silent presence to dominate the screen, encouraging us to study his face for signs of inner feelings.

The teenage outcast: Dean was described by Elia Kazan as a 'pudding of hatred'. His image appealed romantically to the 'hurt' children of post-war upheaval.

character's 'animal joy in his being' and his pride in 'everything that is his, that bears his emblem of the gaudy seed-bearer'. He saw Brando as a 5 foot, 9 inch, muscular mesomorph with building biceps and a powerful chest. 'He was just about the best-looking man I had ever seen,' sighed Williams. It was as if, the playwright thought, Brando had been born to play Stanley. Brando certainly seemed to live the part. He became more crude and aggressive off-stage, and did little to endear himself to the rest of the cast. During each evening's performance there was a twenty-minute period when Brando was not needed on stage, and he spent the time working out with weights, jogging outside the theatre or, sometimes, making love to 'whoever was handy'. On one occasion he took part in a boxing match in the theatre's boiler room and broke his nose; he went back on-stage with blood dripping on to his white T-shirt. Ironically, the accident helped his image. Irene Selznick wanted him to have the nose rebroken and set, but later she realized that the 'imperfection' contributed to his sex appeal. The impression now was one of disturbed beauty, the Mid-western ideal unsettled, offset, by the trace of eastern violence.

Brando was a critical success with his performance in *Streetcar*. The movie executives visited New York to see him. *Life* magazine featured a story on the Brando family. A few select reporters were, eventually, allowed to interview him. He hated the experience and did his best to frustrate them by beating away on his bongo drums, mumbling meaningless comments about Spinoza and Schopenhauer, or going for a swim during the middle of a question. He started to feel bored playing Stanley Kowalski. Stanislavsky said, 'You must live the part every moment you are playing it', and Brando no longer felt able to do so. He left the play in the middle of 1949. He travelled across Europe – first to Paris, then to Rome, Naples and Sicily. It was a disorienting period for the young man from Nebraska and he returned to New York full of doubts about his reasons for acting as a career. Elia Kazan encouraged him to try psychoanalysis and, after some hesitation, he did so. 'I was afraid of analysis at first,' he recalled. 'Afraid it might destroy the impulses that made me creative, an artist. A sensitive person receives fifty impressions where somebody else may get only seven.' He added: 'I just put on an act sometimes, and people think I'm insensitive. Really, it's like a kind of armour because I'm too sensitive. If there are 200 people in a room and one of them doesn't like me, I've got to get out.'[5]

The performing ego is a delicate one; it requires tremendous nerve to appear in front of an audience. Too many errors, too many rebuffs, sometimes a single show of disapproval, can shatter that requisite combination of skill, experience and egoism – a combination that has to be reconstituted on schedule. Brando developed his talent for acting only to discover that he was being applauded for something inside him that seemed, to some extent, outside his conscious control. An actor in the older, more contrived, style would have found it much easier to take. Brando, however, considered his acting skills to be the product of psychic weakness. It was hoped that analysis would provide a direction for the art. With the success of Clift and Brando in achieving that tense balance between emotion and repression came the more insupportable image, nurtured by the publicists, which directors and colleagues responded to with charges of 'temperament'. Self-protection and retreat became the answer in private life as well. Montgomery Clift had, unwittingly, acted as a guide to Brando. His career, and its pressures, were carefully followed by Brando.

Brando admired Clift's economy of gesture, his graceful spontaneity and subtle inventiveness. Indeed, Brando spent a great deal of his free time during this period studying actors who possessed a gift for gentle suggestion, which he felt he lacked. He was particularly impressed by such actors as Paul Muni, Cary Grant, Gérard Philipe and Spencer Tracy ('The way he holds back, *holds back* . . .'). 'An actor is at most a poet, and at least an entertainer,' said Brando. 'You can't be a poet by really trying hard. It's like being charming. You can't be charming by working at it. Also, if an actor holds back 20 per cent, he'll always be honest with his audience. Try to show more than you've got to give and they catch on right away.' Brando was never someone who enjoyed acting simply in order to exhibit himself. On the contrary, he acted in order to impersonate, asserting himself without revealing too much of his own insecure self. 'Actors have to observe, and I enjoy that part of it,' he said. 'They have to know how much spit you have in your mouth, and where the weight of your elbows is. I could sit all day in the Otimo Cigar Store telephone booth on 42nd Street and just watch the people pass by.' Stage acting, he felt, sometimes undermined his desire for a more intimate, subtle style. He was often obliged to seem unnatural, projecting his voice and exaggerating his gestures. The movie offers he had been receiving grew more tempting. As he said:

No stage actor's training can be considered complete until he has first made a picture. It is the toughest form of acting, and anyone who can come through it successfully can call himself an actor for the first time. When you have to portray a shattering emotion while realizing at the back of your mind that if you move your head an inch too much out of focus and out of frame, that's acting.[6]

Brando began with a good actor's instrument: his body. Not a huge man when young, he was both solid and lithe. He seemed to carry in him a silently humming dynamo of energy, bridled and instantly ready. Whenever he moved, something seemed to impend. His face was more expressive than one first expected. Even his somewhat unrefined mouth could become sensitive, not with make-up or clever lighting but with the artist's method: imaginative suggestion (one of the tricks he learned from watching Clift). He worked to develop more delicate vocal colours, and his command continued to increase. From the very beginning, he was never so effective as when he was in motion. He was an actor whose very shoulders seemed to speak, to suggest a sense of energy always about to explode (in affection or aggression), a frame packed with theatrical power. The constraints imposed by the movie camera, pinning him down, forcing him to stay within a very tight frame, served only to accentuate this sense of explosive physicality. Whenever the camera moved in on him, his eyebrows arched, his face tightened into a grimace, and he looked set to break out and flee. Language itself, with its own kind of laws, was something

Brando rebelled against. He continued to mumble his lines, or revise them, or omit them. He explored the spaces between words, the unspoken graces and the muted despair. Although it was sometimes hard to understand what he was saying, it was impossible to misunderstand what he was thinking and feeling – this was its own kind of realism, a kind that was more potent than could ever be conveyed through mere words, however clearly and passionately enunciated.

As an actor Brando would prepare for his performances with tremendous self-discipline and a kind of hunger for stimuli of any kind. When he was searching for a quality he felt was crucial to his characterization, he could be unscrupulous. For example, during the making of *Mutiny on the Bounty* (1962), Brando befriended an English actor who had a small role in the movie. Although they appeared to have very little in common, they were inseparable for the entire shooting. When the last scene had been completed, the actor went to Brando and suggested they arrange to meet again in the very near future. Brando stared at him incredulously, as though he had never seen him before, and then muttered, 'Fuck off!' The actor was stunned and recounted the incident to a friend. His story was greeted with laughter. 'Don't you see?' said the friend. 'The accent! The accent!' Viewing the finished version of the movie, the demoralized actor recognized the cruel imitation of *his* voice coming out of Fletcher Christian's mouth.[7] Another incident illustrates Brando's cavalier attitude towards other actors. When filming a scene for *Guys and Dolls* (1955), Brando concentrated on perfecting his own performance and ignored the other actor in the scene, Frank Sinatra. Sinatra was known as 'one-take Frank' for his somewhat minimalist approach to acting. He would get worse with each successive take and therefore expected his fellow actors to try to complete their lines without any mistakes. Brando, on the contrary, preferred to ease his way into each scene, mumbling the lines until the timing and the rhythms seemed to suit his character's mood. In one scene Brando had to talk while Sinatra ate some cheesecake. Brando could not master the odd rhythms of the sanitized Damon Runyon dialogue, and kept changing some phrases and stopping mid-way through. Each take brought Sinatra another cheesecake to eat, and each take brought another of Brando's unscripted revisions. Eight takes were ruined and Sinatra was feeling nauseous. When the ninth take was scrapped, Sinatra moaned, hurled the plate of cheesecake to the ground, stabbed his fork into the table and screamed at the director: 'These fuckin' New York actors! How much cheesecake do you think I can eat?'

On other occasions (when there were no rival egos to tame) Brando's approach did not interfere with his colleagues. For example, when he was preparing for the role of Sakini in *The Teahouse of the August Moon* (1956), he studied Japanese and mastered the language; he also altered the look of his eyes, nose and cheekbones, his expressions and the sound of his voice. No detail was too insignificant for him. Brando (like Clift) acted with his eyes, his hands and his body, as well as his voice. The movie camera could capture for cinema audiences what only the first few rows of a theatre could hope to see. It was an impressive (and perhaps rather ironic) achievement: Brando used all his intellectual sensitivity to bring to life a series of brutish, aggressive characters. Few actors have ever used their bodies with such a cunning sense of revelation in reflex. He expressed emotion through motion. As his acting became more subtle, his slightest gesture assumed a significance that had been conceived with meticulous care. For example, there is a scene in *On the Waterfront* featuring Brando's character and his new woman friend. They are walking along when she accidentally drops her glove and Brando picks it up. By holding on to it, Brando makes the glove into a symbol of his desire to take hold of the woman. He is too nervous to articulate his sexual feelings for her, so the desire is displaced on to the glove. First he strokes the fingers and then he slips his hand into her glove as he looks at her, as though his body is employing a language his words cannot convey, his gestures charting the curve of his concerns from possession to penetration. It is the kind of expressive, sensual acting he had been working towards during his years in New York.

The Hollywood producer Stanley Kramer, known at the time for his movies on contemporary social issues, finally persuaded Brando to accept the challenge of the cinema. Brando later admitted he left for California with mixed feelings. He feared he would not photograph well, and he certainly felt he would be at odds with the LA life-style. From his first day in Hollywood, he made it very clear he was unwilling to conform to the conventional code of conduct for aspiring young stars. 'There are no artists,' he often told reporters. 'We are businessmen. We're merchants. There is no art.' The basic sentiment may have been heartfelt, but its expression was clearly well rehearsed. These remarks were just as formulaic and glib ('an actor is a product, like Ford cars or Florsheim shoes') as the publicists' blurb for their latest movies. Hollywood was, he declared, 'a cultural boneyard', and its producers had 'the manners of ants at a picnic'. 'The only reason I'm here,' he said, 'is because I don't yet have the moral strength to turn down the money.' Brando's first movie, *The Men* (1950), was directed by Fred Zinnemann, who felt that it was difficult for Brando to make the transition from stage acting to screen acting: 'When he has troubles he likes to withdraw within himself. It's not easy to reach him . . . But he struck me as a man of extreme and exciting talent.' Brando did not sign a long-term contract; he would work as a free agent, and *The Men* was in many ways an experiment with a new medium, not a commitment to it. Brando was cast as a paraplegic, a victim of war. The performance involved great physical control as the character, Ken Wilozek, deprived of the use of his legs, exercised the muscles of his arms and torso. Equally, the screenplay by Carl Foreman delineated the mental stress and self-pity of a virile man reduced to virtually half of his former self.

Brando prepared for *The Men* by living at the Van Nuys Hospital for Paraplegics, spending his time in a wheelchair, trying to live as though he really was paralysed. He worked hard at gaining the trust of the other men in the hospital. On one occasion, as he sat with some of his fellow patients, a religious fanatic gave an impromptu lecture on the healing powers of the True Faith. 'You mean,' said Brando, 'if I believe, I'll be able to walk again?' He rose totteringly to his feet, his face full of concentration, took two stiff steps forward, then, suddenly, went into a manic tap dance. 'Now I can make a living again!' he shouted. The wheelchair-bound men, apparently, were highly amused.

When it was time to perform in front of the cameras, Brando was extremely self-disciplined. The physical constraints imposed on him stimulated his search for a more restrained, subtle form of gesture. Brando's character is first seen being shot in battle and for the rest of the movie his attempts to reconcile himself with life as a cripple are intertwined with the doubts his condition sows in his relationship with fiancée, Ellen (Teresa Wright). They do get married, but on their wedding night all the pent-up anxieties come pouring out in a torrent of hatred. He returns to the hospital, but is soon discharged once again. The doctor believes that making the marriage work is Ken's only possible salvation. There is no happy ending, merely an affirmation that the search for one is worth the effort. Wilozek is physically *and* emotionally injured; his impotence seems complete, his manhood in doubt. Before the 1950s it was not considered masculine to concede to suffering, but Wilozek ends the movie with a look of utter desolation on his face as he waits for his wife to manoeuvre him up the steps of their house. One reviewer described Brando's appeal in the role as a 'radical masculinity'. As a test piece in another medium, *The Men* was a success for Brando, although his full quality was not to be gauged until several years later, when the sensitivity of his performance could be compared to his more aggressive characterizations.

The 'tap-dancing' incident during the making of *The Men* was the first of a long-running series of eccentric pranks which Brando (in stark contrast to Clift) indulged in on and off the set. On one occasion he placed a piece of paper down the side of his shoe, crossed his legs and waited until someone's curiosity forced them to bend down and examine the note. 'What the fuck are you looking at?' it read. Sometimes he would place a cigarette up each nostril in order to amuse or upset the actor who was delivering a speech. He also had an enduring fascination for 'mooning': he liked to pull down his trousers and expose his bare buttocks to shocked cameramen and technicians. On the set of *The Godfather*, he held a 'mooning contest' with his co-stars. It seems he never tired of the joke. One of Brando's former colleagues, director Donald Cammell, remarks: 'His sense of humour is erratic. Everybody blesses his bizarre sense of humour but they're not really talking about that. They're talking about their own extreme insecurity in the face of great cruelties that come from Marlon which have to be interpreted as humorous, or else everyone's going to suffer.'[8]

Whenever Brando tried to be funny on screen, the results were crude and clumsy. He was much more amusing when bringing out the eccentricities and cosy habits of serious characters (there are, for example, several comic moments during *Streetcar*). In the early years of his movie career, the unpredictable 'jokes' and elaborate pranks helped him to rebel against the stereotypical images of stardom disseminated by the studio publicists. He gave out conflicting (and increasingly fanciful) details concerning his family background and career. He said he had been born in Calcutta, that his parents were 'early tea planters' and had once been 'gymnasts' together. He signed his name as 'Lord Greystoke' or 'Dr Miles Graham, dentist from Omaha'. If the magazine profiles described him as 'scruffy' or 'unkempt', he would make sure that he was next seen wearing an expensive suit; if a reporter suggested he was 'mellowing', he would start behaving violently. The tactic eventually became a rather tiresome cliché, but for a time it contributed to his highly intimidating public image.

Brando was determined to resist assimilation into 'conventional' Hollywood society. He broke every rule for the aspiring movie star: he astonished the most influential newspaper columnists by going out of his way to insult them (he called Louella Parsons 'the fat one' and Hedda Hopper 'the one with the hats'); he thought nothing of criticizing other stars (Brando said of Sinatra, 'Frank is the kind of guy, when he dies, he's going to heaven to give God a bad time for making him bald'); he flouted convention by ignoring the publicity managers and mocking the profile writers (when one journalist exclaimed, 'You're just like everybody else', Brando ran to the corner of the room and stood on his head); he refused to cooperate with his studio when a movie needed promoting, and sometimes even went on record as disowning his own work. 'The only thing an actor owes his public,' he said, 'is not to bore them.' Hollywood never understood Marlon Brando. As Alexander Walker has observed, 'He remained a "Why" actor in a "Who" society.'[9]

During the shooting of The Men, Brando had been offered an opportunity to do the screen version of Streetcar, but he was not particularly interested in repeating the performance. He felt he had dredged up everything there was to be found in the part (of course, he may also have felt apprehensive about the risks involved in returning to the role that made him famous). He decided to delay his decision until Warner Brothers had resolved the numerous censorship problems. During the summer of 1950 Warner Brothers concluded a deal with Elia Kazan and Brando, and the movie version of Streetcar was prepared. The role of Stanley Kowalski assured Brando of movie stardom. Reunited with his Actors' Studio director Kazan, and faced with the rare opportunity to revise an old performance for a different medium, Brando (despite his earlier doubts) worked well to make his characterization even more intense than before. Kowalski was crass, calculating and materialistic – a type that was a factor in every aspect of American life in the twentieth century.

The story begins when Blanche DuBois (Vivien Leigh), having lost her youth, her husband, her inheritance, her ancestral Southern mansion, her teaching job and nearly all of her family, arrives in New Orleans to stay with her younger sister, Stella (Kim Hunter). She is appalled by the appearance of Stella's home: a small, dingy apartment on a slum street in the old part of town. Stella has married a louche, uncouth automobile-parts salesman of Polish origin, Stanley Kowalski, whom she met when he was a soldier during the war. Blanche cannot comprehend how Stella could have 'married beneath herself' and 'betrayed' the DuBois tradition of Southern gentility and aristocratic pretensions. She is shocked by Stella's unashamed admiration of Stanley's uncultured sexuality ('I can hardly stand it when he's away for a night!'). It seems that, after the trauma of losing the family home, Blanche became an alcoholic and, it is hinted, a prostitute, yet she clings to her former demure self-image ('I don't want realism. I want magic !').

Stanley unsettles Blanche, for his lack of pretension and his raw physicality are qualities she strives to repress in herself. She hides behind a variety of masks: heavy make-up and soft lighting to hide the ageing of her skin; expensive dresses to disguise her poverty; a mannered aristocratic accent, decorated (in the way that rotting meat is disguised with rich sauces) with a few French phrases, to obscure her loss of status; and a contrived gentility and coyness to obscure her boundless sexual appetite. Stanley behaves without any fear of social censorship; his is a thrusting self, a sweaty, soiled, sensual self. Stella and he *enjoy* each other. There is sex and sanity in their interaction, in contrast to Blanche's sleazy past. He rejoices in his physical nature: he chews gum as he speaks, eats with his hands, wipes the grease on to his old T-shirt, picks his teeth, scratches his crotch, strikes a match on the back of his thigh, holds a bottle of beer between his legs and stares openly at any woman he finds attractive. He learned his inventiveness on the factory floor and the battlefield; he responds to threats and danger. Slurred, nasal, guttural, rising to a growl in bursts of temper, descending to an insinuating purr in moments of calm, his voice has a jolting blue-collar coarseness. Blanche likes to hide behind appearances and feels that actions are a kind of exposure, an obscenity ('funerals are pretty compared to deaths', she says), and she feels safer with flirtations than with physical relationships. Stanley has no time for Blanche's 'magic', which to him seems 'phoney' and tiresome (magic is a trick that takes one in, and Stanley hates being taken in). He wastes no time with the formal aspects of society, eschewing talk of beauty and culture, never complimenting his wife except for a grudging 'You look OK.' In a sense, both Blanche and Stanley are emotional cripples, suffering from their self-inflicted repressions. Blanche cannot admit her 'basic' desires, her sexual hunger; Stanley cannot accept his own need for tenderness and respect. As the movie progresses, we come to see Stanley's crude behaviour as another kind of contrivance, another pose: his masculinity is overpowering in order to obscure his 'feminine' qualities. He must dominate and scare all those he cares for in order to ensure that they will never hurt him; he cannot trust, for he fears betrayal. When Blanche's radio is too loud for him, he hurls it through the window. When Stella asks him to clear the table, he sweeps everything on to the floor and smashes the plates. When someone disagrees with him, he punches them out. It is the overdramatic behaviour of a child demanding attention, the desperate aggression of a man unsure of his manhood (as opposed to his strength).

In an effort to make a new start, Blanche finds a possible husband, Mitch, from among Stanley's friends only for Stanley to come between them. At the end, having been raped by the man of the house in which she sought refuge, her mind becomes unhinged and she is removed for an indeterminate future to a mental asylum. The movie censors demanded that Kowalski be punished for his behaviour and so (in a change from the stage play) we see Stella leaving with her baby, ignoring Stanley's pleas. Like Strindberg's *Miss Julie*, Williams's *Streetcar* combines class conflict and sexual warfare. However, in Williams it is not so much the woman as the man whose desire is mixed with hostility. Strindberg's suave Jean aspires to the aristocracy, whereas Williams's unrefined Stanley aspires to destroy the aristocracy. He cannot make contact with other people in any way other than physically; his penis is his weapon, his emblem, his trademark. He goes to bed with his own orgasm and is unconcerned about his 'partner'. He takes the same sexual pleasure in degrading Blanche as he has already taken in pulling Stella down from the columns. Stanley's animal vigour, his pragmatism and solid connection to the living present seem at first to contrast favourably with Blanche's neurosis, delusion and her nostalgic relation to the dead past. He is cast as the defender of hearth and home against an intruder whose imperious attitude is evident from the beginning. Yet, as the story develops, our sympathies shift. Stanley's cheap physical abuse and his asinine lecture on the regal command of the male in the home outdo Blanche's own delusions. He is a rebel because he lacks the courage to trust anyone. His rambling explanation of the Napoleonic Code (a convenient recourse to the law) merely reveals his panic when he realizes that his marriage to Stella has doubled his chances of being betrayed ('It looks to me like you been swindled, baby, and when you get swindled under the Napoleonic Code *I* get swindled too.

And I don't like to be swindled!'). By the time he rapes Blanche, while his wife is giving birth in the hospital, bestiality and cunning have all but obscured his engaging directness, humour and physical wellbeing.

Stanley Kowalski's economic status may be working class and his outlook on life – 'to hold front position in this rat race you've got to believe you're lucky' – may undermine the belief that each man is essentially responsible for his own fate, but he is nevertheless ambitious, believes in himself and is obviously loyal to America as a land of opportunity. He bristles when Blanche refers to him as a 'Polack', for he sees himself as 'a 100 per cent American . . . and as proud as hell of it'. His emphasis on luck and male bonding has strongly traditional overtones, but he usually sees no reason to doubt himself either as a man or as a real American. The doubts are largely repressed, occasionally exploding into his consciousness when Blanche makes her most pointed observations. This tension and ambiguity beneath Stanley's show of uncomplicatedly one-dimensional masculinity are precisely the elements illuminated by an actor with the subtlety of Brando (and for all the aggression and arrogance, this *is* a very subtle performance). He draws one in, seeming at first to be so simple a character, then alerting one slowly to how the sexual mask constrains the individual's expressions.

The movie (even more so than the play) revolves around Blanche and Stanley's mutual desire less for love (which both have left far behind as a preoccupation of the trivial-minded) than for immolation, a total devouring of one another. Stanley is thus both predator and prey. He is wild and fierce, but his freedom is problematic. The contrast between his unconventional beauty and the literally cocksure qualities of the character he is playing makes the audience understand how Stella fell under his sexual thrall. Brando gave Williams's character something more – an instinctive intelligence, a satiric humour and, most important, a yearning quality that informs his thrashing bafflement with Blanche and the airs she puts on. On stage, from a distance, this was harder to discern; with the aid of the movie camera, moving in so close as to catch sight of the beads of sweat on Stanley's flesh, it is there for us to glimpse at.

Kazan saw Stanley's brutality as springing from self-hatred; he was 'deeply dissatisfied, deeply hopeless, deeply cynical'. To escape from his quiet desperation, he has built a hedonistic life that he would defend to the death. He bombards his consciousness with food, drink, sex and sport. Brando uses all kinds of props in order to illustrate this. He takes enormous (perhaps rather childlike) pleasure in opening a bottle of beer, finishing a meal or even changing a T-shirt. He likes to feel his clothes on his body: his T-shirt, a size too small, is sweat-soaked and clinging; his jeans are cut tight, revealing the outline of his genitals. 'Where's my dinner?' he yells. 'Where's my woman?' He is a Lawrentian fantasy of the earthy, animal, proletarian male. None the less, although the sensual male is captivating, Brando's complex performance makes it clear that Kowalski, with his drunken all-night poker games which always seem to degenerate into mindless brawls, is not the most desirable sexual partner. When his hedonism fails him, his tactic is to destroy everyone else's dignity. For example, he violates Blanche's wardrobe, hurling her fine dresses over his shoulder, and then he violates Blanche's body, devouring her overwhelming illusions of Southern gentility. Outwardly, he is assured, contained, insolent; he has an extraordinary physical presence. However, at times the mask drops – only for a moment, but, for that very reason, all the more enlightening. Kazan felt the scene where Kowalski smashes all the dinner plates was particularly significant: 'I doubt that Williams found that act vulgar; he'd have found it thrilling. I can recall his cackling over the way Brando did it in rehearsal. It was kind of a release for Tennessee; perhaps they were his mother's plates.'[10] Stanley and Blanche are Williams's self-image riven in two and subsequently exaggerated. Blanche is the repository of all the repellent qualities Williams wanted to disavow – narcissism, vanity and the fear of growing old. Kowalski's brutality is a reaction to his actual powerlessness; all he really has is himself, a self that is confused, uncertain and threatened.

The reviews of the movie were full of praise for Brando. C. A. Lejeune in the *Observer* described Brando's performance as 'one of the strongest and most selfless I remember seeing in the cinema'.

Otis L. Guernsey Jr, in the *New York Herald Tribune*, found him giving a performance 'as close to perfect as one could wish'. The movie received a cluster of Academy Award nominations and was an international success. This was the way the world got to know Marlon Brando. It was not the way Marlon Brando would have chosen to announce himself. The image of Stanley was following him around. Brando, disliking the way Kowalski was being presented as his *own* personality, ignored the subtlety of his acting and deliberately caricatured his old role. 'Kowalski was always right, never afraid,' said Brando. 'He never wondered, never doubted himself. His ego was very secure. And he had the kind of brutal aggressiveness I hate. I detest the character.' It sounded as though Ishmael had been forced to play Ahab. Sam Spiegel, the movie producer, recalled: 'He was a tortured man in the early days and he was great on the screen. When he ceased being tortured, he had to pseudo-torture himself in order to function.'[11] During the 1950s there were enough problems to keep him feeling tortured: his agony over his mother, his hatred of his father and his own complicated emotional life.

As the shades of the 'sex symbol' prison house closed around him, Brando was thrown into confusion. In many ways he enjoyed his image of the super-potent male (at least for a while), and was amused by the way younger men (such as James Dean) started to hero-worship and copy him. In other ways, he felt even more insecure than before, because people expected him to be this hyper-masculine male in everyday life, and it became a role from which he could not easily extricate himself. 'Deep down,' he admitted, 'I feel a bit ambiguous.' Donald Cammell recalls how Brando felt in competition with other male sex symbols: 'Marlon was always fascinated with Presley – his greatest rival. He was envious and in slight awe. They looked amazingly alike. Peas in a pod.'[12] Unlike Presley, however, Brando revealed in his performances that the traditional masculine role and its various quirks were actually utilized to shield male insecurities rather than to present the masculine norm.

Brando's first wife, Anna Kashfi, has claimed that Brando's own sexuality was always highly ambiguous while they were married: 'He cheated on me with both men and women and was quite proud of his huge appetite for sex of all kinds . . . He would start mincing about [in their home]. Here was Marlon, who appeared the soul of masculinity, behaving like a fairy.'[13] She says that Brando was careful of his public image, and limited his unconventional behaviour to the privacy of his home: 'Marlon was terribly discreet. He lived in terror of anyone finding out.' Although Kashfi has a reputation for sometimes being untrustworthy in her comments about her former husband, these remarks went unchallenged. She has always refused to call their son by the name Brando chose for him, Christian, because she insists it was inspired by Brando's male friend of the time, the French actor/director Christian Marquand. It is certainly true that Brando was very close to Marquand at this time, and several of Brando's old friends imply that the relationship was probably, for a short while, sexual.[14] 'Marlon and Marquand,' said Kashfi, 'displayed an affection towards each other that far overreached the usual expressions of friendship.'[15]

Kashfi has encouraged a cheap and prurient fascination with Brando's private life. This is a misleading approach to what was possibly a brief and confusing period. When he was in public, it sometimes seemed that he was parodying his Stanley Kowalski performance. He would refer to his penis as 'my noble tool', and it was known for him to take a woman into his dressing-room, remove his clothes, make love to her, replace his clothes and return to the set without at any time speaking a single word to her. At the same time as he was announcing his disgust for Kowalski's machismo, he was doing his best to emulate him. Speaking to Adriano Botto in *L'Europeo* in March 1973, Brando recalled this contradiction:

I have loved a lot in my life. I still do. I have had many women. I like love. I insist on enjoying sex. Should sex and desire die in me, it would be the end. It doesn't matter if I have almost never been happy with a woman . . . I face love every time as a necessary good or a necessary evil. Sometimes I even approach sex and love with boredom. But I must make love and give love, whatever the price. It is a matter of life and death.

Despite the fussed-over, rehearsed tone of this declaration, it conveys a sense of the genuine melancholy that seems to feature in Brando's attitude to sex (on and off the screen). Actor Roy Scheider once said of Brando: 'He's pansexual, beyond normalcy of any kind. He's so delicate. He can out-feminize any woman in any scene.' Kazan, recalling directing Brando in *Viva Zapata!* (1952), notes that he instructed him to play the love scenes with the leading woman with complete romantic detachment: 'Don't mix it up with love,' he said. 'He loves his *compadres.*' Kazan observed: 'That wasn't hard for Marlon to understand. He was that way in life . . . Perhaps this was discretion or shyness, but the warmest relations I've seen him involved in have been with men.'[16] Brando could always present the appearance of masculinity when it was necessary; it was machismo as *maquillage*, an undeniably impressive performance. At such times as these Brando seemed a dandy, a shrewd stylist of affectations. Though society is the very atmosphere he breathes, the dandy audaciously turns its conventions against itself. He often carries the expectations of society to such an extreme that they rebound upon themselves in self-parody. The attributes of masculinity, generally admired and encouraged by society, when taken to their extreme, rebound with apocalyptic effect.

In Hollywood probably the one fellow actor who could fully understand this aspect of Brando's performances, and sympathize with his private anxieties, was Montgomery Clift. Although Brando tried to resist such comparisons with his most important rival, he appreciated the tensions they shared. Clift said, 'One year, Marlon and I were both nominated for Oscars – he for *Streetcar* and I for *A Place in the Sun*. I voted for him, I thought him that good.' Clift could always find Brando's insecurities, and enjoyed playing on them when Brando seemed overly vain. One call from Clift informing Brando that his buttocks were looking chubby, or that his waist was going to fat, or that his face was beginning to look haggard, and Brando would depart to a health clinic or increase his visits to the gym. In many ways the two men saw each other as their alter ego, their hidden self (Clift envied Brando's ability to be so physically direct, while Brando envied Clift's principled defence of his own sensitivity). Clift's career was haunted by unresolved tensions he felt in his relationship with his mother; Brando's career was similarly affected by his ambivalent feelings for his alcoholic mother. He told Truman Capote, with Oedipal anguish:

My mother was everything to me. A whole world. I tried so hard ... I thought if she loved me enough, trusted me enough, I thought, then we can be together, in New York; we'll live together and I'll take care of her. Once, later on, that really happened. She left my father and came to live with me. In New York, when I was in a play. I tried so hard. But my love wasn't enough. She couldn't care enough. She went back. And one day ... I didn't care anymore. She was there. In a room. Holding on to me. And I let her fall. Because I couldn't take it anymore — watch her breaking apart, in front of me, like a piece of porcelain. I stepped right over her. I walked right out. I was indifferent. Since then, I've been indifferent.[17]

None the less, Brando was there when his mother died, and he wept as he sat by her bed. After her death he kept a life-sized portrait of her in his house. Several of his women friends have said that he continued to analyse his relationship with his mother and felt embittered by what he saw as his failure to sustain it. He told Patrice Chaplin, 'I hated my father so much I once wanted to tear out his throat. For what he did to my mother.'[18] In the spring of 1972 Brando told the Italian magazine *Oggi* of these feelings: 'That's why I make women suffer. They give me a feeling of taking revenge on my mother. I have tried to act normally but I have not succeeded.' Such remarks cause one to wonder whether analysis did much more than provide Brando with a number of comforting theoretical justifications for some discomforting feelings. The women in question must have found them quite chilling. 'I can't trust anyone to give myself to them,' he told Capote. 'But I'm ready. I want it.'[19] Clift was struggling more obviously to protect himself from the dangers of being so sensitive (a quality he believed was essential for a good actor). Brando was engaged in the same struggle: 'Sensitive people are so vulnerable; they're so easily brutalized and hurt just because they *are* sensitive. The more sensitive you are, the more certain you are to be brutalized, develop scabs. Never evolve. Never allow yourself to feel anything, because you always feel too much. Analysis helps. It helped me.'[20] For Clift the task was to 'uncallous' oneself, to strive to remain in precisely that vulnerable condition which threatens to destroy one. Kenneth Tynan's well-known observation concerning the bisexuality of the finest performers (combining sensual and sensuous gifts, striving for transcendence of the prosaic) seems apposite here: both Clift and Brando used their ambiguity to enrich the realism of their roles.

Throughout the 1950s Brando and Clift felt themselves drawn together professionally and personally. It was an intensely ambiguous relationship, a mixture of admiration, affection, envy and resentment. In their approach to acting there were obvious differences; their respective screen personalities spark from opposite ends of the emotional scale. Clift was the aristocrat, the humane spirit whose delicate sensitivity served to indict the harsh world around him. Brando possessed a crude, almost animalistic force, moist with urgent desires, and the principal interest in many of his movies lies in the process whereby this force is civilized. Clift was the more European, the more subtle of the two; Brando was more 'American', impatient and direct. Each actor seemed to play off the other. The rivalry sometimes tended to bring out an uncharacteristic pettiness and paranoia in Brando. He once claimed that Clift was copying him ('He's more fucking me than I am myself!'), which sounds unnecessarily defensive as well as rather implausible. Sometimes they were happy to relax with each other. In home movies taken by Kevin McCarthy, Brando and Clift can be seen dressing up in women's flowered hats, falsies stuffed into their shirts, flirting and laughing at each other. 'We're not tough guys,' said Clift. 'We're real.' Both men felt that on screen they were helping to transform people's perceptions about modern men; in various ways, they did so.

Brando's 1950s rebel male is someone who has had to become a man despite his weakness, whether physical, economic, social or intellectual. *The Men* has Brando as a paraplegic struggling to remain a man (more accurately, someone whom he recognizes as a man) despite this handicap; he remains confined to a wheelchair, a man who 'cannot make women happy'. Stanley Kowalski is someone who has been denied economic and political power, education and culture, a family, and has consequently founded a 'manly' identity upon brute strength, physical attractiveness and sexual prowess. *Viva Zapata!* has Brando as a revolutionary who loses his faith in the revolution (an obvious – and conscious – allegory of Elia Kazan's dismal submission to McCarthyism). The movie reads as a kind of displaced Western: the bandit Emiliano Zapata (Brando), who took part in the successful guerrilla campaign that overthrew the Mexican dictator General Diaz, is portrayed as a simple, honest soul, a natural man of the Southwest who struggles to read just as he struggles to learn the laws and lessons of power and leadership. It is a Rousseau-like story (as many Westerns are) of the corruption of innocence, rather than any account of the politics of revolution. Kazan's 'message' stresses the oppressiveness of political power, as Zapata, once inside the presidential palace, intimidates the peasants just as Diaz did before him. Its emphasis is on the tortured loner who decides, after retiring from politics and being betrayed by a friend, to return to the land. Brando's Zapata is a quiet man, subtly projecting the dedication and anguish of a young rebel who (as Lenin once observed of himself) cannot afford to expose himself to the cultural beauties of the world. Zapata says to his lover as he strokes her forearm and caresses her fingers: 'I believe a man is fire and a woman is fuel.' However keen he is to be simply a husband and father, Zapata defines his manhood in terms of his inability to stand by without intervening as people are being tormented (the fact that women might share this attitude is ignored). Brando's performance makes Zapata appear a man of contradictions, and therefore a whole man, a creature of strengths and doubts, humble and yet imbued with the spirit to fight injustice.

Brando's next rebel figure, Marc Antony in *Julius Caesar* (1953), was given a modern interpretation. He is a rather tired, disenchanted character, articulate yet restrained. Brando's Antony spanned the centuries and became meaningful in relation to twentieth-century struggles for power. It is a forthright, uninflected interpretation. He is impressive with his vow over Caesar's dead body, and with the application of rhetoric and psychology in the forum. However, neither of Antony's great set pieces had sufficient respect for the verse; and while each of them compelled admiration (from Olivier, among others) for Brando's empathy, they were embodied in a movie that strained to incorporate a bewildering variety of acting styles, with Gielgud's typically eloquent, ethereal Cassius at one extreme, Brando at the other, and in between them a diversity of talents that could not be fused.

The Wild One featured one of Brando's most famous rebel figures, Johnny, the teenage biker. Although the movie was relatively tame, it was judged an incitement to teenage rebellion by the British Board of Film Censors, who refused to give it a certificate from 1954 to 1969. Brando's character epitomized an entire subculture that was fast spreading in America at that time — the drifting gang. 'Johnny' inspired many young men in search of a role model, including Dylan, Presley and Dean. The cool, self-confident pose adopted by Johnny disguises a person who is actually profoundly insecure and confused, which explains why he treasures a stolen racing trophy and fights a rival gang leader to protect his popular emblem of masculine virility. 'It begins here for me on this open road,' he says on the opening voice-over. 'Mostly I remember the girl ... She got to me, something changed in me ...' From his first appearance, leading the swarm of motorcycles, this man/boy lone ranger is established as a figure of considerable force. Johnny appeals to men and women alike, and while this is never openly expressed by the character himself, there are unmistakable signs that he needs the adoration of both sexes.

Johnny leads an all-male gang. In their complete conformity to the norms of this surrogate family, these young men announce their need to win approval and affirmation, even as their posture of defiance is a complaint against a society that regards them merely as victims to be forced to conform. Johnny's credo is a kind of petulant self-assertion: 'Nobody tells *me* what to do.' Beneath his violence is his vulnerability, a personal configuration through which Brando creates a new sexual ideal. The romantic triangle lurking just below the surface of *The Wild One* is completed by a wholesome, virginal type (Cathy) and a street-smart hoodlum (Chino) — both of whom, it is implied, are in love with Johnny. Chino is really Johnny's brother under the skin — a crude embodiment of a latent aspect of Johnny. They used to belong to the same gang, and now Chino follows him everywhere, crying out to him mockingly, 'I love ya, Johnny!' The only sequence in the movie that comes close to realizing the sexuality implicit in the story is Cathy's long motorcycle ride with Johnny through the dark countryside. The fact of her virginity is not communicated with any subtlety: 'I've never ridden a motorcycle before,' she says with wondering admiration. Johnny picks her up, saying only, 'Get on,' then, when they have reached a quiet spot in a park, he says, 'Get off.' The ride seems to liberate her (a kind of sexual journey), and she reveals her secret desire to go away with him, away from her father (a law man). At this point it is not difficult to see Cathy as the unrealized and unacknowledged *anima* — the feminine principle, or what is turned towards the unconscious and, once acknowledged, must be left behind again. However, the narrative (or at least the censor) pulls back and Johnny becomes insulting, causing Cathy to run away in tears. A group of male townsfolk assume that she has been assaulted and descend on Johnny to administer a savage beating ('to pound a little respect for law and order into the guy's thick skull') — a punishment he bears stoically until he escapes and weeps beside his bike. 'My old man used to hit harder than that,' he mutters, his face contorted with pain. It is part pathetic boast, part lament. As a low-angle close-up emphasizes Johnny's upturned, anguished face, one wonders why he is crying now — because he has been reminded of his father's brutality, or because of his loss of Cathy, or because he wishes both the old *and* the young folk would leave him alone.

Johnny is a true harbinger of James Dean's troubled adolescent of the mid-1950s. While presenting the tough surface of the adolescent male, Brando allowed us to see how thinly veiled this image really was and how tormented and anguished the real person was beneath the superficial machismo. The role established Brando as an actor whose roles expressed the type of rebel hero who, feeling trapped and alienated by society, withdraws into a world of his own where he can feel comfortable as an individual of importance, with ideas not to be dismissed and emotions not to be questioned.

On the Waterfront witnessed the affirmation of Brando's unique gift as an actor and, in the character of Terry Malloy, introduced one of Hollywood's definitive rebel males. The movie is set on the New York waterfront, where the dockers' unions are festering with corruption. The gangdom rule of the ironically named Johnny Friendly (Lee J. Cobb) brought death to anyone who signified an individual will to resist. Forces of law and religion alike were powerless, and the ideals of solidarity among workers had been exploited with a cynicism and ruthlessness that assumed the significance of a metaphor (again, the self-serving work of director Kazan). Beyond its immediate subject, disturbing in itself and a prime example of sociological comment rising above the confines of expedient political pigeonholes (note the well-known 'fascistic' undertones), *On the Waterfront* crystallized the strongest theme to emerge in American movies of the 1950s: the rights of the individual – one's entitlement to eschew conformity and one's suffering in the process. The point was brought home by the simplistic case of Terry Malloy, a docker who had done some boxing in his time and was somewhat slow-witted yet possessed the instinct to distinguish wrong from right (he seems the lowlife brother of Clift's Private Prewitt). Easily led, he had permitted himself to be a pawn in lethal games on behalf of Friendly. 'Which side are you on?' he is asked at one point. 'I'm with me,' he replies. 'You wanna hear my philosophy of life?' he asks. 'Do it to him before he does it to you ... Everyone's got a racket ... Down here it's every man for himself.' The real drama of the movie is an internal one – what goes on in this young man's mind. Malloy's one-man rebellion at the climax is incited by personal relationships: a forlorn kind of love for the young woman whose rebel brother was murdered by Friendly's thugs (with the complicity of Terry himself); and a primal urge to avenge the killing of his brother Charlie, formerly a legal aide to

Friendly and a sharp-witted opportunist, but one who relinquished favour. Thus Malloy is transformed into a solitary redeemer, beaten to a bloody pulp by Friendly's men while his fellow dockers stand by and do nothing. His battered, blood-soaked body struggles through the conformist crowd, a loser of the modern world whose passion touches the spectator's heart. The defiance shown by Malloy in the face of the tyranny of a corrupt majority reaffirms the traditional ambivalence shown by the American individual towards the law. Malloy's brother was a lawyer, and he had cynically manipulated the rules in order to cheat rank-and-file union members. The Crime Commission is shown to be a fumbling, lethargic bureaucracy whose inability either to make or to enforce laws represents society at its most ineffectual. Terry's friend urges him to flee to the Midwest, to a farm (away from the city and its laws), but he cannot really escape. Confronted by the stock inadequacy of the legal system, Malloy can only take the standard outlaw hero course: individual action.

The rebellious gesture – part sacrifice, part salvation – is superbly set up by Brando's finely paced performance. Kazan has said: 'Brando gives the best male performance I've ever seen by an actor. Period. I do not add "in the country". It is a perfect performance. And everything we learned in Group Theater bore fruit here.'[21] It is certainly an arresting (and charming) *tour de force* from Brando, capturing that strange combination of fear and fury that makes the character so memorable. There is an ex-athlete's bounce to his walk, a lonely look on his face. Malloy is, at first, almost anti-human: he is unable to speak clearly and is unaware of who or what he is. As an ex-boxer he has conventional male credentials, yet these are not presented as grounds for pride but rather as an indication that his rebel self, his potential self, has been repressed. As his future lover observes, 'He *tries* to look tough.' He appears for much of the narrative as an inner-directed man in an outer-directed world. He spends most time with his pigeons: 'They're faithful,' he says, as though no other creatures are capable of fidelity. Sitting in a cab with his brother, reeling from the shock of yet another betrayal, he exclaims:

You remember that night in the Garden you came down to my dressing room and said, 'Kid, this ain't your night. We're goin' for the price on Wilson.' You 'member that? 'This ain't your night.' *My night!* I coulda taken Wilson apart. So what happens? He gets the title shout outdoors in a ball park and what do I get? A one-way ticket to Palookaville. You was my *brother*, Charlie. You shoulda looked out for me a little bit. You shoulda taken care of me just a little bit so I wouldn't have to take them dives for the short-end money ... I coulda had *class*. I coulda been a *contender*. I coulda been *somebody*. Instead of a bum ... which is what I am, let's face it.

When Terry Malloy says, 'I coulda been a *contender* ... Instead of a bum', many people saw it as a generational lament, a declaration of betrayal not merely by an individual but by a whole society in which humane values now seemed inadequate to a monstrously complex age. He never had such a receptive audience again.

Brando's final movie role of the 1950s, Val in *The Fugitive Kind* (1960, based on Tennessee Williams's play *Orpheus Descending*), was fittingly uncompromising. Val is an outsider, a fallen angel, a mysterious drifter, who enters the life of a woman (Anna Magnani) tied to humdrum work in a little store and shackled to a cancer-riddled husband. Val is a modern Orpheus, his guitar slung over his shoulder, and he wanders into a world steeped in darkness, where night predominates and death surrounds. He says, 'We're all sentenced to solitary confinement, sentenced to our own little skins.' Significantly, he wears his snakeskin jacket like a (foreskin) symbol of his defiant desire to shed all ties and obligations. He has a grimy, back-room affair with the woman. She is eager for the physical release that is granted, transitorily, by the fugitive who is also destined for burning, leaving behind an exuberant memory to set beside others, and a snakeskin jacket to be donned for a time, perhaps, by another of his own kind. Val is another of Brando's American rebels: 'There's a kind that doesn't belong *anywhere*,' he says, 'like a bird with no feet to land.' That is precisely the terminal point of the mixture of eroticism, love and pain that Brando represented so potently during the 1950s. George Melly described this image as 'a black leather phallus whom it was necessary for society to castrate in its own interests'.[22]

In his roles of the period, Brando conveyed how the traditional toughness and tight-lipped invulnerability of the male hero were actually defence mechanisms as opposed to emblems of masculinity. Through his sensitivity Brando demonstrated that the tougher and more unyielding a man seemed to be, the less in control of himself he really was. At the start of *The Young Lions*, Brando's character can say: 'I am not political at all. Political discussions go round and round and round, and nothing is ever settled.' By the end, he is the victim of this political process. Such rebel males as Stanley Kowalski, Johnny, Terry and Val are disaffected wanderers, often unable to comprehend the social components of their density. Their pain is deeply felt, but so keen that it must be muted in expression. Their love is unclear and so it is often thwarted. In the unambiguous world of the traditional Hollywood hero, right and wrong were given factors, established and agreed upon before the movie started to unwind through the projector. In the 1950s one had to deal with the process whereby these truths were re-established, or sometimes even revised, for the rebel male. Thus we have Brando acquiring the knowledge that aimless violence is wrong (*The Wild One*), that racial prejudice is intolerable (*Sayonara*, 1957), that revenge is feckless ambition (*One-Eyed Jacks*, 1961), that political corruption must be resisted (*On the Waterfront*) and that brutality based on class distinctions is wrong (*Mutiny on the Bounty*, *Viva Zapata!*).

Pauline Kael has noted how Brando became a distinctive *American* hero for the 1950s. 'There was no theory, no cant in his leadership. He didn't care about social position or a job or respectability, and because he didn't care he was a big man; for what is less attractive, what makes a man smaller, than his worrying about his status? Brando represented a contemporary version of the free American.'[23] Even in his distinctive vocal mannerisms, argues Kael, Brando was liberating Americans from the need to sound English: 'Americans mumble!'

Brando's rebel is concerned above all with establishing, as a moral and prevailing quality, an 'original' innocence – and he does not care how much violence this entails. No matter how many fistfights, street brawls or gun battles he wins, he typically remains a fugitive, an outrider; he lives on the loose, unravelled end of life. What he infallibly needs is a 'new start' and what his movies often demonstrate is the violent reaction of the established order when he attempts this rebellion. The ideal is seldom realized, and the rebel sometimes perishes (as in *Viva Zapata!*, *The Young Lions* and *Mutiny on the Bounty*) or suffers a brutal beating (colleagues called this 'Marlon's obligatory messianic scene'). Compared to other rebel males, Brando's character is usually a risk-taker who is unusually sceptical of fatalist arguments. Whereas Montgomery Clift's Prewitt never seems ready to compromise with the existing order of things, and must therefore perish, Brando's Terry Malloy will fight back, claw his way up and struggle on.

Rivals throughout their careers, Clift and Brando continued a relationship Kevin McCarthy once described as 'tentative'. Yet by the end of the 1950s, after they had worked together on *The Young Lions*, the two men seemed ready to acknowledge how productive the old rivalry had been, providing each of them with a rare opportunity of measuring his performances against those of a similarly gifted actor. Clift commented: 'I don't think either Marlon or I are imitators, which is why I guess we respect each other. Maybe because we both have delusions of grandeur.'[24] The problem for Brando as the 1950s ended was that Clift seemed to have lost the will to continue struggling for quality in a system obsessed with quantity. He had been badly injured, alcohol and drugs had seriously affected his ability to cope with major movie roles and many of his friends feared his self-abuse would soon kill him. Brando visited Clift at his home in order to offer his support. He told Clift he had heard all the rumours and was concerned. 'You're too good to let this happen,' Brando said. He offered to go with Clift to therapy meetings, clinics, Alcoholics Anonymous – anything that might help him. He compared the two of them to Olivier and Gielgud, and stressed the need for competition: 'Don't you know the only actor in America who interests me is you?' Brando told Clift: 'In a way I hate you. I've always hated you because I want to be better than you, but you're better than me – you're my touchstone, my challenge, and I want you and I to go on challenging each other.'[25]

Clift told Brando how moved he was that someone cared, and he made a half-hearted attempt to reassure him: 'I'm all right, Marlon. I'll be all right.' It was said that Brando left in tears, resigned to the decline of his friend's career. In the last year of his life, Clift reflected on the critical reports of Brando's faltering career and argued, 'Marlon isn't finished yet. He's just resting up. He'll be back – bigger than ever.' Brando was profoundly upset to hear of Clift's death, but in many ways he had been mourning Clift's acting since the 1960s began. There were, of course, numerous personal reasons why Brando now felt distracted and demoralized: his first wife had tried to commit suicide and involved him in a sensationally acrimonious divorce case; his second wife argued with him over child support; at least two other former lovers criticized him via the newspapers; and both his parents died unpleasant deaths – his father from a malignant melanoma, his mother from the effects of years of drinking. However, another serious contributory factor in Brando's artistic decline during the 1960s was the absence of his old rival. Without new performances from Clift, Brando lost his 'touchstone', and he felt surrounded by younger actors who appeared to be basing themselves on his 1950s model.

Although Brando was still relatively young, he seemed oddly alone, abandoned. There is a photograph from 1955 which features Brando with Marilyn Monroe at a movie première. They both look stunningly attractive, confident and very successful indeed – two famous sex symbols, relaxed in each other's company. In a few years Monroe would die, as would Dean and Clift. His distinguished contemporaries gone, Brando was left with his unsought position as a hero of a peculiarly modern kind, a cultural hero, burdened with the great (if ill-defined) hopes of at least two generations for the renewal of American acting and, through it, of the American theatre, American cinema and perhaps even American culture in general. His rebelliousness turned into public cynicism; the burden was too great.

The critical fascination with Brando made him increasingly

anxious, not just because of those aspects of his private life he preferred to shield from his fans but also, and more important, because he feared the paralysing self-consciousness that might come from the serious analysis of his extraordinary gift for acting. When Truman Capote visited him on location in Kyoto during 1956 to research a profile he was writing, Brando made an error of judgement which he would always regret. Capote, an amoral gadfly of an interviewer, deliberately got Brando drunk on vodka and then recorded the most memorable moments of a long, rambling, often very emotional Brando monologue. Off his guard, Brando discussed the most private of things: his feelings for his mother and father, his love affairs, his childhood and his own sense of inadequacy. 'Do you know how I make a friend?' asked Brando:

I go about it very gently. I circle around and around. I circle. Then, gradually, I come nearer. Then I reach out and touch them – ah, so gently . . . Then . . . I draw back. Wait awhile. Make them wonder. At just the right moment, I move in again. Touch them. Circle . . . They don't know what's happening. Before they realize it, they're all entangled, involved. I have them. And suddenly, sometimes, I'm all *they* have.[26]

When the profile appeared in the *New Yorker* magazine, Brando was horrified at what, to him, seemed a gross betrayal of his trust. Capote enjoyed the controversy but Brando felt humiliated. Recalling his victim's horror, Capote later reaffirmed his belief in its worthiness, describing Brando as 'a wounded young man who is a genius, but not markedly intelligent'. It hardly seemed an apology. Brando went into shock and for years afterwards he would complain about the microscopically cruel story and how it had damaged his image. 'The audience shouldn't know *me*, they should watch the character.' The Capote profile became a popular source for reviewers to exploit for new interpretations of his work.

After the trauma of this unwelcome public self-analysis, Brando seemed consciously to avoid any characters that were too close to his own personality. He sought to submerge his self in other, alien characters – a racist Southern soldier (*Sayonara*), a German officer of the Second World War (*The Young Lions*), a foppish Englishman

(*Mutiny on the Bounty*), an aristocrat (*Queimada!*, 1968), a Sicilian mafioso (*The Godfather*) and a very peculiar mystic (*Candy*, 1968). He even tried the unreality of slapstick comedy in *Bedtime Story* (1964) and Chaplin's dreary *A Countess from Hong Kong* (1966); both performances were dreadful miscalculations. Indeed, as the 1960s went on Brando's performances seemed to be less passionate and more formal, the variety of roles being exploited for their technical challenge rather than the complexity of their emotional skein. He determined to transcend his stardom. He would do whatever he had to in order to become a character different from the image in the public's fancy. He was trying to escape one of the basic traps in the Hollywood system, where being a star can of itself prevent one from acting. If one evades the trap by acting outstandingly, one becomes a bigger star, and one has to think of new ways to escape, and somewhere to escape to. Brando's career demonstrates the terrible irony of this on the grandest scale.

Too often he impersonated characters he had thought out rather than discovered within himself. The characters no longer *engaged* him in the way they used to; he became less inclined to take on those risk-laden roles which involved unappealing or unacceptable personalities (his glib attempt to make his Nazi character in *The Young Lions* into a kind of martyr was an early example of this trend). As Shelley Winters remarked, 'Actors can't bear to be hated and Marlon is no exception.' His one serious attempt at establishing his independence in Hollywood – the formation of his own produc- tion company, Pennebaker Productions (named in honour of his mother), resulted in *One-Eyed Jacks*, a long, wilfully unconventional Western which he directed himself. Brando's movie showed great promise (with some exciting direction), but it originally ran for over four and a half hours, and by the time others had cut it down to a more realistic length he had lost all interest in the project.

Elia Kazan remembers a poignant moment from 1963, when he and Brando were sitting in a room in the house of the dramatist Clifford Odets (who was dying from cancer). Brando seemed overcome with despair: 'Here I am, a balding middle-aged failure ... I feel a fraud when I act ... I've tried everything ... fucking, drinking, work. None of them means anything.'[27] During the 1960s his blunt comments to journalists exhibited not just impatience with them but also, more pointedly, self-contempt. When he agreed to take over the role originally intended for Montgomery Clift in John Huston's *Reflections in a Golden Eye* (1967), he merely said, 'The appeal to me of a neurotic role like Major Penderton? $750,000 plus $7\frac{1}{2}$ per cent of the gross receipts if we break even.' Angela Allen told me:

Did Marlon really just do it for the money? I think he probably did. By that stage in his career, he'd lost something; I don't think he knew what to do. He'd play little games all the time, testing you, seeing how far he could push you. 'I want a motorbike,' he'd demand. He'd get this brand-new Yamaha bike delivered to the set, and he'd never touch it. 'I want to sleep in the studio,' he'd announce. 'You can't.' '*I want to sleep in the studio!*' He was seeing how far you'd let him go. Testing you, you see. It wasn't the director who bothered Marlon. It was the producers who Marlon liked to upset. *They* were the people he disliked.[28]

The movie was, perversely, one of Brando's most interesting of the 1960s and its flaws serve to illustrate the change in his attitude. The story (a kind of American Gothic fantasy) takes place at an Army post in the Deep South, with repressed homosexual Penderton (Brando) becoming progressively obsessed by a mysterious private soldier who exercises the stallion loved by Mrs Penderton (Elizabeth Taylor). 'Is it morally honorable,' asks Penderton (during a lecture on 'Leadership, Strength, Power and War'), 'for the square peg to keep scraping around in the round hole rather than to discover and use the unorthodox one that would fit?' The soldier (an exhibitionist and an underwear fetishist) exacerbates the tensions in the Pendertons' marriage and causes their futile imbroglio of attraction, tolerance, repulsion and rivalry to surface. Mrs Penderton thinks nothing of beating her husband in public: 'That cleared the air,' she tells her startled guests. Penderton's pedantry, his spartan delight in the ego-aligning aesthetics of drill, all the professional qualities which constitute his defence in depth against his strange tangle of animal energies, inferiorities and nostalgia, are not merely negatives. He has a certain splendid obstinacy despite his mutilation by Army life, or rather, by a largely self-inflicted excess of that ethos of unemotional, unyielding, vegetative toughness which is a characteristic abuse of Army life as it underlines the Western myth of the lone rider. He is a character one should have expected Brando to engage with (reminding him, perhaps, of his own father), yet his performance turns out to be a strangely bloodless display, clever without ever being convincing. The Southern accent is mannered, the gestures seem to have been inspired by a slavish reading of Freud on the anal character (the repeated demonstrations of tidiness, the clipped, constipated-sounding voice, the compulsive concern with his appearance and so on). It is the kind of screen acting Olivier sometimes resorted to – full of superb little technical tricks yet with no sense of authenticity, a performance trailing in the cold ashes of a passion that has long been burnt out.

Brando's performance as Penderton showed the occasional, perverse effect of Method teaching: namely, to *draw attention* to the actor's skills. The gestures seem too rich for everyday consumption. They have been positioned to impress the visitor. In many of Brando's later roles (and at times during his best roles), one can 'catch' him acting, one can note his technical genius and lose sight of the character he is portraying. Kael makes a similar point when she argues that 'the non-conformist with no roles to play plays *with* his roles . . .' The organic truth of American movie history is that the new theme or the new star that gives the vitality to the medium is widely imitated and quickly exhausted before the theme or talent can develop. Everything good can be turned into a trick.'[29] Brando, whose acting was always intimately bound up with his vulnerability, did not feel that the emotional risks were still worth taking: 'There comes a time in one's life when you don't want to do it anymore. You know a scene is coming where you'll have to cry or scream and all those things, and it's always bothering you, always eating away at you . . .'

'Acting,' said Brando, 'is an illusion, a form of histrionic sleight of hand, and in order to carry it off well, an actor must have intense concentration . . . When actual shooting commences, I put in ear plugs to screen out the extraneous noises that inevitably prick at one's concentration.'[30] The contempt he felt, for himself and for movies, continued to show itself. Not only did he ignore his fellow actors, he sometimes failed to learn his lines (for *The Godfather* they were scribbled on his shirt cuffs and on strategically placed pieces of paper and 'idiot-boards', while for *Last Tango in Paris* they were sometimes written on the unfortunate Maria Schneider's breasts and buttocks). When acting in *The Formula* (1980) he had his lines wired to him via a fake hearing-aid his character wore. In *The Missouri Breaks* (1976) he decided to really ham it up, using more than one accent and switching costumes for no apparent reason (one moment he is dressed as a preacher, then he is wearing the clothes of a pioneer woman). The challenge seemed to be: 'If you're foolish enough to pay me for this, I'll do it.' His favourite comment was, 'I'm only doing it for the money.' He filmed a cameo role in *Superman* (1978) for a fee of $3.7 million and a brief mumbled scene in *Apocalypse Now* (1979) for $3.5 million. The handsome physique of the 1950s had, by the 1980s, given way to overindulgence and lethargy (he was always a compulsive eater when feeling depressed and now his weight rose to well over 300 pounds). The more the critics lamented his artistic decline, the less Brando seemed to care. He mocked their ideals and laughed at their seriousness, insisting that movies were 'not worth caring about'. Angela Allen recalls the problems she had with Brando during *Reflections in a Golden Eye*:

I don't remember him improvising, but he did this little trick: he'd mumble, and then he would just mouth the words throughout the take – he wouldn't actually *speak* them at all. The sound man, naturally, would be going mad, wondering why he wasn't picking up any sound. Sometimes he would speak, other times there'd just be this *mouthing*. I'd say, 'Marlon, *why*? Why do you do it to your fellow actors?' He'd be sheepish ... give me this embarrassed little-boy grin. He wasn't used to anyone challenging him. He was just playing games. Marlon could be a very childish person at times.[31]

His behaviour was intensely self-contradictory: for example, as soon as he made *The Freshman* in 1989, he told the newspapers it was 'a stinker' and that he was 'retiring from acting'. Shortly after this outburst, he issued a lengthy statement declaring he was 'proud' of the movie and was planning another acting project. Since the 1950s it appears that even Brando has found Brando enigmatic.

He once said, upon reaching middle age, that he felt 'a gloomy regret. Self-hatred. All men, when they reach my age, unless they are complete idiots, must feel an emptiness inside, a sense of anguish, of uselessness.' He spoke of the need to lead a 'responsible' life. However, a responsible life requires ethical and social intricacies of involvement for the political agent – precisely the kind of qualities that Brando's blithe chameleonism avoids. He forever runs the risk of protecting his freedom so dazzlingly, behind multiple masks and postures, that his autonomy becomes anonymity, his liberty homelessness and he himself ceases to be an emotionally involved participant in, and contributor to, the human community around him. Performative prowess may become not a means of finer self-expression but a screen behind which the vulnerable self hides in order to avoid self-disclosure. Brando's career prompts one to consider whether such fluidity of selfhood is also the destruction of selfhood. The director who surely knew him better than most people, Elia Kazan, has argued that the political events of the 1960s (especially the assassination of Martin Luther King) shocked Brando and led him to drift away from movie acting. Kazan recalls trying to persuade him to appear in *The Arrangement*:

He was so intense . . . that I didn't realize he'd walked me back to my car and opened the door to help me in. Before I got behind the wheel, he informed me that he simply couldn't do the part in my movie. At which he kissed me and looked so sorry I didn't ask any questions but drove away, planning to call him in a few days. I saw the man in the rear-view mirror, walking to his house and going in; he looked desolate. I never saw Marlon again, haven't seen him to this day.[32]

In 1966 Brando had bought the small atoll of Teti'aroa, twenty-five miles north of Tahiti, as a retreat. Later, he began construction of a settlement where waste would be recycled and solar energy would provide power. He continued to be involved in political campaigns for civil rights and the plight of the minorities (support-ing the Black Panthers, the American Indian Movement, anti-apartheid groups and UNICEF). His conduct left much to be desired. If he cared so much about these issues, why was he so uncritical in his support of activists he often had little knowledge of? Are the 'poor and honest' people he celebrates the same people who consume the 'junk culture' and the 'moronic' mass media he detests? For the working class, political concerns are intrusions, things to be overcome – there is nothing intrinsically enjoyable in them. For the middle class, political activity is a *choice*, and for the insensitive it can become an end in itself. Brando is middle class, and as earnest as he might feel, he can be remarkably patronizing at times. Being an indifferent political agent is not any more admirable than being an indifferent movie actor, and the moral cost is certainly greater. In 1974 he sent a starlet, Maria Cruz (dressed as an American Indian and calling herself Sacheen Littlefeather), to reject his Oscar and disrupt the Academy Award ceremonies by trying to read a fifteen-page speech about Hollywood's racial stereotyping of Indians. It was a gesture by a man too impatient to think really seriously about politics, but too proud to be silent. More recently he filmed his 1989 cameo in *A Dry White Season* for the Screen Actors Guild minimum wage and a contribution by the production company to an anti-apartheid organization (he then spoiled the gesture by making his disappointment with the movie public knowledge). The director, Euzan Palcy, said: 'The man I had on my set was still the Brando whose films revolutionized the whole relationship between actors and audience ... I felt that if Brando loves the project, he can still sustain a role. But I'm not sure he could sustain interest in a purely commercial enterprise.'[33]

Two of Brando's roles from the latter part of his career reveal how much of the early brilliance remains: *The Godfather* and *Last Tango in Paris*. Not only did these two performances prove that Brando was still, when he wanted to be, a great actor; they also provided him with a new challenge – the mature rebel, the outlaw in middle age. In *The Godfather* Brando's Don Corleone is a tough old Sicilian peasant who has risen to become a chieftain in an empire of Italian-American crime. He is an outlaw who has always craved acceptance by the ruling class and is proud of his apparent approbation. He tells his son, 'I *refused* to be a fool, dancing on a string for all those big shots.' Thematically, the movie manipulates the identification process by isolating its heroes in a moral vacuum in which they appear as forces of justice (the enemies include a crooked policeman, a venal movie producer, family traitors and drug pushers – the ideal context for Brando's sympathetic portrayal). They are endearing characters who 'just happen' to express themselves through brute violence. Corleone has taken literally the American success myth and done everything in his power to achieve it. Whereas the radical outlaws had struggled to escape from carefully conceived ambushes, the Corleones themselves set the traps, using the law to escape punishment. Thus in this movie the outlaw heroes have corrupted themselves with the most debased of society's institutions. One is reminded of Balzac's remark that behind every great fortune there rests a crime. As Brando told *Life* magazine, 'The picture made a useful commentary on corporation thinking in this country.'

Brando's acting in *The Godfather* was widely praised (winning him his second Academy Award), and, indeed, there is much to admire: his voice, which, after his near-fatal illness, moves up from the chest to the throat; his Italian gestures – the defiant/apologetic shrug, the slant of the head, the hands that shoot helplessly up; and that peculiar combination of sentimentality and ruthlessness, a toughly articulated benevolence, which makes Corleone so intriguing a presence. None the less, it is not an entirely fulfilling performance. Once one has worked out how the wheels go round, most of the charm has gone. It is hard to be moved by him, because one cannot help noticing the vast technical trick he is performing.

The Godfather was certainly a timely project for Brando, but it was not a dangerous one for him as an actor. *Last Tango in Paris*, on the other hand, is Brando at his most daring, producing precisely the kind of performance that underlined his unique acting gifts. In the movie a man (Paul) and a woman (Jeanne) meet in a Paris apartment which they are each inspecting with a view to renting it.

They copulate – the choice of verb is difficult, the act too brutal and detached to be called 'making love' – and, rising from the bare floorboards, silently, separately, they leave. Soon they return, and set up a series of meetings, which the man stipulates should be kept totally isolated from their past and present lives, even their identities ('No names'). The apartment is the theatre in which they have sex, sex shorn of all social conventions (by abbreviating the act, one abbreviates the experience – one can circumvent it, observe it). Inside the apartment, they work out the dynamics and subservience in an increasingly unconventional series of erotic acts. Outside the apartment, they are plagued by relatives, lovers, material concerns, politics and religion. The arrangement inverts all the values of the Judaeo-Christian tradition in that sex emerges as the positive aspect of human life, whereas civilization, restraint and self-control are presented as negative traits.

Brando's character represents, in his own words, 'the best fucking around'. He has mostly negative memories – drunken parents, humiliation, vagrant wanderings, meaningless marriages. Paul's forty-five years have brought him the full measure of suffering and humiliation: his wife is dead, his hair is thinning and his waistline growing thick. Paul recalls an earlier American tradition of rebellious individualism. Like Ahab, he has travelled the world, pursuing his vision in the face of repeated defeat, detour and disaster. He is the culmination of the twisted fringe characters that Brando has always been drawn to. In one scene, when Jeanne tells Paul that she has fallen in love, he makes a speech that is at the centre of this vision:

Is this man going to love you, build a fortress to protect you so you don't ever have to be afraid, lonely, or empty? Well, you'll never make it . . . It won't be long before he wants *you* to make a fortress of your tits and your smile and the way you smell till he feels secure enough and can worship you in front of the altar of his own prick. You're alone, you're all alone, and you won't be free of that feeling until you look death in the face.

The famous sodomy scene is thematic, summed up in the remark about 'looking up the ass of death to the womb of fear'. The woman's wedding to her lover approaches, and Brando's character begins to admit he feels involved. The spell is over, and she sees him less erotically and more as an ageing romantic. Even though Paul cannot relinquish his aggressive dominance, he tries to transcend the machismo of his 'whorefucker, barfighter, super-masculine' father and unite sex with love. He begins to realize, probably for the first time, that what breathes beneath him has a soul. Hitherto, sex has been a survival technique for him, but now it motions him towards a fuller commitment. During their last tango together, she shoots him with her father's revolver. 'I didn't know him,' she tells the police. 'I don't know his name.' The rebel figure – one of Brando's finest – is dead.

It is, by any standards, extraordinary acting, more about nerves, sinews and essences than about skin and appearances. Director Bertolucci observed that Brando 'loved and hated improvising his scenes. He loved it because it was new for him and hated it because it seemed a violation of his privacy.' This highlights the dialectic at the heart of Brando's career; the desire to break down the boundaries of his art battling with the desire to preserve the barriers that shield the private self. Bertolucci said that 'Brando is an angel as a man, a monster as an actor'. Brando's finest work comes from this very conflict; that is why he felt so painfully ambivalent about the results ('I felt violated from the beginning to the end'). After *Last Tango* he said, 'That's the last time I use up my energies.'

Brando brought the spirit of modernism to movie acting, including in his performances both visible self-consciousness and evident self-doubt. Like Clift, he was forever questioning the worth of his work: 'Why does anybody care about what any movie star has to say?' he exclaimed. 'Freud, Gandhi, Marx. These people are important. But movie acting is just dull, boring, childish work.' And again, 'We have no real theatre in America,' he always insists. 'If there were an art form in America, it would be making money.'[34] Only by the assertion that acting has a moral dimension, that it may have at best social and political effects, can one still these nagging doubts and fears, and salvage one's soul. Brando, along with Clift, showed the audience its own anxieties. The spirit of rebellion was taken into acting itself, challenging the form as well as the content of expression. For more than four decades Brando continued to struggle against all the conventions of stardom. 'It may seem peculiar, but I've spent most of my career wondering what I'd really like to do.' Kenneth Tynan remarked of Brando: 'He doesn't mind bruising his soul.' Elia Kazan, who has witnessed the development of Brando's career from the very beginning, continues to be in awe of his talent:

Marlon had everything. Not only was he, at one time, the most beautiful man in films, both in face and body, but he had all the essential talents. He had emotion of a terrifying and awesome intensity. He had great imagination but never eccentric, that is to say always within the bounds of reality ... He was a great mimic, could astonish with his voice as well as with his postures. He had an abundant and always ready humour. And he was capable of surprise – the dearest quality an actor can have for his director ... With Brando the director was always hoping for a miracle and he often got it. Finally he had what few actors have, a surprising intelligence. He would understand a role, yes, but also the theme and direction of an entire production. He was a true collaborator too.[35]

'An actor must interpret life,' said Brando, 'and in order to do so he must be willing to accept all experiences that life can offer. In fact, he must seek out more of life than life puts at his feet ... To grasp the full significance of life is the actor's duty, to interpret it his problem, and to express it his dedication.'[36] Marlon Brando became the template for the modern anti-hero, the virile but vulnerable male disenchanted with the traditional notions of masculinity. He used acting to express, with unprecedented power, the anxieties of the modern rebel male. Why does he remain such a memorable figure? In part, because he was so gifted and so concerned with the best ways to use those gifts. The torn T-shirt, the blue jeans, the mumble, the stutter, the stare, the sweaty sexuality: these are part of the Brando we remember. His 1950s image is still with us, stubborn and unstoppable, in light and shadow. 'I suppose,' says his character in On the Waterfront, 'some people just got faces that stick in your mind.'

4

James Dean

Only the cry of anguish can bring us to life; exaltation takes the place of truth

Albert Camus

James Dean was the ultimate teenage rebel, the definitive neurotic boy outsider. His career was over almost before it had begun. He spent less than two years in Hollywood, and when he died in 1955 (at the age of twenty-four) only one of his three movies had been seen by the public. His image, more than thirty years after his death, seems richly symbolic of the culture of 1950s America: youthful, anxious and angry, insolent yet innocent, a Narcissus in denim, forever young. Andy Warhol described Dean's image as 'the damaged but beautiful soul of our time'. His movies show him coping with the perennial teenage problems of coming to terms with sexuality, establishing a working relationship with parents and trying to find a place in the world, all against a background of a vague and generalized air of discontent with the family, authority and the status quo. More than any other actor, Dean distilled the essence of youthful non-belonging – in the same sense as Holden Caulfield meant it – for teenagers in the West. His life was as alienated as that of the characters in his movies. His appeal was not so much to a sex as to an age group. What he offered was a rallying-point against the adult world of corruption and disenchantment.

Dean was a child of the American Midwest. He grew up in Fairmount, Indiana, the quintessence of the small, quiet, intimate town. 'Hush,' says a character in *Picnic* (one of the first plays to highlight the Midwest), 'the neighbors are on their porches.' Twenty miles to the south of Fairmount is Muncie, the town selected by Robert Lynd for his classic study of Middle America, *Middletown*. Twenty miles to the north of Fairmount one finds a town called Normal. Fairmount was a Quaker town and Quakers have described themselves as people 'who praise the zero in themselves'. The mood was captured in Bob Dylan's 1967 song 'With God on Our Side':

> Oh my name it is nothin'
> My age it means less
> The country I come from
> Is called the Midwest
> I's taught and brought up there
> The laws to abide
> And that land that I live in
> Has God on its side.[1]

Fairmount is in the heartland of America. Its original name, 'A-1', reflected the surveyor's coordinates. In every US Census from 1890 to 1940, the national centre of population has been Indiana; Fairmount is central. The frontier is the border, the rim, the cutting-edge of consciousness; on the border between the old and the new, it is a zone of transition where America realized itself. It was in Fairmount that some of the archetypal images of America were born: the hamburger and the ice-cream cone. In the 1950s it was in places like this that the young sons of Mom and Pop Culture were born. While James Dean was making his first movie, a one-time truck driver called Elvis Presley was recording rock 'n' roll songs in the Sun Studios in Memphis.

James Byron Dean was born on 8 February 1931, in Marion, Indiana, the only child of Winton and Mildred (née Wilson) Dean. Both parents were native Indianans: Mildred came from a Methodist family, Winton a Quaker from a line of original settlers that could be traced back to the *Mayflower*. The family home was part of Green Gables Apartments, on 320 East 4th Street. Winton Dean, a quiet, dour man, was a dental technician employed by the federal government. Mildred was in many ways the opposite of her husband in outlook; she was gregarious, good-humoured and positive in her view of the world around her. Their son Jimmy seemed as ordinary a boy as ever came out of Grant County. He looked healthy enough, although in fact he was delicate by constitution, often suffering from nosebleeds and internal bleeding, which caused black and blue marks on his arms and legs.

In July 1935 the family was forced to uproot itself. First, they moved to a 300-acre farm at Fairmount, ten miles south of Marion, owned by Winton's sister Ortense and her husband, Marcus Winslow. Later that year they moved again, this time to a cramped bungalow in California, 3,000 miles away, where Winton took a job as a dental technician at a Santa Monica hospital. Unlike the families of Clift and Brando, who moved around out of financial fortune and volition, Dean's family travelled out of financial misfortune and necessity. Jimmy spent most of his time with Mildred; he always had an extremely close relationship with his mother. She was a farmer's daughter, a warm, sensitive woman with an interest in poetry, theatre and music (it is said she chose 'Byron' as her son's middle name in honour of her favourite poet, although this is debatable – Byron was a fairly common name in the Midwest, pronounced 'B'arn' further south). She would read to him, help him act out plays in a toy theatre, and sent him to tap-dancing, violin and piano lessons. She taught him to think imaginatively, to entertain the grandest of notions, the greatest dreams. Overprotective and vicariously ambitious, Mildred cocooned her son throughout his formative years.

Early in 1938 Mildred was diagnosed as having advanced breast cancer and Winton was obliged to sell the family home to meet the cost of the hospital bills. Mildred died in 1939. His financial resources exhausted, Winton was unable to afford the fare to accompany his wife's body back to Indiana (nor could he drive to Marion, having been forced to sell the family car). He sent the body by train with Jimmy and his grandmother.

Mildred was only twenty-nine years of age when she died. Jimmy reacted by withdrawing into himself, hiding his pain and his fear. 'Jimmy said nothing – just looked at me,' his father told

Modern Screen later, in 1957. 'Even as a child he wasn't much to talk about his hurts.' A cousin observed: 'He shut it all inside him. The only person he could ever have talked about it with was lying there in the casket.'[2] There followed a succession of mother substitutes to whom he attached himself: first Ortense Winslow, his aunt, whom he always called 'Mom'; then his high-school teacher Adeline Nall; in later years there were his agent, Jane Deacy, and his co-stars Julie Harris, Mercedes McCambridge and Elizabeth Taylor. Barbara Glenn, one of Dean's New York friends, recalled:

The only person I could believe was really close to him as a person was his mother . . . He never really had anybody, because at that point I think Jimmy lost everybody. It was such an irrevocable loss that it could never be filled . . . In a strange way she was this fantasy creature even to him. He loved her very much and I don't know that he had not fantasized a lot about her . . . Jimmy had a terrible anger for his mother. *She died.* He was a nine-year-old child saying how can you leave me? When he talked about her, it wasn't a twenty-one- or twenty-two-year-old. It was a child and he was deserted. He'd loved her desperately. He'd loved her desperately and she left him. I think it had a profound effect on him. And he expressed it in terms of his art.[3]

Separated from his father by geography and from his mother by death, Jimmy began to assume that complex mixture of toughness and vulnerability that would eventually help make him such an intriguing actor. The rage and the aggression were always undermined by a helpless desperation. Each time he described his feelings about his mother's death and that journey back home with her coffin, he made the story sound increasingly reminiscent of William Faulkner's classic *As I Lay Dying.* All the family tensions came back with vivid and urgent images. 'My mother died on me when I was nine years old,' he would often say. 'What does she expect me to do? Do it all by myself?'

Jimmy was sent back to Fairmount to live with Marcus and Ortense Winslow. Fairmount was a retreat for him; it matched his frame of mind. Geographically remote from the sectors of change in America, Fairmount, because of its isolation, preserved a way of life that had disappeared from the cities almost a decade before. It was one of the quiet little towns, built from the basic formula of white wooden school, post office, garage, diner and two or three small churches to suit varying tastes. For a young boy keen to shut out the painful memories of travel and transformation, Fairmount was a small, warm, protective shell. He took to farm life and, by the end of his first year with the Winslows, he could drive their tractor as well as perform all the chores of a young farm worker. 'Now, this was a real farm I was on,' Dean later told Hedda Hopper. 'I worked like crazy – as long as someone was watching me. The forty acres of oats was a huge stage, and when the audience left, I took a nap and things didn't get plowed or harrowed.' Although such memories have to be treated with suspicion (Dean often enjoyed depicting his younger self as a Huck Finn character if he thought journalists would warm to such an image), the evidence tends to support the idea of a playful farm life. Jimmy was a boy who seemed to be constantly reinventing himself, a habit and a process that had begun very early in a rather unconventional childhood.

At the local school he was, to begin with, a lonely figure. Misunderstanding (exacerbated by his grudging recognition of his poor eyesight) led to apathy, and apathy led to restlessness. His self-consciousness was heightened when he broke his front teeth and had to wear false ones. Sometimes he would make an effort to establish friendships at school, but more often he preferred to return to the farm and resume his solitary role-playing games. The first person to really have an influence on Dean after his mother's death was James DeWeerd, pastor of Fairmount's Wesleyan Church. DeWeerd was an odd mixture of worldly sage and wry Midwestern storyteller. He had been a distinguished war hero and was one of the few people in Fairmount to have travelled abroad. Dean would listen as DeWeerd told him of the exotic places he had visited and showed him home movies of bullfights in Mexico. He encouraged the romantic in Dean. He cited the right sources, instilling the desire to 'live deep and suck out all the marrow of life', to explore and examine, create and appreciate. The small-town context highlighted DeWeerd's particular appeal, and in Dean he had a most impressionable student. He taught Dean to drive, and then took him to watch the Indianapolis 500. 'Conformity is cowardice,' he told the boy. Dean was inspired to buy his first motorcycle – a Czech model, with a top speed of fifty miles per hour. He often joined a small group of neophyte bikers at Marvin Carter's Cycle Shop on Fairmount Pike, just two doors away from the Winslow farm, where they would race each other and talk about fast cars and fashion. It seemed that the young Jimmy Dean was beginning to enjoy the company of his peers. He became, despite his lack of height, a fairly talented basketball player and did well at other sports, especially track and field events. It was, none the less, the drama class and the debating society in which he made his mark. Adeline Nall, his teacher and drama coach, urged him to do a reading for the Women's Christian Temperance Union. He won a prize and became one of her most enthusiastic students. She led him into the school plays, and in his senior year he played Grandpa in *You Can't Take It with You*. He graduated with honours and left for California. True to the pattern of the classic American hero, he began his adventures from the outskirts.

Dean returned to Santa Monica in 1949. Winton Dean had remarried four years after Mildred's death and, it seems, was looking forward to re-establishing a family environment for his only son. Jimmy and his step-mother, Ethel, circled each other warily. They were both too cautious to make waves, although the atmosphere was often tense in their modest little house. The nine-year separation of father from son had created a painfully evident communication problem. The resentment Jimmy felt towards his father was hardly ever articulated, and was never something he liked to show in public, but it was undeniable and insuperable. The idea of a father was an abstraction to him. Winton Dean was just the man who had sent him away with his mother's coffin. Ethel looked on as Winton struggled to win back his son. He bought him a 1939 Chevy in a final attempt to bridge their differences, but it was obvious the tensions remained. Winton disliked his son's acting pretensions, regarding the theatre as an unpredictable and rather effeminate profession. After a year of attempting to please Winton by attending Santa Monica City College and dealing indifferently with a pre-law course, Jimmy left both his father's house and the local college to enter UCLA. He was attracted to the university because of its wide range of courses on the performing arts – theatre, movies and music.

UCLA was a privileged arena for young students to learn their craft, with a teaching roster which could always be enlarged with guests culled from Hollywood's leading producing, writing, directing and acting talent. Dean appeared in only one play at UCLA, cast as Malcolm in the university's major production of *Macbeth*. He was not a success, with critics being particularly distressed by his strong Midwestern accent and his inability to deal with the play's distinctive rhythms. However, Isabelle Draesmar, a Hollywood agent, thought he showed enough talent to take him on to her books. He subsequently lost interest in UCLA and concentrated upon making a living as an actor.

His first paid job came when an advertising agency hired him to play (or, more accurately, pose as) an all-American boy in a one-minute television commercial for Pepsi-Cola. Dean, wearing a manic grin, could be seen pushing to the front, looking more hungry for the camera than thirsty for a coke. He was then asked to appear with Roddy McDowall and Gene Lockhart in a semi-religious play especially filmed for broadcast on Easter Sunday. Dean, playing (rather incredulously) John the Apostle, had a mere three lines, but it seems they were sufficient for the girls of the Immaculate Heart High School to form a James Dean Appreciation Society.

In 1952 Dean appeared in the movie *Has Anybody Seen My Gal?* and delivered his longest line yet: 'Hey, Gramps, I'll have a chocolate malt, heavy on the choc, plenty of milk, four spoons of malt, two scoops of vanilla ice cream, one mixed and one floating.' He looked like any other young American of the period: rather short; somewhat frail perhaps; and with an expression that might have seemed impish, but was generally carefree and thoroughly optimistic. After *Has Anybody Seen My Gal?*, Dean was keen to move on. He had long discussions with the actor James Whitmore, who agreed to give him lessons in Method acting, which had made its way from New York to California as the students of Strasberg and Kazan came west. Towards the end of the summer of 1951 Whitmore urged Dean to move to New York City, study at the Actors' Studio and try stage acting and live television work. Never one to give credit to anyone but himself for his ascendency, Dean none the less considered Whitmore a great catalyst. 'Whitmore,' he said, 'made me see myself and gave me the key.' He borrowed money from Marcus and Ortense and James DeWeerd back in Fairmount, and soon he was heading east to Manhattan.

During the winter of 1951–2 Dean started work in New York – auditioning for theatre and television roles, studying with a number of acting coaches and, once again, creating a new 'self'. He read Kerouac and the Beat poets, Rimbaud and Gide, Sartre and Camus. The farmboy craved culture. He started to copy other people's mannerisms, styles of dress, speech patterns and opinions. He was never a political person, but if it was fashionable Dean was happy to embrace the 'cool' views of the day. His role models were Montgomery Clift and Marlon Brando. He studied their movies, sat and gazed at them at the Actors' Studio and worked hard at assimilating their styles. The fascination bordered on the obsessive. He would follow them along the street, he would note down the addresses of their friends and he paid money for their unlisted telephone numbers. For a while he must have seemed a suspicious, perhaps even sinister, figure, trailing the young movie stars and assuming their mannerisms. Clift started hearing about the young man with the obsessive interest in his work, and said, 'Who *is* that fucking creep, anyway?' Soon the telephone calls came. Clift would pick up the phone and sometimes hear nothing except the nervous breathing of Dean, and he started changing his number to escape the eccentric calls. Brando would listen to Dean talking in a quivering voice to the answering service, leaving messages and expressing hero worship for him. Dean would sometimes go through periods when he resented their lack of interest and he 'retaliated' by phoning them up to play 'Hound Dog' to them as loudly as possible. The extraordinary fascination with his two idols appeared to many people as a pathetic condition (some felt it was pathological). On one occasion, Dean persuaded Sammy Davis

Junior to take him to a party where Brando was expected to be. Dean arrived dressed up in an exact replica of Brando's *Wild One* outfit, only to find Brando wearing an expensive three-piece suit. Later on, at another party, Brando took Dean to one side and asked him if he 'realized he was sick'. He gave Dean the name of an analyst. 'At least his *work* improved,' Brando recalled. The hero worship, however, continued. In letters to friends he sometimes signed himself 'James-Brando-Clift-Dean'.

Dean's appearances at the Actors' Studio were irregular, partly because he resented the criticisms of his work (particularly from Strasberg), partly because he needed to earn a living. City life encouraged a change in Dean's appearance. The country child's soft, rounded face gave way to tauter, thinner lines; his jaw and cheekbones became more prominent; and his torso looked leaner and more muscular. Wandering around Broadway, he would see familiar faces, like Roddy McDowall's. In casting line-ups he would be vying for roles with Paul Newman and Steve McQueen. It was an exciting, yet ruthlessly competitive, period for young actors.

Dean was living with his friend Bill Bast at the Iroquois Hotel on West 44th Street, which was situated in a relatively attractive area (with the Algonquin and the Harvard Club as neighbours). It was not the obvious place for an impoverished young actor to reside, and it remains something of a mystery how he and Bast managed to pay their rent. During the day Dean could usually be found in 'the actors' drugstore', Cromwell's, in the NBC building at Rockefeller Plaza – the place where many young actors met to drink coffee, talk about work, discuss deals, dream up new projects and check the lists in *Variety*. It was in Cromwell's that Dean met most of the people he later regarded as his closest friends: Bill Gunn, Martin Landau, Barbara Glenn, Leonard Rosenman and Billy James.

A young agent called Jane Deacy became intrigued with Dean and guided him into several television projects. His initial job was as a standby comic for *Beat the Clock*, a popular quiz show. His task was to act out the sight gags and comedy material the contestants were assumed to have improvised and he did so with tremendous energy. It may have been a poor showcase for his talent, but when the camera was on him, he was determined to keep it there. There followed several bit-parts in weekly series such as *T-Men in Action, The Web, Tales of Tomorrow* and *Martin Kane*. He also had a walk-on part in an early 'Studio One' teleplay. Records show that in 1953 he had at least fourteen screen credits – a very successful year for a young actor. A reputation was established. He became fairly well known as an extremely capable juvenile, a little limited in his dramatic range but, none the less, rather memorable. Dean appeared in two shows written by Rod Serling (known for his work on *The Twilight Zone*); one was entitled *A Long Time Till Dawn*, in which Dean played a character described by Serling as 'terribly upset and psyched out, a precursor to the hooked generation of the 1960s, the type that became part of the drug/rock culture'. Serling recalled, 'Jimmy Dean played the part brilliantly. I can't imagine anyone playing that particular role better.'

In the autumn of 1953 Dean went home to Fairmount, but he had spent some of the summer as a paid member of the crew of a luxury yacht owned by Broadway producer Lemuel Ayres. Both Ayres and his wife were impressed with Dean, and Ayres promised to consider him for a part in a play he was preparing: *See the Jaguar*. Ayres decided to cast Dean in the key role of Wally Wilkins, a bewildered youth who has been completely shut off from the world by an overzealous mother and who, set free, has his eyes opened to a world of beauty and brutality. The advance publicity described the work as an 'allegorical Western without a horse'. It was not a successful play, although Dean received several favourable notices.

Dean's second (and final) Broadway appearance occurred in 1954, when he was signed by producer Billy Rose to play a scheming Arab youth involved with a homosexual tourist in Ruth and Augustus Goetz's dramatization of André Gide's semi-autobiographical novel *The Immoralist*. Dean's character, Bachir, is the catalyst for a French archaeologist's succumbing to his latent homosexuality when the youth introduces him to a native homosexual. The Frenchman, who is on vacation with his wife, is left alone to redefine his identity after his marriage collapses. Dean won all the best notices (and received a 'Theatre World Award' as one of the most promising actors of the year), but he handed in two weeks' notice on the opening night after a run-in with the director. The defiant gesture was, in reality, not as principled as Dean liked people to think. He knew that his agent was considering several movie offers and he was keen to ensure he was not committed to any long-running New York jobs in case the 'right' offer was made. Even the most prudent of decisions could be made by Dean to seem the outcome of pent-up frustration and confusion.

His agent felt he was perfect for the part of Caleb in the Warner Brothers movie *East of Eden*. The director, Elia Kazan, had seen Dean at the Actors' Studio and had serious doubts about his ability. He did, however, agree to give Dean a screen test. Kazan has recalled the first impression he had of Dean at the audition:

When I walked in he was slouched at the end of a leather sofa in the waiting room, a heap of twisted legs and denim rags, looking resentful for no particular reason. I didn't like the expression on his face, so I kept him waiting. I also wanted to see how he'd react to that. It seemed that I'd outtoughed him, because when I called him into my office, he'd dropped the belligerent pose. We tried to talk, but conversation was not his gift, so we sat looking at each other . . .[4]

Kazan, not the most even-tempered of people, felt more enthusiastic after he studied the screen test. Dean won the role. There had been rumours during the previous year that Kazan had been trying to persuade Clift and Brando to star as brothers in the movie (a fascinating idea), and now Dean was set to emulate their success. He moved to Hollywood in March 1954 and lived at the Warner Brothers lot.

Kazan did not regard Dean as an actor with the potential to equal the achievements of Clift and Brando, although he recognized it was prudent to allow Dean to think otherwise. This was the great irony: Dean, the ambitious young actor who dreamed of matching the finest work of his idols, impressed Kazan by being himself – not, like Clift or Brando, adapting himself to a role, but rather adapting the role to himself. When Clift had played a young soldier in *The Search*, people had asked the director where he found a 'soldier who can act'. When Brando played Kowalski in *Streetcar*, his friends observed how much the character differed from the actor's own personality. When Dean played Cal, people (including his closest friends) said he seemed to be playing Dean. His reputation preceded him. For Kazan, Dean was right for the part of Cal because 'he *was* Cal'. He said: 'Jimmy was it. He was it. He was vengeful, he had a sense of aloneness and he was suspicious. He let you into a private club that had only a few members.'[5] Bill Bast, Dean's room-mate from New York, claimed that watching Cal Trask in *East of Eden* was the closest any movie-goer ever got to seeing 'the real James Dean' (not, one would have thought, a comment that an actor would regard as a desirable reaction). Adeline Nall, Dean's old teacher, remarked: 'Many of the movements of "Cal Trask" were characteristic movements of James Dean. His funny little laugh which ripples with the slightest provocation, his quick, jerky, springy walks and actions, his sudden change from frivolity to gloom – all were just like Jim used to do.'[6] What 'Cal' used to do, no one knows; Dean's personality completely overwhelmed the character.

East of Eden was John Steinbeck's metaphorical postscript to the biblical drama of the world's second generation, Cain and Abel. Cain killed his brother, Abel, thus committing the first violence of man against man, destroying the biblical world's first nuclear family. Although the Steinbeck allegory (set in the Salinas Valley of California around 1918) was not directly concerned with social problems, it struck a nerve in its confrontation between generations, the son who questions his father's values as opposed to the son who follows them. Cal (Dean) is the younger of two motherless brothers, brought up by their strict and law-abiding father, Adam (Raymond Massey). Dean's Cal is the 'bad' twin who aches to be loved for himself by his authoritarian father. He is a confused, anxious youth: 'I gotta know who I am. I *gotta* know!' He is the young male demanding confirmation of himself from his parents. He pleads with his cool, conventional father ('*Talk* to me!') and, when he learns of her existence, he pleads with his whorehouse madam mother ('Let me *talk* to you!'). Cal is an outcast, an outlaw, an outsider, who cannot please his parents in a culture where, traditionally, parents demand that their children conform to their own adult needs and values. His father is a Freudian nightmare of a man: repressed, obsessively religious, stern, demanding and cold. Nothing Cal does seems to please him.

Adam dreams of freighting his lettuce crop to meal tables in the east by means of refrigerated wagons. He sinks all his savings into the project, but the experiment fails and he is ruined. This financial disaster further erodes Adam's status within the close-knit farming community. Cal tries to gain his father's affections by replacing, through a business venture of his own, the capital which his father has lost.

His love for his brother's fiancée, Abra (Julie Harris), underlines his alienation. Like Brando's characters, Cal prefers a 'good' woman, not a rebel like himself (he wants someone stable to hold on to). His impulsiveness unnerves everyone around him: 'He's scary,' Abra says. 'He looks at you sort of like an animal.' At one point Cal goes into the barn where his father has stored some blocks of ice and, in a sudden fit of anger, starts hurling chunks down the chute. 'Why did you push that ice down?' his father asks. Cal mumbles, 'I don't know.' Their estrangement is evident at the dinner table, where Cal and his father sit far apart, the space and the silence dominating the scene. 'You kept on forgivin' us,' says Cal, 'but you never *loved* us!' During their arguments the camera tilts up and down to reflect the differences in power and perspective. When Cal persuades his father to tell him about his mother, he is told, 'I wanted to save you pain.' '*Pain?*' Cal exclaims, his voice trembling, his body twisted in anguish. Cal's mother denies him her affection, just like his father. When he visits her she tries to send him away. She finally relents by giving him money, but financial assistance is all he gets ('Go on, get out of here,' she snarls).

Money and love do not go together. When Cal presents his impoverished father with money he has earned from the sale of a bean crop, the gift is rejected. Adam construes Cal's efforts as profiteering by selling the beans during the wartime shortage. Cal says, 'I'll keep it for you, I . . . I . . . I'll wrap it up. I'll just keep it in here and then you'll . . .' Adam interrupts: 'I'll *never* take it! Son . . . I'd be happy if you'd give me something like . . . well, like your brother's given me. Something *honest* and human and good . . . Don't be angry, son. If you want to give me a present, give me a good life. That's something I could value.' Cal hugs his father, clinging to him the way he has held on to walls and doors and other objects throughout the action. Inarticulate with grief, he runs from the house, expelled from Eden, seeking shelter beneath the branches of a large tree. 'You're mean and vicious and wild,' Aaron (Richard Davalos) taunts the outcast. 'Don't touch Abra again.' He turns against the others, accusing his father of having failed him utterly: 'Tonight I even tried to *buy* your love. But now I don't want it. I don't *need* it any more . . . I don't need *any* kind of love.' He tries to hurt the others as they have hurt him. 'I did an awful thing,' Cal confesses to his father, who has had a stroke brought on by Aaron's sudden drunken departure for the war after Cal has shown him their mother's whorehouse. When his father wants to speak to him, Cal leans in to hear the man's enfeebled voice. At last, his father talks to him, asking him to stay and take care of him. As Abra opens the door to leave, Cal, his face alight, gives her a look of confirmation. The unconvincingly penitential ending does little to erase the memory of the conflict that preceded it.

East of Eden, although overblown and sentimental, reveals much of true human feeling and behaviour, communication and the failure to communicate, the tragedy of jealousy and the gap between youth and maturity. As Steinbeck's tortured anti-hero, Dean gives a performance notable in its physical and vocal intensity. It is an extraordinarily risk-laden approach, and there are many moments when Dean's expressive style seems almost comic in its straining for effect (for example, the scene in which Cal tries to give Adam some money). None the less, the scenes in which it works are remarkably dynamic. Although *East of Eden* is a First World War period piece, it has a distinctly 1950s glaze to it; in Dean's moodiness and isolation and his battles with language, he makes Cal seem vividly contemporary. Dean's image confirmed and rendered acceptable the fact that men are as tormented by feelings of rejection and loneliness as women. The movie admits that what makes a man whole is approved by the first male in his life, his father. The narrative shows how the enslavement of a son to an authoritarian father emasculates the young man unless infantile ties can be broken and the unresolved need confronted and relinquished. It was one of the key characterizations of the teenage rebel male. *East of Eden* is such a crucial youth movie because it indulges the young person's unprincipled and shameless yearning to be the centre of attention and affection. As François Truffaut commented: '*East of Eden* is the first film to give us a Baudelairean hero, fascinated by vice and contrast, loving the family and hating the family at one and the same time. James Dean, the freshly plucked "*fleur du mal*" . . .'[7]

Dean's acting in *East of Eden* shows how indebted he was to Clift and Brando. He was working, quite consciously, to synthesize the sensitivity of Clift with the brooding physicality of Brando. Whereas Clift and Brando communicated the moral strength of the rebel, Dean kept the world at a distance, his body huddled as if against the cold. His resignation underlined the restricted personality of the world he inhabited. 'Brando,' said Kazan, 'was Dean's hero; everyone knew that, because he dropped his voice to a cathedral hush when he talked about Marlon. I invited Brando to come to the set and enjoy some hero worship. Marlon did and was very gracious to Jimmy, who was so adoring that he seemed shrunken and twisted in misery.'[8]

When Brando eventually got to see the finished movie, he was distinctly displeased with Dean's performance: 'Jim and I worked together at the Actors' Studio in New York, and I have great respect for his talent. However, in that film, Mr Dean appears to be wearing my last year's wardrobe and using my last year's talent.'[9] The mumbling delivery, the bowed head and upward-turned eyes, the fidgeting hands – all are there in Dean's performance, and they made it extremely easy for people to describe him at the time as 'Brando's kid brother'. The photographer Roy Schatt recalls Dean asking him why he was always being compared to Brando:

I gave him the obvious answer . . . both were anti-establishment characters. I also told him that maybe part of it was publicity, plain and simple, and that someone might have figured that Dean could cash in on Brando's success. Jim faced me without anger, and said, 'I don't want that kind of help.' I regretted my comment immediately, as he looked genuinely hurt. His character cracked, for just a second, and the vulnerable being underneath shone through . . . At times he seemed almost obsessed with Brando. Occasionally, for no apparent reason, he would begin quoting *A Streetcar Named Desire*. One time, during a discussion of Method acting, he took off his shirt and ripped his undershirt to shreds, yelling 'Stella!' in imitation of Marlon Brando.[10]

Kazan, who worked with them both, is keen to resist the equation:

People were to compare them, but they weren't alike. Marlon, well trained by Stella Adler, had excellent technique. He was proficient in every aspect of acting, including characterization and make-up. He was also a great mimic. Dean had no technique to speak of . . . On my film, Jimmy would either get the scene right immediately, without any detailed direction – that was 95 per cent of the time – or he couldn't get it at all.[11]

Dean does not often show off or act out. Rather, he beckons us into his recessive self, with a discreet flourish as sly as it is compelling. His face corresponds to a dominant physiognomic type: blond hair, regular features. Further, the fluid mobility of his expressions reflects the ambivalent nature of the adolescent face, still hesitating between childhood's melancholy and the mask of the adult – a smooth-cheeked subversive. John Dos Passos wrote of 'the resentful hair . . . the deep eyes floating in lonesomeness, the bitter look, the scorn on the lip'. The photogenic quality of this face, even more than that of Clift or Brando, is rich with all the ambiguity of an ageless age, mixing scowls with surprise, delinquent glamour with rustic innocence, disarmed candour with sudden coldness, resolution with collapse. As Edgar Morin put it, 'The face of James Dean is an ever-changing landscape in which can be discerned the contradictions, uncertainties, and enthusiasms of the adolescent soul.'[12]

Roy Schatt's famous 'Times Square' photograph of Dean is a fine illustration of the actor's iconic appeal: he looks a shadowy, fugitive figure on that rainy, cold city street, his shoulders hunched, slouching along the iron railing that divides Broadway and Seventh Avenue. It tells Dean's story the way he wanted it told: the loner in the city. Dean became a living sign, codifying the uniform of youth. His clothes were carefully chosen to express a whole attitude towards society: faded blue jeans, scuffed cowboy boots, leather jacket, T-shirt — so many ostensible signs of a resistance against the social conventions of the adult world, selected with a painful self-consciousness that symbolized his youthful insecurities more tellingly than anything else he did. As Truffaut observed at the time:

In James Dean, today's youth discovers itself. Less for the reasons usually advanced: violence, sadism, hysteria, pessimism, cruelty and filth, than for others infinitely more simple and commonplace: modesty of feeling, continual fantasy life, moral purity without relation to everyday morality but all the more rigorous, eternal adolescent love of tests and trials, intoxication, pride, and regret at feeling oneself 'outside' society, refusal and desire to become integrated and, finally, acceptance — or refusal — of the world as it is.[13]

The power of his screen image is often remarkably impressive. At his best he seems *nearer*, more tangible than his fellow performers. 'Perhaps part of this power,' said his acquaintance Mike Wilmington, 'came because he was nearsighted, because, in all his films, he couldn't *see* much of what was happening — and, therefore, fell back on himself; created a universe out of his body, his face and his words that *forced* the other actors to adjust to his rhythm — enter his world.'[14] His poor eyesight was one reason for his appearance of being a stranger among familiar faces; another factor was the selfish nature of his acting. He knew all the tricks employed by actors to catch the camera eye. He was also quick to adopt another's striking mannerism. One of his friends recalled: 'I don't think he did it so much as it overtook him because he was so impressionable.' He was an observant person when he was not working. He would wear his glasses and sit quietly, studying people's physical characteristics and their speech patterns. When he was living in New York he would try, as an exercise, to imitate a variety of characters on the street, and noted the movements of down-and-outs in wino alleys.

The careful observations seemed only to heighten Dean's concern for his own personality and appearance. Kazan recalled Dean's narcissistic fascination with his new image: 'He used to stand in front of the mirror in his room and take roll after roll of close-up photographs of his face, with only the slightest variation of expression.'[15] It was as though he was seeking a soul beneath the skin, an answer to the appearance. Dean's technique was designed, like psychoanalytic therapy, to release emotional lava, thereby enabling him to become acquainted with his depths and then to possess them enough to be taken over by the role. Yet the virtue of Dean's method was also its professional shortcoming: the worse the role, the more one needs an external style to project. Dean could only squander energy in a bad role, consuming his precious hoard of identity and tarnishing his hard-earned style by offering charm to lines which never began to probe his personality. Unlike Clift or Brando, Dean was often found wanting when faced with alien qualities in a character.

Dean's directors were forced into taking highly unconventional or aggressive action when he lost his hold on a role. For example, during the shooting of a scene in *East of Eden*, Dean found it impossible to respond to any direction. Kazan decided the only way to get a performance from Dean was to get him drunk on Chianti and then commence filming. Kazan also noted how Dean seemed to rely upon genuine, off-screen feelings for his characterization. He thus encouraged the animosity that was evident between Dean and Raymond Massey, so that by the time the movie was shot, the two men really detested each other. Kazan sought to make Dean embody the theme of rebellion, and he exploited Dean's nervous system to make his most radical point: Cal as juvenile delinquent, a symbol of youthful self-pity. Kazan and Dean had a common cause in confrontation with the father, the father as repressive society and society as an oppressive patriarchy. 'He had a grudge against all fathers,' said Kazan, and he exploited this feeling. Kazan also worked on the tensions between Dean and his 'brother', Richard Davalos, in order to enrich the movie's sibling rivalry with a sexual ambivalence between the brothers. Thus he insisted that the two actors live together while the movie was made. The tensions on the screen were charged with real emotions. According to Dennis Hopper, Dean used every means possible to generate the appropriate mental *and* physical state for his perform-ance. For one scene, Hopper recalls, 'he really wanted to look uptight. So to get himself really uncomfortable, he told me he didn't pee all day until they did the shot.'[16] Kenneth Anger has claimed that some of Dean's screen mannerisms were the result of living the character's life rather too passionately – the famous scratching of the crotch, Anger says, sometimes came about because Dean was suffering from 'crabs'. 'I can't divert into being a social human being when I'm working on a hero like Cal, who's essentially demonic,' Dean argued.[17]

Dean's personality at this time reflected a pathetic wish to ingratiate himself tempered with an ingrained distrust of others. His close friends all seemed to have stories of how Dean had tested their affection for him. It was, as he said himself, as though he had Montgomery Clift saying, 'Forgive me,' at the same time as Marlon Brando was saying, 'Fuck you!' Actor Bill Gunn said, 'Jimmy was affected by Brando, but he was more moved by Monty. Jimmy dug Monty's fractured personality – his dislocated quality. Brando was too obvious. Monty had more class.'[18] Clift's characters, such as George Eastman in *A Place in the Sun*, captured a particularly poignant vulnerability, which often showed itself in the young man's relationship with women – especially his mother. The theme was of obvious interest to Dean. Dennis Hopper recalls a very enlightening conversation with Dean:

I told Jimmy I *had* to know what he was doing because acting was my whole life . . . I asked him why he became an actor and he said, 'Because I hate my mother and father. I wanted to get up on stage . . . and I wanted to *show* them. I'll tell you what made me want to become an actor, what gave me that drive to be the best. My mother died when I was almost nine. I used to sneak out of my uncle's house at night and go to her grave, and I used to cry and cry on her grave – Mother, why did you leave me? Why did you leave me? I need you ... I want you.' OK, well that eventually turned into Jimmy pounding on the grave saying, 'I'll show you for leaving me ... fuck you, I'm gonna be so fuckin' *great* without you!'[19]

Watching Clift, Dean learned how to draw on this feeling in a constructive way, finding meanings and motions in the space between words and in the slightest of gestures. The concern was not with the style of expression but rather with the justness of it, its happy injuries, its ecstasies of exactness. Clift liked to reduce his lines to the barest minimum, preferring to imply what others tended to put into words. Brando would switch, mid-way through a scene, from the epic to the intimate, allow his emotions to dominate his lines, often rendering the actual words almost incomprehensible. Dean, again, tried to emulate his two heroes in his delivery of important dialogue. He would mumble, pause, turn away from the camera, alter the rhythms of certain lines and phrases and sometimes revise (or even omit) entire speeches. Dean had a reading problem, and this may have been one of the reasons for his tendency to improvise, freeing himself from the script. The effect was certainly dramatic, helping Dean in his attempt at, as he put it, 'ripping away layers to find roots'. Mercedes McCambridge described Dean as 'the runt in a litter of thoroughbreds'. Dean made his inadequacies into his stylistic strengths.

'Ex-farmboy now making hay in movies,' announced the *Fairmount News*. As an 'instant' star, Dean's private life became the focus of considerable attention from the gossip columnists and fan magazines. The more complicated he appeared, the more his moods fluctuated and his attitude altered, the more the public embraced him, particularly young people, who easily identified with him. They saw themselves, a generation of misunderstood youths, rebelling against the values and the authority of their elders. He had arrived at a time when the movie industry desperately needed a new star for its teenage audience. Martin Sheen remarked:

In the mid-fifties, young people didn't have a voice; they were just null and void. No one dealt with them seriously until James Dean came along.

I was just fifteen and living in Ohio at the time Jimmy died, but he left me with the impression that anything was possible. Dean was a genius at a time when one was needed.[20]

Dean rebelled, but became rich and powerful in the process of rebelling. He thereby combined the teen dream of non-conformity with the American dream of financial success, and was the idol of his generation. Dean became the adolescent incarnate, articulating the unspoken causes of countless young Americans. The image was a seductive one, so much so that it even seduced Dean himself. He spat at the portraits of Bogart, Cagney and Muni that adorned the walls at Warner Brothers. He sought to shock. He was known as 'the complete non-conformist' in Hollywood. Carroll Baker, who worked with Dean on *Giant*, recalls an occasion when he deliberately made her late for an appointment with the studio executives:

When I told him I was worried, he just shrugged and said, 'You have to treat 'em like shit – it's the only thing they understand!' It wasn't that he thought he was bigger than the studio, he just felt that by coming to Hollywood he had sold out – all of us from the Actors' Studio felt a bit like that, including Marlon – and behaving outrageously was Jimmy's way of saying to the studio, 'OK, you've got me, but I still call the shots!'[21]

Dean's visible contempt for what the studio executives represented was counterpointed by a compulsive desire to enjoy the adulation and power which only they could assure him. Dean was not the first young actor to arrive in Hollywood to face this peculiar dichotomy. He came to terms with it by giving the outward impression that stardom was meaningless to him, while secretly he thought of little else. 'Jimmy wanted very badly to be a star,' said Carroll Baker. 'So badly, in fact, that he would never admit how important it was to him. He was single-minded about becoming [a star], and when it happened, he loved the attention it brought him – not just with audiences, but on the set. It was "Jimmy this" and "Jimmy that" and everything revolved around him . . . and he loved that, really.'[22]

Julie Harris remembers going to say goodbye to Dean after the last day's shooting of *East of Eden*. She heard what sounded like a little boy sobbing and then she saw it was Dean, with his head in his hands, tears streaming down his face. 'It's all over,' he said. 'I never wanted it to end.' Harris had never seen a fellow actor so distressed at the prospect of returning to an off-screen existence.

Dean was already known as a 'Hollywood rebel' when he was signed to make his second movie, *Rebel Without a Cause*. Warner Brothers had owned the property since 1946 (and offered it to Brando), but it was shelved as 'unsuitable' until the changes in the composition of movie audiences and the new concern with 'social problems' in the early 1950s provided a more congenial climate for its production. The director, Nicholas Ray, was convinced that Dean was the only actor who could play the leading role of Jim Stark, a young man at odds with the adult world, a soulful pilgrim in search of sincerity. Robert Lindner's original study, *Rebel Without a Cause*, defined this rebel figure as a 'religious disobeyer of prevailing codes and standards . . . an agitator without a slogan, a revolutionary without a program . . . incapable of exertions for the sake of others'.[23] Lindner's psychotic male subject had been oppressed by a brutal, sexually threatening father. Lindner himself believed, in keeping with a dominant motif in American culture, that 'no great man in history ever aspired to get married'. Ray's movie adaptation retains only the bare outline of Lindner's case study: Jim is no recalcitrant 'psychopath', but a sensitive and attractive middle-class teenage boy whose *weak* father has failed to provide him with a strong, clearly defined masculine image. The movie thus inverts the meaning of Lindner's insight by placing Jim in need of the very kind of dominant, aggressive, self-confident father who caused Lindner's subject to become psychopathic in the first place.

The youths are always in the foreground and the adults are, for the most part, shown only as the youths see them (the camera looks up, not down). Because everything takes place within a twenty-four-hour period, Jim Stark's development is accelerated through a series of symbolic scenes: a ceremonial battle (Jim is forced into a knife fight with one of the school's thugs); a test of nerve and courage (he is challenged to race against Buzz, the gang leader, in a 'chickie run' − they drive their cars towards a cliff and have to dive out of the door just before their vehicles fly over the edge; Buzz gets his jacket caught on the door handle and he perishes); a constitution of a new order (Judy transfers her affections to Jim and, with the younger Plato, plays 'house' in an abandoned mansion); a confrontation of hostile forces (a rival gang invade the mansion, the police move in and parents arrive); and a final reconciliation (Jim and Judy are embraced by their parents). A crucial scene occurs when Jim, just before leaving home to take part in the 'chickie run', exchanges his drab wardrobe (brown-flecked jacket and flannel trousers) for his battle colours (blood-red jacket and bright-blue jeans), leaving behind the compromised 'Jimbo' for the anti-hero Jim Stark.

The movie's central scene takes place in a darkened planetarium where the teenagers view, as part of their science class, a representation of the earth's eventual destruction, while the casual, unemotional voice of the scientist explains that our world 'is not missed in the universe' and that human beings are ultimately 'of little consequence'. Jim Stark and Plato are deeply affected by this thought. They are members of the first generation to grow up with the constant threat of the complete annihilation of the human race and this sober lesson makes the fact seem unbearably urgent. The 'chickie run', symbolically, depicts these teenagers' chaotic but headlong rush towards an oblivion which, in a frightening way, is oddly seductive to these impressionable young people trapped in a world seemingly without meaning and beyond human control. Jim and Judy find a temporary diversion when they act out their role as surrogate parents to Plato's helpless child. Their make-believe domestic bliss is shattered when Plato is startled by the invading gang and shoots at them with his gun. He flees to the planetarium, pursued by Jim and Judy. Jim manages secretly to remove the clip from Plato's gun and then persuades him to give himself up to the police outside the building. On the steps of the planetarium, Plato panics when he sees all the spotlights trained on him. He tries to escape, but the police (seeing the weapon he is holding) gun him down. Jim's parents, having witnessed his futile attempt to save the other boy, respond with a new-found respect. As the movie closes there is an indication that both he and they have come to a better understanding of each other.

The theme of *Rebel* is the evolution of a new generation. The process is mythic (it takes place in a single day) and the young generation grows up at night (it is a night journey). The characters depict the biological, sexual and moral shifts of adolescence, the changes from child into adult. Jim Stark is a loner in the spirit of adolescent retreat that reinterprets its isolation as a function of the world's defects. Everything around him seems 'phoney'. The clash between the teenage rebel and the adult conformists is highlighted when Jim, coming home after the incident in which his rival has perished, makes it clear that he wants to make a confession to the authorities:

MR STARK: You can't be idealistic all your life, Jimbo.
MRS STARK: It isn't good to get involved.
JIM: I am involved. We are *all* involved! Mom – Dad – just once I want to do something right!

Jim's rebellion is thoroughly emasculated by the backsliding notion that firm authority offers the solution to a tormented, alienated adolescent's quest to learn how to be a man: 'What can you do when you have to be a man?' In *It Happened One Night* (1934), Clark Gable said of an independent woman: 'What she needs is a guy that'd take a sock at her once a day whether it was coming to her or not!' *Rebel* works hard to keep that thought alive: 'If he had the guts to knock Mom cold once, maybe she'd be happy and stop picking on him ... I don't *ever* want to be like him.' Jim's parents never understand his rage: 'Don't we give you everything you want?' Materially, certainly, he wants for nothing; spiritually, however, he is a pauper, since there is no family inheritance of a sense of value, honesty, decency or love. The contradiction was obviously a topical one in a post-war period in which the affluent teenager was discovering the inadequacies of materialism. 'I want

answers *now!*' Jim screams, almost strangling his father as he pulls
him close. 'We don't have *time!* . . . I'm not interested in what I'll
understand ten years from now!' Many teenagers could identify
with that kind of impatience.

Jim bonds with a young woman, Judy, and a younger boy, Plato,
each of whom has also been deprived of parents who can accept
them. Judy's father is so overwhelmed by his sudden sexual attraction to her that, projecting, he calls her a 'dirty tramp'. Plato's
mother leaves him in the care of a maid. Together the three waifs
try to create a family, bestowing upon each other the tenderness
and support denied them by the adults in their lives. Their new
family is not really in a genuine social space; it is only a fantasy, a
community of the imagination, just as their inhabitation of their
'home' (an old mansion) is only a matter of play-acting adult
behaviour. The movie presents free and creative imaginative expressions as possible only as alternatives to, or escapes from, actual
social forms of organization and understanding. Jim tells Judy, 'Each
day I'd look in the mirror and I'd say, "What? You still here?"' The
teenagers search themselves for an inner ballast, a sense of moral
constancy, in an evanescent culture. 'If I had *one* day when I didn't
feel confused, didn't have to feel ashamed of anything . . .' *Rebel
Without a Cause* recognizes that however sensitive and fragile and
tender-hearted a young man may be, he must confront a brutal,
deforming masculine culture outside. Jim has to play the game – at
least until he survives the 'chickie run' test. Plato says of his new
hero, Jim: 'He doesn't say much, but when he does, you know he
means it. He's sincere.' He is also gentle: 'Your lips are soft,' Judy
says as he kisses her.

Jim and Judy are not really seeking a 'counter-culture'; they just
want a conventional 'grown-up' life *now*, putting an end to the
confusions and anxieties of adolescence. He falls for her like Tom
Sawyer fell for Becky Thatcher: 'without firing a shot'. Jim feels his
own identity as a man begin to sharpen when he comes to see Judy
as the object of his desire. In her presence, Jim becomes the child he
could not be with his parents, yet simultaneously he discovers his
responsibility as a man. The eroticism is uneasy and equivocal. Judy

offers a new definition of an ideal male: 'One who can be gentle and sweet, like you are ... who doesn't run away ... Being Plato's friend – *that's* being strong.' Significantly, their relationship is not undermined because they express how they really feel. On the contrary, it is strengthened and enriched by their openness. *Rebel Without a Cause* finally reverts to the old belief that traditional male authority can assuage the pain of the young and the weak: Plato is dead, Jim weeps on his father's shoulder and his father says, 'I'll try to be as strong as you want me to be.' Jim had given his jacket to Plato as a sign of his protectiveness; now Jim's father gives his jacket to his son. It is a reactionary conclusion. The ways of the old become the ways of the young.

As long as the rebel remains without a cause – a real concrete grievance rooted in structural contradictions within society – his search for a rational and humane compromise must end in failure. At best, it will resemble Jim's: the rhetoric of mutual responsibility will serve as a cloak for authoritarian manipulation, which ultimately delivers its children to the purposes of the state. Thus despite its popular image, *Rebel Without a Cause* is a profoundly conservative movie. True, the parents have changed by the end of the story, but in a regressive direction: Jim's father has learned to play the orthodox male role and his mother has learned to subordinate herself to it. The movie, which started out as a critique of the family, finishes by reaffirming its vitality. Yet Dean's performance remains an undeniable irritant, an antinomy. He emphasizes his inability truly to conform when he complains, 'I don't know what to do any more, except maybe to die ... If I had *one* day when I didn't feel confused ... and felt I belonged somewhere ...' When Jim asks, 'How can a guy grow up in a circus like this?', he touches a nerve; he is genuinely anxious. Dean's first few scenes are power-fully constructed. In them he shows an explosive, tortured nature that makes the subsequent 'resolution' seem thoroughly implausible and forced. His character always seems half-cocked (in every sense of the word). Just before the 'chickie run', he asks his opponent: 'Why do we do this?' The reply – 'Well, you gotta do *something*, now don't you?' – captures the pointless yet addictive machismo of

Dean denuded of costume. He is often pictured looking up at
people, plaintively or adoringly, with a yearning quality in
the eyes.

The quest for culture: Brando, stripped but serious, the body
straining to maintain its poise, with empty ice-cream cartons
nearby . . .

The thinker: Clift portrayed men who seemed to be in a state
of constant inner conflict and isolation.

On the set of *East of Eden*: Elia Kazan, Brando, Julie Harris and Dean. According to Kazan, Dean was so much in awe of Brando that when they met 'he seemed shrunken and twisted in misery'.

On the set of *The Young Lions*: 'You're my touchstone, my challenge,' Brando told Clift, 'and I want you and I to go on challenging each other.'

On the set of *A Streetcar Named Desire*: 'When one stops seeking to find out who one is,' he said, 'one has reached the end of the rope.'

A carefully staged off-duty pose: 'Acting is just interpretation,' he said. 'I want to create myself.'

The celebrity Bohemian: at times Brando seemed determined to ignore the contradictions in his image as the successful rebel.

The Bohemian boy: once as tragedy, twice as farce – even this moment of release is carefully recorded for posterity.

Dean in his final role – Jett Rink in *Giant*. Brando would later create a remarkably similar look for his role in *The Godfather*.

The anxiety of influence: Al Pacino with Brando in *The Godfather*. 'I'm acting with *God*,' said Pacino.

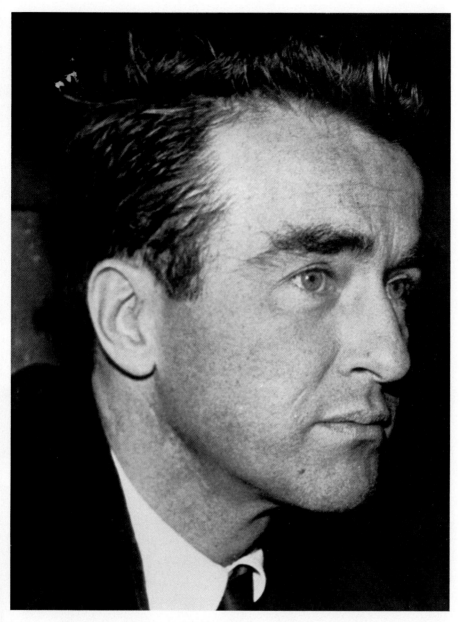

The *Times* obituary portrait of Clift. 'Heroes usually become bores,' he had once remarked. When he died he was forty-five years old.

Brando alone: the prisoner of his own past.

the group, as well as echoing *The Wild One*'s 'Whaddya got?' alienation.

In many ways *Rebel Without a Cause* served to highlight Dean's talent at the expense of the story. Nicholas Ray, unlike Elia Kazan, was happy to give Dean an unusual degree of autonomy in the way he shaped his character and approached his scenes, prompting co-star Jim Backus to remark (favourably) that Dean deserved to share the director's credit. More than any other movie, *Rebel* indulged Dean; here is his distinctiveness at its most blatant. It is not the place to see his acting gifts *in extenso*: *East of Eden* is the finer context, because Kazan made him play against equally competitive performers. *Rebel* is uneven and, at times, too uncritical in its use of Dean's stellar appeal. None the less, it contains, for better or worse, a number of moments of typical Dean 'business': the masochistic, two-fisted attack on the police desk after his arrest; the sly glance he gives the police officer after his father's placatory offer of a handful of cigars is turned down; the mumble away from the camera as he shyly talks to Judy; rolling the chilled milk bottle over his forehead after returning home from the 'chickie run'; and the slow wounded-animal movements around Plato's body after the shooting. Of course, most actors strike certain poses in the course of a performance, but few have done so as memorably as Dean.

Sal Mineo, who played Plato in the movie, later described the character as 'the first gay teenager in films. You watch it now, you know he had the hots for James Dean. You watch it now, and everyone knows about Jimmy, so it's like *he* had the hots for Natalie and me. Ergo, I had to be bumped off, out of the way.'[24] Indeed, the ambiguous sexual identity of Jim Stark reflected the genuinely unconventional tastes of Dean himself: during the making of the movie he had affairs with Natalie Wood *and* Sal Mineo. Bill Bast, who was probably one of Dean's closest friends, has confirmed that Dean had sexual relationships with both men and women: 'Gay as a descriptive term would categorize Jimmy in such a limited manner. He tried a lot of new things and he was always open to new experiences . . . He was so many things.'[25] Barbara Hutton, the Woolworth heiress, had a brief affair with Dean, although, being twenty years his senior, she felt he saw her more as a mother figure than as a lover: 'I couldn't help but wonder about his sexuality. He talked so fervently about men and adventure and masculinity.'[26]

There had always been something intriguingly arbitrary about Dean's sexuality. When he accepted the role of the boy in *The Immoralist*, he was very conscious of the implications of playing a homosexual, but homosexuality was, at least in the theatre, no longer considered quite such a taboo subject. Dean was also aware of the androgynous qualities in his own personality and appreciated that they would make his private life a subject for speculation in the gossip columns. However, he possessed a capacity for keeping his intimate life to himself and, generally, was not inclined to fuel speculation. Unlike Clift and Brando, Dean was adept at charming the powerful (and highly conservative) Hollywood columnists, flattering them by calling them his 'confidantes', researching their interests and tastes before he met them. 'I look at it as protective coloration,' he explained. He even managed to ingratiate himself with the redoubtable Hedda Hopper, who had frequently printed thinly veiled allusions to Clift's bisexuality and had done her best to damage Brando's public image after he had offended her during an interview. Dean took *all* public appearances – even (perhaps especially) interviews – as opportunities for acting. His private self, along with his sexual preferences, remained matters for conjecture. He did not openly associate with the 'homosexual scene' in Hollywood, except for a brief period at the start of his career when he was desperate to find work. A friend once remarked of Dean during this period: 'Jimmy would fuck a snake to get ahead.'[27] He registered for the draft as a homosexual, although he sometimes claimed this was merely a ruse to ensure he remained a civilian. Shortly after arriving in Los Angeles, Dean moved in with an older man – television producer Rogers Bracket. The fan magazines referred to their 'father–son' relationship. 'If so,' said Kenneth Anger, 'it was touched by incest.'[28] Dean was, at least in his first few months in Hollywood, a regular visitor of The Club, a leather bar where he was introduced to the world of S & M. According to Anger, a drunken Dean was known to ask lovers to stub out their cigarettes on his bare chest (and the coroner's report after his car crash tends to support this story, noting the 'constellation of keratoid scars' on Dean's torso).

In Hollywood Dean's behaviour became so eccentric that the columnists found it hard to be certain what was real, what was simply for effect and what was merely apocryphal. He was friendly with a television personality named Vampira (real name Maila Nurmi), who travelled in a hearse and wore make-up that made her appear corpse-white. He told journalists that he sometimes slept in a coffin and he had photographer Dennis Stock take pictures of him lying in a casket at the local funeral parlour in Fairmount. Visitors to his apartment in New York were surprised to see a noose hanging from the ceiling and various books and objects associated with black magic scattered around the rooms. It seems doubtful that Dean read many of these books, but he knew how to drive home a message. All kinds of individuals seemed to live in the apartment. Some of his friends recall visiting his home and finding an assortment of beatniks, bongo players, dope smokers and 'aspiring actors', but no sign of Dean himself. He would hide his money in his mattress and then go out and sleep rough. Dean was excited by the bizarre. For four days he was nearly inseparable from a young, one-legged woman who was the leader of a gang of male thieves that burgled the homes of movie stars. She prided herself on her ability to hop, naked, from the kitchen to the bedroom with a full cup of hot cocoa in her hand, never once scalding herself. She liked to have Dean rub her stump.[29]

A lock of his mother's hair, snipped by her son from her forehead while she was in the coffin, was always kept in a small envelope under Dean's pillow. He often discussed his mother and her death with his women friends; it was a subject that he always returned to. The woman who, for a while, seemed set to replace his mother as the object of his affections was the young Italian starlet Pier Angeli (Anna Marie Pierangeli). She had been born in Sardinia and first travelled to Hollywood to appear in Fred Zinnemann's *Teresa* (1951). Dean said that he was in awe of her from the moment he set eyes on her. At the beginning she was happy to assume the dual role of lover and mother figure. At meal times, claimed Joe Hyams, 'Pier would spoon-feed Jimmy and he, after a few glasses of wine, would become sleepy and fall asleep with his head on her lap.'[30] During the shooting of *East of Eden*, Dean and Angeli shared a room next to Elia Kazan: 'My front door opened on to his front door, and I could hear what went on through the walls. What went on was Pier Angeli, but clearly that didn't go well for Dean ... I could hear them boffing but more often arguing ...'[31]

Angeli's mother eventually persuaded her daughter to reject his proposal of marriage, primarily because he was not a Catholic, but also because he had recently acquired a reputation for beating up his women friends when he was intoxicated with a mixture of alcohol, amphetamines and marijuana. Angeli hastily married the crooner Vic Damone. Although Dean was devastated by the betrayal, the rebel image never faltered: he sat astride his motorbike as the bridal couple left the church, made his presence felt and then disappeared into the desert for ten days. This was not the sort of behaviour one associated with, say, Victor Mature. Dean always behaved impulsively, brashly, boldly; it was one of the reasons Dennis Hopper called him 'the first guerrilla artist to work in movies'.

According to Carroll Baker:

Jimmy was very difficult to get to know. He kept very much to himself. At parties, he would arrive late and disappear early, and not mix at all. He spoke in monosyllables ... He could be really strange at times. I got the impression right away that he felt awkward in other people's company. I think in some ways he was an unloved child and that affected his judgement of people. There hadn't been any way to turn that insecurity outwards, so it had gone in, and taken hold of his personality.[32]

Dean's behaviour was erratic, certainly: intense and impulsive one moment, dismissive and distant the next. The hip, street-smart movie star never managed to overcome the insecure, Midwestern farm boy; the two co-existed, but never peaceably. As Dean himself said, 'I'm a serious-minded and intense little devil — terribly gauche and so tense that I don't see how people can stay in the same room as me. I know I couldn't tolerate myself . . .' He had a low boredom threshold and anyone dipping below simply ceased to exist. Danger seemed to have an intoxicating effect on him but, unlike Steve McQueen (who risked his life driving at speed for the thrill of it), Dean's passion for powerful motorbikes and fast cars had, to some, a more sinister connotation. 'There *was* something suicidal in his nature,' said Carroll Baker. 'But I doubt if it was a conscious desire. One can only speculate about the fast cars and so forth, but I suspect there was some psychological connection with all that.' Many critics saw Dean's behaviour as a mannered imitation of the rebel biker Brando portrayed in *The Wild One*. One director who knew both Brando and Dean remarked: 'The major difference between Brando's behaviour and Dean's was that Brando's was very often a put-on. If people didn't realize that, Marlon always did. But Dean was self-destructive, masochistic. It was no act with him – he was sick.'

Although Dean spent a relatively short period of time in Hollywood, his unpredictable behaviour was the cause of innumerable arguments, confusions and feuds. On one occasion, Dean was with a friend when a Warner Brothers executive came over to greet him. Dean refused to shake his hand and then threw a fistful of coins on the ground in front of him. Turning to his friend, Dean said, 'I'd like you to do me a favour. If you ever find out why I acted the way I did today, please tell me.' There was something rather deliberate and tiresome about Dean's irrationality, as though he feared the responsibilities and obligations of adult life and chose to hide from them behind the guise of an incompetent. He once, absurdly, screamed at a lover who abandoned him: 'And when I die, it'll be your fault!' There was no time for Dean to grow up, or, if there was time, he did not take it. A writer friend once told him, 'You've never given anyone a chance to really like you or not like you, because you never even let them in past the first wall. So what's hiding in the middle, Jimmy? Why do you shut people out? Do you think you're empty? Is *that* why you're so scared?'[33]

Dean was certainly more authoritative when he was playing someone else. He went through life like Baudelaire's dandy, in

155

desperate pursuit of stimulation and selfish reassurance. As Camus observed:

The dandy is ... always compelled to astonish. Singularity is his vocation, excess his way to perfection. Perpetually incomplete, always on the margin of things, he compels others to create him, while denying their values. He plays at life because he is unable to live it. He plays at it until he dies, except for the moment when he is alone and without a mirror. For the dandy, to be alone is not to exist.[34]

Dean was drawn to those activities which offered the shock of novelty, the promise of a temporary release from the anxieties of social life: 'fast culture', drugs, rock music, sex and, especially, fast cars. Speed, described by Aldous Huxley as the only genuinely *modern* pleasure, thrilled the young actor. Dean never settled in any one place, with any one person or any one ideology. His life seemed intoxicated with the idea of the evanescent. It is a distinctive characteristic of American culture, one noticed by de Tocqueville when he describes how the American individual seems so peculiarly restless and impatient:

The recollection of the shortness of life is a constant spur to him. Besides the good things that he possesses, he every instant fancies a thousand others that death will prevent him from trying if he does not try them soon. This thought fills him with anxiety, fear, and regret and keeps his mind in ceaseless trepidation, which leads him perpetually to change his plans and his abode.[35]

The pursuit of happiness is urgent and unending for such individuals: 'Their prevailing frame of mind, then, is at once ardent and relaxed, violent and enervated. Death is often less dreaded by them than perseverance in continuous efforts to one end.'[36] The car enabled Dean to feel self-accountable, an extension of Emerson's cowboy self-reliance which remains so central to the American male. Driving fast involved control, and the real possibility of losing it, with facing (even relishing) fear, injury and death. The excitement of the activity involved weighing the odds between danger and safety, suspense and relief. Thus it is the excitement of sex (but a very selfish kind of sex). American culture had the accumulated associations of virile sportsters, libidinous limousines, back-seat petting and mobilized amorality. He wrote to a friend: 'A new addition has been added to the Dean family . . . a red 53 MG. My sex pours itself into fast curves, broadslides and broodings, drags, etc. . . . I have been sleeping with my MG. We made it together.'

While making *Rebel*, Dean bought a white Porsche Speedster – the first car he ever raced. During his time in Hollywood he owned an MG roadster, a Ford station wagon, a Triumph motorbike and a Lancia motor scooter. He entered the California Sports Car Club races and spent most of his free time practising his driving. Eventually, his search for his 'ideal' car ended when he exchanged his Speedster for a silver-grey Porsche Spyder: a two-seater with a lightweight aluminium body, no windshield and no top. It was the car, he said, he 'had always dreamed of'. It became his proudest possession and the most tangible sign of his success. He painted his racing number, 130, on the side of the car and then added a nickname, 'Little Bastard'. An auto mechanic who often observed Dean's races said, 'Jimmy wanted speed. He wanted his body to hurtle across over the ground, the faster the better. Jimmy was a straightaway driver. His track was the shortest distance between here and there.'[37] His friend Leonard Rosenman recalls: 'Jimmy was absolutely suicidal with a car. People just stayed away because they didn't want to get killed. I'm not saying that he wasn't gifted as a race-car driver, but that extra-irresponsible attitude towards his own life, I think, influenced his winning very often.'[38] Another observer described Dean as 'a dreadful driver. He would hit a hay bale every time he went round a corner.'

By the time of his third (and final) movie, *Giant* (which was filmed during the summer of 1955), Dean's obsession with fast cars was regarded as a serious insurance risk. A clause was added to his contract, preventing him from indulging in his passion for race-car driving until completion of his work. *Giant* was Dean's only encounter with a Hollywood production in the grand manner. The film was the third of director George Stevens's trilogy on American history: *Shane* (1953) reflected the transition from open ranges to fenced-in plots; *A Place in the Sun* noted the transition from rural to urban living; and *Giant* was set to chart the transition from cattle as the source of wealth to the 'new money' of oil. The movie was based on Edna Ferber's epic novel of Texan life, but the screen adaptation subordinated Ferber's social concerns to an emphasis upon a personal story: the rise of a Texas millionaire over a thirty-year period. Stevens assembled a high-powered cast, headed by Dean, Elizabeth Taylor and Rock Hudson, and featuring Mercedes McCambridge and Carroll Baker. Dean was cast as Jett Rink (the inspiration, it has been said, of the later figure of 'J. R.' in *Dallas*). In Ferber's book, Rink is a conventional ranch hand who benefits from extraordinary good fortune. However, by the time Dean and Stevens finished with him, the character had been stretched to the point where he dominated the entire story. It reduced the epic to a portrait of a social reject who bides his time, becomes part of the establishment, ruins those around him and, at the same time, destroys himself.

The movie begins in 1923, when a strong-willed woman, Leslie (Elizabeth Taylor), falls in love with a young Texan ranch owner, Bick (Rock Hudson), who visits her father's farm in Maryland. They marry and return to Texas together. Leslie finds the eye-wearying bleakness of Texas almost unbearable and is appalled by the dictatorial way in which the ranch is run. Against the wishes of her husband, she sets up a medical centre for the Mexican workers and servants. She does her best to civilize the business. A young ranch hand, Jett Rink (Dean), is employed by the couple. After the death of Bick's domineering sister, her will reveals that a thin wedge of the land has been bequeathed to Jett. He determines to turn this land into oil-dollars, and he succeeds. As the years go by, he becomes a millionaire and shows his contempt for the old figures of authority. At the age of fifty he attempts to seduce Leslie's nubile daughter in the deserted bar of his own luxury hotel.

Bick is presented as the ideal male figure: strong, industrious, straightforward and steadfast. Jett is an unreliable male, unable to control his desires and his temperament. He becomes an alcoholic and a crude materialist; as a rebel he lusts only after the positions and property of others. He has no new values, no new visions, only old vices. The story makes little attempt to involve the female characters in the serious action. Leslie does not want to give up her privileges or change the economic and political structures; she merely wants the élite to be more paternalistic and to demonstrate some kindness to the impoverished workers. She is given limited opportunity to show some critical independence: 'What is so masculine about a conversation that a woman can't enter into it?' The protest is, in practice, ignored. The movie thus does little to undermine the traditional image of the indomitable male.

Jett Rink defines the ontological drifter, the malcontent who inadvertently seeks his own destruction by attempting to bring down the powers that be. Although physically unsuited to play a surly, proletarian role that in many ways would have been more appropriate for Brando, Dean saw in Jett Rink the conflicting elements he felt in himself: rebel, loner and anti-hero. Jett has no parents, no family; his anger is directed at everyone else. He may, magically, acquire property and economic power, but social accept-ance is always beyond his reach. At the peak of his success, he is still an outsider. Like Cal, with his profits from his business venture, Jett finds that his recent wealth does little to satisfy his hunger for respect and recognition. He cannot cease his rebellion, even when he wants to. The movie plays poetically with the image of the rebel: stylized still lifes fragment the narrative (such as the classic 'crucifixion' pose, with Dean standing with his head hanging down, a rifle threaded like a cross through his arms, and Taylor kneeling at his feet).

The character of Jett Rink offered Dean his most demanding movie work (he had to age thirty years from start to finish). He was obliged, for the first time in his career, to use special make-up and alter his appearance by moving his hairline. In terms of his characterization, he had to evolve from a compassionate Jim Stark figure to a ruthless capitalist (a transition the uninspired narrative has us believe is inevitable for such an idealist). His on-screen appearances were rare – barely twenty minutes in total in a movie lasting over three hours. The later scenes, it must be said, are poor and unconvincingly acted. The final image of him is of an affluent middle-aged drunk – a sad and deeply ironic figure.

Dean was clearly extremely anxious about the task. He spent hours trying to telephone Montgomery Clift and Marlon Brando, seeking their advice and support, but the messages he left on their answering machines remained unanswered. On the set Dean rebelled – in part out of frustration, in part out of insecurity. His persistent questioning of George Stevens's direction, his insistence upon knowing the character's motivation for each line of dialogue, destroyed any rapport the two men may have felt or hoped for. Dean started arriving late and sometimes would not appear at all. Stevens grew to hate him. The actor would now use every trick to steal attention once a scene was being shot: while others were talking, he fiddled with his hat, shuffled his feet or giggled and twitched. Rock Hudson, who had a very limited technique, suffered when working with an increasingly self-obsessed Dean. He recalled, 'While doing a scene, in the giving and taking, he was just a taker. He would . . . never give back.' Significantly, Hudson felt very strongly that Montgomery Clift would have been a more successful Jett Rink: 'If Monty had done the part he would have acted the bejesus out of that role . . . Dean broke down as the older man. He was brilliant in the early part . . . I keep thinking that if Monty had done that there would have been nobody else in the movie. He was such a brilliant actor.'[39]

Dean's attitude, as shooting came to an end, had never seemed so disturbingly unpredictable. His famous giggle, always on the verge of sounding manic, now became a shrill, nervous mannerism. Even those people who still felt some warmth for him found it hard to understand his sudden mood changes. Sometimes he would seem helpless and fragile, while on other occasions he would be aloof and intimidating. Elizabeth Taylor said, 'One felt that he was a boy one had to take care of, but even that was probably his joke. I don't think he needed anybody or anything – except his acting.'[40]

Before he finished his contribution to *Giant*, Dean took part in a thirty-second road-safety television commercial which, in retrospect, seems remarkably, almost unbelievably, ironic. At the end he turns to the camera and says, 'The road is no place to race your car. It's real murder.' He was supposed to sign off with the safety committee's slogan: 'Drive safely, because the life you save may be your own.' Instead, he chose to say, 'And remember, drive safely ... because the life you save may be *mine*.' The self-obsession showed up in everything he did.

After his final scene in *Giant*, Dean and a friend, mechanic Rolf Wutherich, departed for a weekend race at Salinas. By 6.00 that evening (30 September 1955), Dean was dead. His silver-grey Porsche Spyder had crashed into a Ford sedan. Dean's last words, said Wutherich, were, 'That guy up there's gotta stop. He'll see us.' The driver of the Ford and the sports car passenger suffered superficial injuries; Dean was killed instantly. His body was still in the car. He had been lifted from his seat and thrown backwards; his head hung over the passenger door and his foot was entangled in the clutch and brake pedals. He was rushed to hospital, where it was discovered that he had suffered a broken neck and forearms, had fractured one leg and had lost a great deal of blood. It was decided that he must have died on impact. The sports car would not, it was judged, have been very easy to see with its grey colour against a dull, grey background. Was Dean wearing his glasses when he was driving? The evidence was, it was said, 'ambiguous'. Dean's body was claimed by his father, who accompanied it on the train to Fairmount, where he was buried next to his mother.

The 1 October 1955 issue of the *Los Angeles Examiner* announced: 'Death overtook speed-loving James Dean, 24-year-old film star and newest idol of the bobby-soxers, at a highway intersection, 28 miles east of Pasa Robles last night.' The rumours began almost immediately: that Dean had committed suicide, that the accident had been faked to allow him to quit the movie business, and that he had been given plastic surgery after surviving the crash. Hollywood had not witnessed such scenes since the year when Valentino died. Montgomery Clift said of Dean's death: 'The instant I heard about it, I vomited. I don't know why.' People started to theorize as to why the accident occurred, and Dean's apparent self-destructive impulse was underlined by many of his colleagues. Lee Strasberg commented: 'His behaviour and personality seemed to be part of a pattern which invariably had to lead to something destructive. I always had a strange feeling that there was in Jimmy a sort of doomed quality.'[41] It fast became the popular interpretation: Dean as the doomed rebel, the American Dorian Gray, the good-looking corpse, the eternal teenage icon. There were endless anecdotes about Dean that encouraged such a myth: for example, in one of his last interviews, when asked what he respected, Dean replied: 'That's easy. Death. It's the only thing left to respect. It's the one inevitable, undeniable truth. Everything else can be questioned. But death is truth. In it lies the only mobility for man, and beyond it only hope.'[42] The morbid story haunted those who knew Dean: Pier Angeli died of a drug overdose in 1971; Sal Mineo was murdered in 1976; and Natalie Wood drowned in 1981.

Rebel Without a Cause and *Giant* were both released posthumously. *Rebel* opened on 3 October 1955 – three days after Dean's death. One studio executive is said to have looked at the posters of Dean's movies and said, 'Great career move, kid'. The date '9/30/55' was painted on walls, carved into school desks and printed on to T-shirts. 3,000 people attended his funeral in Fairmount – dwarfing the local population. A year later, Dean's studio was still receiving 2,000 fan letters per week addressed to the dead star. Twenty-six fan clubs were established in Indiana alone. At one point 3.8 million people in the United States were paying members of Dean fan clubs created after his death and given such names as 'Dean's Teens', the 'James Dean Death Club' and 'Lest We Forget'. Records like 'Jimmy Dean's First Christmas in Heaven', 'The Ballad of James Dean' and 'His Name Was Dean' were released and, to the distress of many, sold well. The ghoulish media coverage continued: magazines carried articles such as 'Jimmy Dean's Ghost Wrecked My Two Marriages', 'I Almost Married James Dean', 'I Was James Dean's Wife' and 'Here Is the Real Story of My Life – By James Dean as I Might Have Told It to Joe Archer'. For fifty cents one could sit behind the wheel of Dean's wrecked Spyder and have a picture taken, and pieces were sold as relics (it seems to have been an abnormally large vehicle). *Picture Post* commented: 'America has known many rebellions but none like this. Millions of teenage rebels heading for nowhere, some in hot-rod cars, others on the blare of rock 'n' roll music, some with guns in their hands. And at their head a dead leader.'[43]

Dos Passos placed him as an 'age type' in *Mid-Century*, one of 'the Sinister Adolescents' who were 'box office'. At Dean's funeral Pastor Xen Harvey had said, 'The career of James Dean has not ended. It has just begun. And God himself is directing the production.' Plans were made for a movie based on Dean's life, with Elvis Presley playing the part of his hero: 'I know by heart all the dialogue of James Dean's films. I could watch *Rebel* 100 times over.' The movie was eventually abandoned in favour of a documentary, which Marlon Brando seriously considered narrating: 'He wasn't a hero,' said Brando. 'He was just a lost boy trying to find himself.' Brando's aim was to use the documentary as a way of showing how a talented young man, in a short space of time, came to destroy himself. When it became clear that the movie was going to encourage Dean's 'legendary' status, he withdrew. *The James Dean Story* was released in 1957 and, as expected, depicted Dean as 'the First American Teenager', the hero of youth culture.

As Carroll Baker said:

His timing was immaculate. There was a growing awareness around the mid-1950s that children had certain kinds of rights, and that parents had an obligation to show them some sort of sensitivity. Nobody had expressed that from the kids' side of the fence before Jimmy, so he had the advantage of being the first to put on to film a kind of contemporary catalogue of their needs and desires ... And, you know, kids everywhere immediately began to identify with him. His acting was so convincing, so real. He played the lost boy, the kid up to his neck in trouble, challenging authority because he wanted to do things his way. And it came across very powerfully on the screen, because Jimmy carried it off beautifully.[44]

Dean's awkward, inarticulate, volatile screen character touched a raw nerve at precisely the right time. Its effect on his generation, and on subsequent generations, was startling.

James Dean's short career made of him a most peculiar myth. The majority of his admirers – even at the time – saw his work only after he had died. Dean was dead upon one's discovery of him; his presence projected an absence – in many ways the postscript *was* the script, the life of the star followed on from the death of the actor. The photographer Dennis Stock perceived in Dean's life the imminence of death's closure: 'Cradle, cocoon, car, coffin'. The image remained, freezing the fast life for ever, the cool corpse, allowing Dean to personify an idealized, eternal teenage in which manhood and responsibility are forever postponed. After Dean, it suddenly seemed old to be twenty-five. For Dean there was no agonizing physical and emotional decline, as there had been for Clift; there was no period of frustration and stagnation, as there was for Brando. Had he lived, the potency of the rebel image might have been damaged by too much wealth and success (this is not a culture that worries about the human cost of its mythologies). As things turned out, he did not grow old and overweight, and neither did his dreams. Death had purified what Dean represented, and the real person could no longer set any obstacle to those who sought personal salvation through a fragment of his car or a piece of his tombstone.

Dean's friend Kenneth Kendall remarked: 'One wonderful thing about dead movie stars – they can't disappoint you. And that's about *all* the live ones ever are capable of doing.' Dean represents the ultimate casualty of popular culture in the 1950s: driven by studio pressures, as much as by his own ornery pouting, to live in an emotional shell, and then to die once he has briefly entered society and gone too fast for those travelling in the opposite direction. Dean's dream came true: he lived fast, died young and left a good-looking corpse that stares out at a new generation of teenagers. The *idea* of James Dean carries a heady cultural resonance. In 1972 Warhol's *Interview* magazine summed it up with appropriately callow overstatement:

James Dean made just three pictures, but even if he had made only one he would still be the greatest male star of the Fifties . . . James Dean was the perfect embodiment of an eternal struggle. It might be innocence struggling with experience, youth with age, or a man with his image. But in every aspect his struggle was a mirror to a generation of rebels without a cause. His anguish was exquisitely genuine on and off screen; his moments of joy were rare and precious. He is not our hero because he was perfect, but because he perfectly represented the damaged but beautiful soul of our time.

5

The Legacy

Another hour passed. Dreams hung in fragments at the far end of the
room, suffered analysis, passed – to be dreamed in crowds, or else
discarded.

F. Scott Fitzgerald

Robert De Niro in *Taxi Driver*: a dark, angry, confused figure in a
hostile urban environment. 'All my life needed,' he says, 'was a
sense of somewhere to go.' Matt Dillon in *The Outsiders*: someone
asks him, 'Whaddya wanna do?' He replies, 'Nothin' legal, man.' He
could be any one of a succession of alienated young rebel males
from a number of movies made during the past thirty years. They
are all faced with a set of problems that were still taking shape
when Clift, Brando and Dean were at the peak of their fame.
Brando's character, in the early 1950s, could say, 'We don't go any
one special place, we just go.' By the end of the decade, the
optimism of that remark had come to seem painfully misplaced;
there seemed nowhere left to go to. America was changing, and
struggling to come to terms with those changes. As Clark Gable's
bewildered character says at the end of *The Misfits*: 'They changed
it. Changed it all around.' Although the 1950s came to an end with
Eisenhower in the White House and Doris Day in *Pillow Talk*
(1959), there was also a sense of disquiet, a fear that the period of
consensus (never very stable) was already disintegrating. 'The
time's running out,' warned an influential movie of the 1960s. The
last great mass audience for movies had fragmented into many
smaller, specialized audiences, with distinct tastes and values, while
some people stopped going out at all. The rebel figure, once so

shocking, became increasingly familiar. There were plenty of causes now. The question was which ones were worth fighting for and which ones one should fight against.

By the end of the 1950s Clift, Brando and Dean had replaced the old male heroes. Young actors now aspired to act like Brando, think like Clift and feel like Dean. The Actors' Studio, and in particular the increasingly opportunistic Lee Strasberg, made the most of its old (and in some cases rather troubled) associations with the three new idols. The old guard was defeated; the new guard had yet to be tested. For many years after Dean's death, the youth of America did not have one particular actor who captured their imagination to such a remarkable degree of intensity.

The early 1960s witnessed the growing popularity of a number of young actors drawing more or less consciously on the image and technique of Clift, Brando and Dean. Paul Newman, in such movies as *The Long Hot Summer* (1958), *The Hustler* (1961) and *Cool Hand Luke* (1967), continued the tradition of the young anti-hero. The early years of his career were haunted by the influence of Brando, with Newman (as he later admitted) sometimes seeming, in role and image, remarkably similar. Like Brando, he relished scenes of physical pain and degradation, for the same sense of stigmata they endowed him with. His choice of roles encouraged the aura of 'apartness' that seemed to surround him – the alienated rebel who is in control of himself, but stands at an angle to society, looking on. He might withdraw, or passively observe, or intervene, or perish trying; his expression gave little away and a sense of danger played around his eyes.

Steve McQueen, dubbed by the fan magazines the 'King of Cool', recalled James Dean in his non-conformist life style and his fascination with fast cars and motorbikes. Such movies as *The Great Escape* (1962) and *The Cincinnati Kid* (1965) provided him with eye-catching roles as the young rebel male. He was, however, an isolated male – his relationships with women were typically lacking in commitment. His most important partnerships were with machines, helping him escape from social constraints and master his own environment.

Warren Beatty, perhaps the most image-conscious actor of this period, was certainly one of the most self-conscious actors of his generation, and one of the most deliberate imitators of the 1950s rebel figures. After *Splendour in the Grass* (1961), *Time* magazine noted the impressive presence of the young Beatty: 'With a facial and vocal suggestion of Montgomery Clift and the mannerisms of James Dean, he is the latest incumbent in the line of arrogant, attractive, hostile, moody, sensitive, self-conscious, bright, defensive, stuttering, self-seeking and extremely talented actors who become myths before they are thirty.' The speed and the ease with which *Time* categorized Beatty reflected the new problem facing the next generation of non-conformists: namely, non-conformity had become something one conformed to, or at least a certain kind of non-conformity had become another kind of cliché. The blue jeans and white T-shirt were, by the early 1960s, the conventional clothes of the movie teenagers; little trace remained of the old working-class connotations. Everyone had their own version of the Clift gaze, the Brando mumble and the Dean fidget. The rebels had become role models. 'Don't follow leaders,' sang Dylan, although he had started his own career imitating the look fashioned by Brando and Dean.

The movies could boast countless rebel figures, but few offered anything new or threatening. From being dangerous individuals, taking real risks, the movie rebels became idols of consumption, objects of passive admiration or slavish imitation. As the original teenagers grew up and had children of their own, the nature of the teenager came to be understood better and indulged in (note the success of *The Graduate*, 1967), and teendom was incorporated into other genres, in some cases giving them a new lease of life (note the horror movies of the 1970s and 1980s), but seldom with the old familial tensions. The idea of the young rebel continued to figure prominently in movies, but with a noticeable darkening of tone and an increasingly ambiguous perspective (consider, for example, the recent *Dead Poets Society*, 1989). The enduring theme in American culture is the rebel who must leave society (alone or with one or a few others) in order to realize the moral good on the margins of settled community. Sometimes the withdrawal involves a contribution to society, as in James Fenimore Cooper's *The Deerslayer*. Sometimes the marginal figures realize ethical ends precluded in the larger society, as in the interracial harmony between Huckleberry Finn and Jim. Sometimes the withdrawal from society is irrational and culminates in disaster, as in *Moby-Dick*. In more recent times, the possibility of withdrawing is itself a problem; there is nowhere to withdraw to.

The movies of the late 1960s and early 1970s returned, explicitly or implicitly, to the frontier's continuing significance in American life. Movies with a relatively radical outlook at this time suggested that America (notwithstanding the exploration of outer space) was no longer living in a frontier age and that, with the frontier gone, the basis for certain life styles, institutions and values premised upon the existence of unlimited space had also crumbled away. This view's most poignant and self-conscious treatment occurred in the Western genre, relocated from its traditional period in the 1880s to the decades preceding the First World War (a period significantly later than the Bureau of the Census's official announcement of the frontier's passing). Thus *Butch Cassidy and the Sundance Kid* (1969) used a New York interlude in order to suggest progressive urbanization and *The Wild Bunch* (1969) has a member of the gang killed by being dragged behind a car, while the others are slaughtered by Mexican bandits armed with machine guns. Since *Red River* in 1948, the Western as a genre had been preoccupied with the dying out of radically individualistic life styles: *The Misfits* features old cowboys who are forced to realize that the traditional life ('Better than wages') is over; *The Wild Bunch* has a veteran group of gunfighters admitting, 'We gotta start thinking beyond our guns. Them days is closing fast' (their opponents not only have new technology but also employ their own accountant).

In other genres the vanished frontier was acknowledged with physical settings of intense claustrophobia: *Cool Hand Luke* begins with tight close-ups of its hero destroying a parking meter; *One Flew Over the Cuckoo's Nest* (1975) is set in a crowded, chaotic psychiatric ward; *McCabe and Mrs Miller* (1971) used exceptionally low-ceilinged sets in order to make its characters appear penned-in

169

and pressurized by urban living. Even *Easy Rider* (1969) reflected a west to east movement, implying that the west had run out of room. This spatial anxiety was accompanied by a *temporal* fear, an anxiety about ageing. Was the New World going to end up no different from the Old? An anxiety about age is endemic in a civilization geared to the cult of youth. (Dean may have escaped the problem, but what of those who remained?) *Easy Rider*'s success was based to some extent on its ability to capture on a visceral level many of the key themes of the youthful counter-culture: freedom, the land, drugs and communes. It connected to the disillusionment experienced by many young people about the America of the 1960s. 'This used to be a helluva country,' says one character. 'I can't understand what's gone wrong with it.' If the innocent turns out to be, in reality, merely inexperienced, the situation alters. The rebel male remained the most common image in these movies, although individualism itself was sometimes pictured as chimerical and outdated. Cool Hand Luke's only crime was allowing himself to become inebriated and then vandalizing a parking meter (a long way from the tragic heroism of Private Prewitt or Terry Malloy, or even Jim Stark). 'Luke,' his mother asks, 'what went wrong?' His pathetic, hopeless answer seemed to sum up the rebel's problem in the modern, urbanized America: 'I just can't seem to find no elbow room.'

Movies with a rather more obviously crude and conservative tone, such as *Bullitt* (1968), *Dirty Harry* (1971) and *The French Connection* (1971), took place in a metropolis, and the decaying, overpopulated city implicitly acknowledged the frontier's closing. However, whereas movies such as *Easy Rider* sympathized with the rebel in a corrupt society, a society 'gone bad', the more conservative movies suggested that, if certain non-conformists were eliminated, society could return to normal. By the 1970s the typical male hero is more violent than ever before, and this violence, instead of being projected into an archaic frontier community, is now perceived as the necessary weapon of the male citizen striving to survive in the city. The European idea of culture as a civilizing process has not just been questioned but contradicted: the lone man has to take the law into his own hands because, it is suggested, society has become too civilized, the law too compassionate, the leaders too liberal. As far as the Right was concerned, the modern malaise could be alleviated only by an individual hero strong enough to defeat the villain for the sake of the community. For example, in *Dirty Harry* Clint Eastwood brought his associations with traditional Western heroes – relentless, ruthless gunfighters who just happened to be on society's side. Again, the American fascination with, and suspicion of, the law is very evident: Harry Callahan ignores the constraining legal proprieties (explained by a Berkeley law professor) and deals straightforwardly with the killer (he steps outside the law in order to defend the law). 'I don't know what the law says, but I do know what's right and wrong,' he says, reaffirming a faith in natural law with a glorification of masculine self-confidence. In Callahan's good society, covenants are accompanied by the sword. Eastwood's peculiar brand of manhood typified something cold, aloof and uncongenial. His machismo has the twin edges of violence and sex, but engagement in both is expedient, and there is no moral reflectiveness to the character. He represents a regression to the wild lawlessness that prevailed in the American West in the last century, and thus his modern urban environment serves to highlight the explosive alienation he feels – a cowboy in a closed city. Harry Callahan was a figure who came to serve as a deceptively reassuring role model in a period dominated by American anxieties about Vietnam and Watergate. Eastwood's super-male offered the male spectator a vicarious sense of personal potency (with his notorious 'make my day' snarl, imitated by innumerable macho fantasists, from plump bar-room habitués to US President Ronald Reagan).

The movies of this period thus polarized into rebel-hero movies and legal-hero movies; outlaws and outcasts figured in the former, police and vigilantes in the latter. The more liberal movies celebrated the values and attitudes traditionally associated with individualism: a distrust of institutions, a need for freedom from red tape and restraints, a preference for intuition as a source of conduct, a reluctance to put down roots, an uneasiness about marriage, and a playfulness that suggested a resistance to conventional adult behaviour. Few of these rebels had a settled relationship; some resort to the fleeting physical intimacy of prostitutes (*Easy Rider, McCabe and Mrs Miller*), others to rape (*One Flew Over the Cuckoo's Nest, A Clockwork Orange*, 1971) or disinterest (*Midnight Cowboy*, 1969). Many movies during the 1970s transported their male characters to remote environments free of women, as in *Deliverance* (1972), *Papillon* (1973) and *The Longest Yard* (1974). Other locations selected as secure for these men were those in which women are peripheral, circumstances explored in *M*A*S*H* (1970), *Husbands* (1970), *The Sting* (1973), *California Split* (1974) and *All the President's Men* (1976). Same-sex exclusivity reinforces male identity, and only 'weak' men, it is implied, allow themselves to be 'feminized' by becoming entangled in heterosexual relationships. Any sense of sexual ambiguity is rigorously policed; as Clint Eastwood's character says to a flamboyant gay in *The Eiger Sanction* (1975), 'You have an incurable disease and you haven't got the guts to kill yourself.' The traditional Western hero (such as Shane) had been a loner. Many of these modern anti-heroes came in groups: Bonnie and Clyde, Butch and Sundance, Joe Buck and Ratso, and the Wild Bunch. Again, the polarity shows itself with the more conservative movies and the splendid isolation of their rebels; these figures can trust no one and even view their own society's laws with suspicion.

What unites all these movies, both liberal and conservative in orientation, is their use of that classic myth of the *reluctant* rebel. The policeman discovers that his bosses are corrupt or that his wife or partner is assaulted or murdered, or he is frustrated by a slow-moving bureaucracy; other individuals might come up against violent or irresponsible authority figures. The quiet desperation wells up, exploding into angry rage at moments of extreme provocation. Although the new, complex problems increasingly necessitated more elaborate, permanent, cooperative reforms, Hollywood was, as ever, uneasy with the idea that the situation could not be solved by personal virtue alone. *Dirty Harry's* viewpoint – 'When I see an adult male chasing a female down an alley with nothing but a butcher knife and a hard-on, I don't figure he's out collecting for the

Red Cross. I shoot the bastard' – appealed to this naïve (but influential) individualism. Few movies offered examples of admirable, orthodox law men. This was not too surprising in a society that seems to see little wrong in the routine breaking of laws involving drugs, income tax, automobiles or sexual behaviour. Formally, this was an obedient society; in reality, citizens owned their own hand guns. Crime was no longer exclusively portrayed as a symptom of our aggression or of social malfunction; it now seemed to stem from what the safety-conscious bourgeois feared might be an inherent disorder in crowded democracies. The vigilante became, in popular culture, a necessary evil.

Taxi Driver (1976) represents one of the most unsettling of the 1970s rebel-male narratives. Directed by Martin Scorsese, written by Paul Schrader and starring Robert De Niro, it is the story of Travis Bickle, a returned Vietnam veteran, unable to relate to women or his urban environment, unable to relax or sleep, obsessed with voyeurism and vengeance. Paul Schrader commented, 'I saw the script as an attempt to take the European existential hero, that is, the man from "The Stranger", "Notes from the Underground", "Nausea", *Pickpocket, Le Feu Follet* and *A Man Escaped* and put him in an American context.'[1] Bickle is sickened by the pimps and prostitutes by which the ghetto poverty of New York is now so shamelessly defined. He says, 'Some day a real rain'll come and wash all this scum off the street ... Just flush it down the fuckin' toilet.' His car is his coffin, his city his tomb. Arming himself with blackmarket guns, Bickle begins training, practising fast draws like the wounded Brando in *One-Eyed Jacks*. He looks in the mirror: 'You talkin' to *me*? You talkin' to me? Well, who the hell else are you talkin' to? ... You talking to me? Well, I'm the only one here. Who the fuck do you think *you're* talkin' to? Listen, you fuckers, you screwheads,' he says to himself. 'Here is a man who would not take any more ... Here is someone who stood up.' The 'justification' for Bickle's sick behaviour is his desire to rescue a twelve-year-old whore from her pimp. He is surrounded by shallow, self-seeking politicians and ineffectual police officers (the movie offers no alternatives), and he decides to take matters into his own hands. 'Loneliness has followed me all my life,' he says at one point. 'There's no escape. I'm God's lonely man.' As an extreme isolate, Bickle satisfies de Tocqueville's prediction for American democracy: 'Thus not only does democracy make every man forget his ancestors, but it hides his descendants and separates his contemporaries from him; it throws him back forever upon himself alone and threatens in the end to confine him entirely within the solitude of his own heart.' [2]

De Tocqueville, as a European, distrusted radical solitude. The American mythology, conversely, habitually portrayed it as the means to grace, locating the origin of sound decisions in the isolated heart. *Taxi Driver* represents a rare deviation from this position, treating it with considerable suspicion. The narrative rigorously structures a path to violence that is separate from any rational comprehension or need, separate from community. It is attached to the explosion of an individual attempting to escape from a self-made prison, an individual who – in his insanity – attempts to act the role of a movie hero. His fear is that no matter what efforts are made, an unknowable presence – governmental, corporate or a union of the two – will have its way and exert its ineluctable power. He diverts his feeling of impotence by permitting the fantasy of personal power. Bickle says, 'I just wanna go out and really . . . really *do* something.' We see him stepping out of a cab. The camera moves up until it shows Bickle's head, shaved in a Mohawk haircut. The shock is considerable. The character with whom the audience has been encouraged to identify is now revealed as recognizably insane. The 'reward' Bickle receives, the recognition he gains for gunning down the mafioso and freeing a young runaway from a brothel, is surely ironic, the result of other people's distorted perceptions, and in no way changes him or his stark inability to understand himself. [3]

Taxi Driver's vigilante image had a powerful (and largely unintentional) effect on its audience. Indeed, the most unexpected consequence of the movie was its profound impact on a young American who allegedly watched it fifteen times one summer: John Hinckley moved to New York in search of the movie's female star, Jodie Foster, and started buying an arsenal – just like Travis Bickle.

He toasted the first minute of 1981 with a glass of peach brandy (Bickle's drink) and then prepared to win Foster's attention. On 30 March 1981 he shot and wounded President Ronald Reagan ('Go ahead, make my day'). In the movie Bickle shot the other man and became a hero; Hinckley expected something similar to happen to him. He described his psychotic act as 'the greatest love offering in the history of the world', one that linked him for ever with Foster in the peculiar intimacy of shared celebrity: 'I may be in prison and she may be making a movie in Paris or Hollywood, but Jodie and I will always be together, in life and in death.'[4]

As the 1980s went on further vigilante figures emerged, such as Bernie Goetz and his single-handed attempt at countering the violent element on the New York subways, and (most disturbing of all) Oliver North and his decision to 'go it alone' in his role in the Irangate affair. The differences between the conscientious rebel and the egomaniacal flouter of the law were still there to be noted, but some people had apparently lost sight of the intellectual method for identifying them. 'We're just as bad as the other side,' says one of Eastwood's characters, but he continues with his work. It is all, he suggests, a matter of perspective; it all amounts to the same thing. 'On every street in every city,' proclaimed an advertisement for *Taxi Driver*, 'there's a nobody who dreams of being a somebody' (he could have been a contender).

Coppola's *The Outsiders* (1983) continued the darker themes, yet it was one of the most mannered attempts at the 'juvenile delinquent' or 'teenage problem' picture. It was particularly significant for drawing together so many of the Hollywood 'Brat Pack' – the new generation of 'difficult' young male stars, including Matt Dillon, Patrick Swayze, Rob Lowe, Emilio Estevez, Tom Cruise and C. Thomas Howell. The story concerns a group of troubled teenagers, Dean dreamers, growing up in 1960s Oklahoma, as seen through the impressionable eyes of a boy who has, among other things, an interest in poetry and a fascination with *Gone with the Wind*. Conflict comes in the form of rivalry between two teenage gangs, the 'Greasers' and the 'Socs'. There are no adults to speak of, and little evidence that their absence is regretted. The movie is full of scenes and gestures reminiscent of such 1950s 'classics' as *Rebel Without a Cause* and *The Wild One*. Indeed, it even includes that self-conscious variation on Brando's 'Whaddya got?', a phrase which combines impudent provocation with callow indifference. When Matt Dillon's character declares he wants to do 'Nothin' legal, man', he draws attention to his continual allegiance to a tradition of cultural rebellion. Coppola recognized the association, calling Dillon 'one of the best young actors to emerge since the Brando–Dean era'.[5] The new young rebels drew on Dean without adding anything new or subversive to his style. Typically, they worked in groups, with the comfort of numbers to cushion the impact of adult hostility and resentment. Their rebellion was more obviously bourgeois than that of their famous predecessors. They looked more bored than confused, too comfortable to be angry, often drugged or drunk and too ambivalent to be anxious.

Of those actors recently associated with 'rebel male' roles, three in particular stand out as examples of the enduring influence of Clift, Brando and Dean: Al Pacino, Robert De Niro and Mickey Rourke. All three were inspired by the rebel images of the 1950s; all three began their acting careers at the Actors' Studio in New York. Ambiguous sexuality and the possibility of cruelty and self-destructiveness hover over these actors. They are often violent, yet they are sometimes seen to be vulnerable; they are not really in control of their lives – this is one of the old 1950s themes which has become even more prominent. Pacino, De Niro and Rourke play characters struggling to come to terms with their apparent impotence in modern society. The old social and political channels of protest seem corrupt or closed-down. These rebels live under the threat of anomie, of collapse, of disappearing into the oppressively ordinary world. As a result, they try by every means they can to define and impress their subjectivity on that world, and because that subjectivity cannot be adequately defined, any kind of success they have is deeply compromised.

Al Pacino follows Montgomery Clift in his quiet, understated rebelliousness. Like Clift, he seems modern, rooted in his own era; ten years earlier, he would have been out of place. He was born in

East Harlem in 1940, of Sicilian parentage; his mother and father divorced when he was a child. Acting was an early ambition. Pacino studied with Lee Strasberg at the Actors' Studio, and was one of his most loyal students. His first two movies were not particularly successful and he learned his craft in relative obscurity. He became a star after he appeared with Marlon Brando in *The Godfather* as Don Corleone's son Michael (a role originally offered to Warren Beatty). Michael represents the one, fragile, chance for the Corleone name to acquire genuine respectability in American society. He is the Godfather's youngest son and has achieved considerable success in the armed forces. Ironically, he seems the outsider in a family of outsiders, caught between his old European family and the post-war American Dream. Don Vito had wanted him to escape from the family 'business', but, when the other men are injured or killed, Michael is obliged to take over. The family's oppressively masculine approach to life is a tradition which is highlighted during the Sicilian sequences. Apollonia, Michael's young bride, is cherished by everyone as a delicate, otherworldly icon, and not as a human being who might have a will and desires of her own. Michael still tries to hold on to aspects of the old code – he believes in machismo and the sacredness of the family – but they exist for him primarily as abstract and formal ideals, and he is never able to convey the love for his children which Don Vito basked in. By the end of *The Godfather*, Michael has destroyed or lost almost everything he has cared for, and he can be seen sitting in tragic isolation, with only unreliable sycophants to call on, his face like a death mask.

Pacino's performance in *The Godfather* is again in some ways reminiscent of Montgomery Clift; the acting is centred in the eyes. In successive close-ups, we watch the changes in Pacino's eyes as his character gradually evolves (or deteriorates) from a pleasant and loving young man, aloof from his father's crime syndicate, to a ruthless middle-aged Mafia boss. The nervous, sidelong glances of the anxious young Michael and the steely gaze of the adult leader tell us all we need to know about the character. He seems trapped. He looks tortured. Michael radiates twistedness. The final sequence, in which Michael professes his Catholic faith at a baptism, is intercut with shots of the murder of his rivals, a process he has himself ordered. Michael and the movie are numbed by the contrast. Unlike Terry Malloy, there is no reprieve, no salvation; unlike George Eastman, there is no tragic release through death. Michael is imprisoned in a stronger system now, and the problem grows more complex.

The outlaw figures, such as Michael Corleone, are balanced by Pacino's maverick law enforcers, such as those in *Serpico* (1973) and *Sea of Love* (1990). Pacino manages to highlight the similarities between both types of rebels, drawing on their profound sense of spiritual rootlessness and alienation. For the detective, the connection of moral courage and lonely individualism is very tight. Smart, sceptical and strong, he is none the less unappreciated; yet this marginality is also a source of power. He pursues justice even when it threatens to unravel the fabric of society itself. Sometimes, as in *Chinatown* (1974), the corruption is so powerful, so complete, that the detective (played by Jack Nicholson, a fascinating actor himself but one who owes more to Bogart than to Brando or Clift) no longer has a place to stand and the message is one of unrelieved cynicism. Pacino never goes quite that far, but his characters often seem to be on the brink of despair. In *Serpico*, for example, he plays a character who rebels against his corrupt colleagues in the police department. Serpico relies more on intelligence than pure physical strength to combat crime (an unusual strategy in 1970s movies). He is a non-conformist – a solitary critic and a potential victim (he has enemies either side of the law). The most honest moment in the movie occurs when he is shown in his hospital bed, having been betrayed by fellow policemen and shot through the face, and he suddenly bursts into tears, overwhelmed by the sense of his complete isolation. In *Dog Day Afternoon* (1975) Pacino makes the ambiguities in his image even more evident with his portrayal of bank robber Sonny, a bisexual outlaw. His attempt at a small-time robbery eventually snowballs into a city-wide incident, attracting huge crowds and media attention. Sonny is an unusually positive gay character for a Hollywood movie; virile and strong, he has simply chosen to embrace his homosexuality. He robs a bank in order to finance a sex-change operation for his male 'wife', Leon. Pacino's Sonny is a relatively self-assured masculine figure, more at ease with his body than many more stereotypical male rebels. 'I'm me and I'm different,' Sonny remarks.

The Godfather, Part II (1974) is arguably Pacino's finest movie performance. The earlier appearance as Michael did not ask much of him, but in this sequel he takes control of the character. Michael is now the head of his family. He struggles to make the family 'legitimate', but the goal is hopeless. The circumstances of the family's rise to power in organized crime, the half-century of supremacy and tradition that have put them where they are, make any 'legitimation' quite out of the question. By the end of the movie, Michael is again all alone, betrayed by his brother and abandoned by his wife. His earlier renunciation of religion and the Family, the two bastions of Sicilian life, had symbolized his Luciferian fall. Now he is one of the most powerful men in America, and one of the loneliest. In the final shot we see a withdrawn, utterly isolated cast to that stony expression – the look of one frozen by ultimate power. It is an image that recurs in Pacino's performances. Unlike the previous generation of rebels, Pacino's character is not so sure of what it actually is that he has witnessed, and this makes him a very contemporary figure. He seems to be slightly pitched forward, and there is a certain mental heaviness that appears to press on his eyelids. He has even lost the ability to weep, and he knows it. He is a man who has achieved a measure of control, yet is unsure of the worth of it. Some of Pacino's other movies (*Cruising*, 1980; *Scarface*, 1983; and *Revolution*, 1985) have been deeply disappointing and, arguably, distasteful in their treatment of sensitive issues. None the less, his work in the *Godfather* saga is exceptional; perhaps even he is intimidated by his success as Michael Corleone.

If Pacino conveys the sensitivity of Clift, Robert De Niro captures the more obviously aggressive and physical qualities associated with Marlon Brando. Indeed, in 1977 *Newsweek* declared: 'De Niro is the heir apparent to the post of American Cultural Symbol once occupied by Marlon Brando and the late James Dean. As Brando and Dean did . . . De Niro seems to embody the conflicting, questing energies of his generation, the generation coming to young maturity in the fragmented 70s.' De Niro's screen personae resemble Brando's rebels of the 1950s (and, of course, he played the younger version of Brando's Vito Corleone in *The Godfather, Part II*). However, De Niro's rebel male is often wiser to his discontent, or at least more accepting of it (and De Niro the actor accepted the highly paid cameo roles much earlier in his career). Brando's acting haunts De Niro's work and is a burden as well as a source of inspiration.

De Niro was born in New York City in 1943. Like Pacino, he was very young when his parents divorced. Both his mother and father were artists in their own right, and he benefited from their support for his early interest in acting. He studied with Brando's old acting teacher, Stella Adler, and distinguished himself with some fine stage work. After a number of appearances in low-budget movies, he started to attract attention with his portrayal of a dying baseball player in *Bang the Drum Slowly* (1973) and his incisive performance as a simple-minded, small-time hoodlum (who eventually goes mad on a rooftop, with explosives and a gun) in Scorsese's *Mean Streets* (1973). The following year he won an Academy Award for his portrait of Vito Corleone in *The Godfather, Part II* (a movie saturated with familiar Method references – including a cameo role for Lee Strasberg). It was a remarkably audacious performance, shaping the young Vito's rise through the ranks of crime in his community as he protects his people and rears his family. He radiates an irresistible charm and nobility, with the watchful grace of the closet assassin. De Niro's acting reveals a scrupulous attention to detail, incorporating the mannerisms and inflections used by Brando in the previous movie. 'I didn't want to do an imitation,' said De Niro, 'but I wanted to make it believable that I could be him as a young man.'[6] In *Taxi Driver* De Niro plays Travis Bickle as a man on the edge of insanity, a cocked gun. He is, as many critics were quick to appreciate, another rebel without a cause, except *this* rebel is not so easily tamed (the family has gone). He does not need to find a cause; he found one, and found it was not worth having.

Bertolucci's *1900* (*Novecento*, 1976) placed De Niro outside his usual New York urban setting and, in doing so, highlighted the distinctiveness of his image. The story is of two men born on the same day on the same Italian country estate at the turn of the century. De Niro plays Alfredo, the son and heir of the landowner. Olmo (Gérard Depardieu) is the son of peasants who work the land. As the two boys grow up together, their uneasy friendship reflects the changing climate of Italy's social structure: the gradual fall of feudalism, the country's endurance through fascist occupation, and its eventual socialist rule by the end of the Second World War. Bertolucci exploits the dialectic between American actors and Italian peasants, and between 'Hollywood and the red flag'. Alfredo is a rather passive character: indecisive, weak and sexually unaware. It was the kind of role Brando sought out after his initial success.

The darker and more morally ambivalent the character, the more De Niro seems alive. In *The Deer Hunter* (1978) Michael (De Niro) is a working-class aristocrat, a man who stands somewhat outside society and struggles with nature to define his manhood. Michael is pictured as a silent man, stoical and sexually chaste, a daredevil leader and a strong-willed fighter. In *The Untouchables* (1987) his Al Capone is an extraordinary figure, suddenly exploding into violent action after a period of icy self-control. In *Raging Bull* (1980) Jake La Motta (De Niro) is a man fuelled by guilt, jealousy, gluttony and pride. Like Brando's Kowalski, De Niro's La Motta is often forced to focus on the smallest details of domestic life in order to reassure himself of his power, for outside in society he is frequently reminded of the shallowness of his idea of success. For example, sitting in his home waiting impatiently for his wife to finish cooking his steak, he shouts: 'Don't overcook it! You overcook it, it's no good – defeats its own purpose!' He finds his means of impressing himself on the world in the boxing-ring, the only legal outlet for his aggressiveness. La Motta is a function of his vocation, his physical size and his monolithic jealousy. *Raging Bull* is a kind of tribute to *On the Waterfront* and the work of Brando. In the movie's opening and closing shots, La Motta sits in a dressing-room, staring at himself in the mirror, and utters the famous 'I coulda been a contender' speech. The audience feels as though they are eavesdropping on a private moment, and this improvised intimacy is the keynote to De Niro's idea of realism.

Like Brando, De Niro approached the role with a tremendous attention to detail, putting on fifty pounds in weight for his scenes as the older La Motta. His stomach hangs out, his face is grotesquely bloated and his eyes look bloody and glazed. The performance is in that tradition of proletarian realism that can be traced through many post-war actors, from Garfield and Brando to De Niro himself. They are finely tuned American anti-heroes, drifting rebel males, inevitably flawed human beings. Their plight is both personal and social, private and public, and thus the ultimate responsibility for their situation is hard to locate. The producer Sam Spiegel said of De Niro: 'I think it's Bobby's uncertainty about himself that people relate to. He has a quality of searching for his own identity. Marlon had that in his early thirties, when we made *On the Waterfront*.'[7] Whereas Brando's rebel rarely lost faith in the plasticity of the political order (it might require radical and sometimes painful reorganization, but it was worth reorganizing all the same), De Niro's rebel often doubts it is worth persevering with that order at all. The heirs to Brando have gone beyond mistrust of the word to a mistrust of the knowable. De Niro's Jake La Motta (like Pacino's Tony Montana) remains a mystery. In any humanist sense, there is no one there. De Niro's rebels see no point of entry into society. One either remains outside or one has to proceed through breaking and entering; there is no mediating link, no civilizing process.

Mickey Rourke has self-consciously revived the image and example of James Dean. Unlike De Niro or Pacino, Rourke has blurred the distinction between his screen roles and his off-screen self. Like Dean, he lives his work. He has born in Schenectady in upstate New York in 1954. His parents divorced when he was seven years old and for most of his childhood he stayed with his mother in Miami. After a brief spell as a boxer, Rourke went to New York and studied at the Actors' Studio under the tuition of Sandra Seacat. Rourke was, from the beginning, a non-conformist. He walked out of the Actors' Studio after Lee Strasberg had criticized his work and drifted through a number of stage and television productions. Comparisons with 1950s rebels, such as James Dean, were welcomed by Rourke: 'I had trouble with the sixties and seventies. I'm fifties- and eighties-oriented. Those are times I can get into . . . The fifties and the eighties are cool.'[8] When he had achieved star status, Rourke opened a bar (described as a 'newsstand-cum-soda fountain') in Beverly Hills called 'Mickey and Joey's'. It was a kind of shrine for 1950s culture and characters, with a jukebox and a video of Brando in *The Wild One* playing round the clock, photographs of motorbikes and a picture of Steve McQueen (every day a fresh flower was placed under the portrait).[9]

Rourke cultivated the full 'Deanager' image, with his love of fast motorbikes and loud rock music, and his reputation for on-set tantrums and off-set shyness. He throws himself into each role with a childlike enthusiasm, and then responds to the finished product with the cynicism of an old man ('They ruined it'). He first caught people's attention with a brief but memorable appearance in *Body Heat* (1981), playing a professional arsonist. With the 'rebel' costume of T-shirt and jeans and one pearl earring, he was very reminiscent of Dean's hunched-over and soft-spoken outlaw. In *Diner* (1982) Rourke is placed in a 1950s setting as Boogie, a hairdresser by day, by night a student (reading, rather unsurprisingly, law). In the group of young male friends, Boogie seems an outsider. He is a gambler, a gadfly, an outrageous flirt (on a date at the movies he hides his penis in the popcorn box on his lap). There is evident in Rourke's performance that same sly, knowing quality that made James Dean's acting so intriguingly effective. As Pauline Kael observed, 'He seems to be acting to you, and to no one else.'[10] Small-mouthed and tight-lipped, he emits a high-pitched murmur that sounds simultaneously detached and passionate. He seems too odd to overlook.

Coppola's *Rumble Fish* (1983) features one of Rourke's most significant performances. He stars as 'the Motorcycle Boy' (loosely based, according to Coppola, on Albert Camus) — the leather-clad biker with the enigmatic grin and the sharp eyes. The other teenagers say of him, 'He's a *prince*, you know? He's like royalty in exile.' His father (played by Dean's old friend Dennis Hopper) says his son's flaw is 'having the ability to do anything he wants to do and finding there's nothing he wants to do'. He looks weary, as though he has seen too much of the world, or seen a little of the world too quickly: 'He looks so *old* sometimes,' says one of the young gang. 'I forget he's twenty-one. He looks really old, like twenty-five.' Another character remarks of him: 'He was born in the wrong era ...' He is shot dead by the policeman who has been pursuing him all along, leaving the teenage gang members to make something of his memory. *The Pope of Greenwich Village* (1984) features Charlie Moran (Rourke) and his friend Paulie (Eric Roberts) drifting in and out of the New York Italian underworld. The two outlaws would rather be with each other than with a woman; together they are relaxed and in control, whereas with women they are weak-willed and insecure. Director Stuart Rosenberg remarked that Rourke possessed 'an ingenuous quality I haven't seen since John Garfield stopped making movies. And as an actor, he plays it completely off the cuff – changes his lines from take to take, uses whatever's going on.'[11] Rourke's appearances in $9\frac{1}{2}$ *Weeks* (1985) and *Wild Orchid* (1990) brought him his greatest notoriety, despite the fact that neither movie transcended the cynical titillation of an expensive television commercial. His director described him as 'the most intense movie character to come along since Brando in *Last Tango in Paris*'.[12] It was an unfortunate comparison, for it merely underlined the tameness of Rourke's parodic efforts.

Rourke conceived the original story for *Homeboy* (1989), which features a tired, second-rate fighter called Johnny Walker (Rourke). Walker is a variation on many of the other characters Rourke has portrayed: the self-destructive writer in *Barfly* (1987), the reluctant IRA hit man in *A Prayer for the Dying* (1987) and the disfigured criminal in *Johnny Handsome* (1990) – individuals on the outside of society who rediscover their courage and, to an extent, their integrity in the gutter. This is Rourke's most insistent message: down-and-outs are the only real men around. *Homeboy* is another in a long line of movies inspired by *On the Waterfront*. Rourke's shambling, mumbling, oddly moving misfit is clearly influenced by

Brando's portrayal of Terry Malloy. As a fighter he seems increasingly vulnerable, yet his spirit grows stronger; the soul is imprisoned in its mortal frame, until its final release. The movie spends most of its time on Johnny's increasingly gruelling fights, and the insistent close-ups of bleeding bodies are given an extra, illicit excitement by the fact that the boxer's years in the ring have taken such an obvious toll. A doctor discovers that a single punch could kill him and the inevitable happens when he gets his best bout ever with a top middle-weight. We have to watch him die, slowly, in the ring. At the moment of death, and only then, the movie hails him as a 'real hero, a real man'.

The masochistic element has always figured in this tradition: one recalls Brando's 'ritualistic' beatings in his movies. Boxing movies, for example, tend to celebrate male masochism and subscribe to the myth that manhood has to be proven, again and again, through pain and extreme physical punishment. Indeed, Sylvester Stallone built his career from a reaction against the new cliché of the anti-hero. The atavistic *Rocky* (1976) and its sequels revived the image of the mumbling, physical commoner of the 1950s, but took its ideological inspiration from the older examples of Broncho Billy and William S. Hart – men whose brawn was not a hindrance to inner peace or an obstacle to social achievement, men whose lives were always better at the end than at the beginning. *Rocky* not only revived the Horatio Alger myth; it also created a character who existed as some pre-psychoanalytic being. Rocky was 'the great white hope', making the white working class fashionable again in Hollywood movies (*Saturday Night Fever*, 1977; *F.I.S.T.*, 1978; *Norma Rae*, 1979). Stallone also appeared in what became another movie series, *Rambo* (1985), featuring a Vietnam veteran who returns to rescue POWs from the evil North Vietnamese. Rambo is no more than an impassioned mercenary, roaming the world in search of fresh battles (Afghanistan, Cambodia, the American Northwest). Fighting is his fix, his fortune; it is the sole release for his fury. He starts by destroying a small town because the local sheriff dislikes him. To be tough, *Rambo* suggests, not only must we believe that it is unmasculine to display emotion but also we must rely on violence in order to solve any of our conflicts. The notion of regeneration through violence is an especially enduring myth in American culture.[13] When the country's international supremacy started to unravel in the 1960s, this myth resurfaced in the movies.

In a way, movies like *Taxi Driver* can be seen as allegories of the American experience in Vietnam: detached isolationism followed by violent intervention. Far more than the movies on Vietnam itself (such as *Coming Home*, 1978, or *Apocalypse Now*, which were invariably didactic and self-conscious, the claustrophobic urban movies of the 1970s captured the anxieties of the modern rebel males. Pacino, De Niro and Rourke are among the most memorable of these figures. They share a passionate desire for a freedom their society denies them. They have an animal verve and an immigrant chagrin, wearing their sweat stains like heraldic crests. If there is a common thread, it is that anguished American male soul, and if there is a common manner, it is the domination of whatever grand or squalid space they manage to carve out around them. At their most accomplished, these actors have an honest rage that is striking because it is so rare. At other times, however (and that is most of the time), they seem overwhelmed by the memory of their predecessors. Al Pacino, preparing to play a scene with Brando in *The Godfather*, was pale and shaking. When asked what the problem was, he is reported to have said, 'You don't understand. I'm acting with *God*.' The younger rebels are more susceptible to the power of past images, and less able at avoiding imitation. In *Midnight Cowboy* there are numerous implicit, perhaps unconscious, echoes of the 1950s rebels, and for those with even shorter memories, Joe Buck has his *Hud* poster on display. These characters cannot resist catching sight of themselves; Cool Hand Luke, Butch and Sundance, Bonnie and Clyde – they all obsessively photograph themselves. The danger has grown dimmer, the fire has faded. The younger rebels never entirely resolve their problem. True, they still have a veneer of passion about them, but, when passion is what is needed, a veneer just will not do.

The legacy of Clift, Brando and Dean is double-edged, part

inspiration, part intimidation. Young people continue to be drawn to these actors; their performances remain among the most powerful examples of screen acting in American cinema. They encouraged men in the 1950s to be more sensitive and thoughtful. They showed what was lacking in the increasingly sybaritic culture of their fathers, and insisted on finding their own way, in their own time. Their sexuality was exquisitely ambiguous. Kenneth Anger's *Scorpio Rising* (1964) exploited this fact by featuring a gay hero who models himself after Brando and Dean; a clip from Brando's *The Wild One* appears on a television set and the camera takes in those heavy-lidded eyes and the sensual lips that suddenly curl into a strange kind of smile. Robert Altman's *Come Back to the 5 and Dime, Jimmy Dean, Jimmy Dean* (1982) makes a similar point when the young boy who resembles Dean reappears, after a sex-change operation, as a woman. However, the finest work of these rebel males may be allowed to inhibit the development of new styles of rebellion, new expressive techniques. The notorious 'Brat Pack' is an example of the extent to which the 1950s legacy has been fetishized and reheated (once as tragedy, twice as farce). If parody at this level is sometimes the highest form of flattery and sometimes one of the higher forms of criticism, it is also a signal of ambition repressed. Who will rebel against the old rebels? In a consumer society, they have become a standard brand. Young performers still delight in citing their names and emulating their style. The Clash song 'The Right Profile' introduced Clift to the punk generation:

> Everybody say, 'What's he like?'
> Everybody say, 'Is he all right?'
> Everybody say, 'He sure look funny'
> That's . . . Montgomery Clift, honey![14]

Morrissey filmed a pop video by James Dean's grave. The once-unique images of Clift, Brando and Dean now adorn mass-produced T-shirts, offering teenagers a convenient rebellion, a clean and easy protest. The face of Dean has even been used to advertise bank loans for students; the old sullen expression in the portrait seems increasingly ironic, sadly oblivious to the joke being told at its expense. Clift and Dean have long been dead, and Brando now seems a profoundly melancholy figure. 'I am deeply lonely, alone,' he said. 'I enjoy life, up to a point, but I no longer have dreams.'[15] Part of his sadness, perhaps, is in the recognition that the old dreams meant more to him than he once appreciated.

Clift, Brando and Dean represent the rebel male at his most passionate and principled. While post-modernists revel in the apparent fluidity of the self and what Emerson called the 'most slippery sliding surfaces' of experience, these rebel males display an Emersonian distrust of such fluidity, feeling it to be a betrayal of the fundamental responsibilities and continuities of our emotional and imaginative involvements. These men, with their intuitive panic and alertness, are keen to understand their own minds, their own bodies, their own identities. They are self-questioning beings, questioning not in order to escape or evade, but rather to establish and explain their own individuality.[16] In an age of growing anonymity, these figures were remorselessly rebellious, not out of contempt for society, but rather for a concern for the kind of society they felt was being repressed. ('We are all involved!') The individual is what Henry James called a 'value intrinsic': tone, expression, passion and personality cannot be eliminated. In these movies the actors are not ventriloquized out of their distinctive presence, but, on the contrary, brought into the fullest possible particularity. The energy, intensity and vividness of these performances is an expression of faith in the power and endurance of the individual figure (however flawed and fallible), a vote of confidence in the actor's undeconstructable presence. 'In many people,' a critic observed, 'it is already an impertinence to say "I".'[17] These actors recognized the element of truth in that statement and worked hard to contradict it. As the century draws to a close, such faith is surely refreshing, and while to the cynic it may appear unduly idealistic, it none the less offers a source of hope for people living in an increasingly uncertain culture.

Clift, Brando and Dean have helped to change audience expectations of screen heroes, drawing attention to individuals at odds with society, who through their behaviour have often highlighted what is wrong with society itself. They do not possess a full-blown political theory, but in their own actions and ideals they are thoroughly political animals. All three, in their own respective ways, have encouraged a more responsive and realistic approach to movie acting.

Clift's influence has probably been the most subtle of the three. Marcello Mastroianni has argued: 'The true originator of the rebellious twentieth-century anti-hero was Montgomery Clift ... not Marlon Brando or James Dean ... The restrained performer with the inner tension and those ancient, melancholy eyes ... his presence so unobtrusively strong that it lingered even when he was off-camera.'[18]

Brando's early work is still an obvious influence on young American actors, and many struggle to escape being labelled 'the new Brando'. John Malkovich is typical in his eagerness to extricate himself (unconvincingly and rather ungenerously) from this comparison:

[Brando] had presence, he was ballet-like ... and people wanted to fuck him, which in movies is a thing of paramount importance. I'm just a trained stage actor, and he never was. But I do have more discipline. He would be in desperate trouble if he ever had to play a character without charisma. But that's the element that makes one person a legend, and another merely an actor.[19]

James Dean has had an extraordinary impact on movie actors, but more so in terms of their attitude to their stardom and to their life styles. 'When I was a young actor in New York,' said Martin Sheen, 'there was a saying that if Marlon Brando changed the way actors acted, James Dean changed the way people lived. I believe that.'[20] Dennis Quaid commented: 'Dean is still alive. All young actors tend to think of Dean as something they've just discovered. He's always been around. He always will − and he'll always be young. That's the reason we all relate to him.'[21]

The 1950s rebel males demonstrated that the qualities thought attractive to women and imitable by men were no longer merely a matter of wardrobe, inflection, colouring and physique. These actors produced portrayals which, more closely than before in movies, resembled everyday experience and a concern for recent history and pressing moral issues. Unlike the old heroes, the Waynes and the Gables and the Coopers, these men make mistakes, and get hurt, and harm the people they love as well as the people they dislike. They are sometimes hard to admire, and often hard to understand, but they usually seem unnervingly realistic. No matter how extreme or psychically bruised their characters are, they never remove themselves from them by technique, investing them instead with a rich, empathetic dignity which forces one, on some level, to identify with their plight.

'All my life needed was a sense of somewhere to go.' As Terry Malloy said, when recalling his past in a children's home: 'Some home . . .' The spiritual outlaws remain. 'We all carry within us our places of exile, our crimes, and our ravages,' wrote Camus. 'But our task is not to unleash them on the world; it is to fight them in ourselves and in others.'[22] There is no real need for yet another reprise or revision of Terry Malloy's 'I coulda been a contender' speech, or Jim Stark's attack on his parents, or Private Prewitt's rejection of demotic conformity. We now need something else, something more, something wild. Not all the answers can be found. Other hearts will no doubt be broken, and other dreams are bound to run dry, but the passionate questions will continue to be asked. Questions about identity, responsibility and respect. Questions about how one lives one's life, and what one lives it for. The rebel asks such questions. The legacy of Clift, Brando and Dean reminds us how rare these rebels can be. It now prompts another question, so far unanswered – the question asked by Emerson: 'Where are the old idealists? . . . Did the high idea die out of them?'[23]

Notes

1 Rebel Males

1 J. Dewey, 'Individualism, Old and New', *New Republic*, 19 February 1930, p. 14.
2 H. Bloom, *The Anxiety of Influence* (Oxford, Oxford University Press, 1973), p. 80.
3 For an account of Garfield's career, see Larry Swindell, *Body and Soul: A Biography of John Garfield* (New York, William Morrow, 1975).
4 A. C. Kinsey *et al.*, *Sexual Behavior in the Human Male* (Philadelphia, W. B. Saunders, 1948).
5 For a discussion of this characterization, see M. Haskell, *From Reverence to Rape* (Harmondsworth, Penguin Books, 1974); and G. McCann, *Marilyn Monroe: The Body in the Library* (Cambridge, Polity Press, 1988).
6 In 1954 Hoover listed no fewer than nine major causes of juvenile delinquency, including a lack of religion and growing permissiveness. He also noted the relative ineffectiveness of the school system and the family (see 'Conditions Conducive to Youth Crime', *Congressional Digest*, 33, 1954, p. 291). The tension was widely felt. In 1949 a national sample of high-school children was asked whether they considered it 'all right for young people to pet or "neck" when they are out on dates'. Only 10 per cent of boys thought it was always wrong to do so, but 39 per cent thought their mother would think so and 26 per cent thought their father would think so; among girls, 26 per cent thought it was wrong to 'pet', but 59 per cent thought their mothers believed it wrong (see H. H. Remmers and D. H. Radler, *The American Teenager* [Indianapolis, Bobbs-Merrill, 1957], p. 106).

7 'Coke for Breakfast', *True Love*, December 1959.

8 M. Wood, *America at the Movies* (New York, Basic Books, 1975), p. 37.

9 C. Baudelaire, *The Painter of Modern Life and Other Essays* (New York, Da Capo, 1986), p. 29.

10 M. Sinclair, *Those Who Died Young* (London, Plexus, 1979), pp. 80–81.

11 E. Kazan, *An American Odyssey* (London, Bloomsbury, 1988), pp. 220–21.

12 J. A. B. d'Aurevilly, *Of Dandyism and of George Brummell* (London, Dent, 1897), p. 18.

13 Baudelaire, op. cit., pp. 27–8.

14 A. Camus, *The Rebel* (Harmondsworth, Penguin Books, 1971), p. 23.

2 Montgomery Clift

1 J. Parker, *Five for Hollywood* (London, Macmillan, 1989), p. 9.

2 P. Bosworth, *Montgomery Clift: A Biography* (New York, Harcourt Brace Jovanovich, 1978), p. 65. Bosworth's biography is the most illuminating full-length study of Clift, drawing on many interviews with his colleagues and close friends (and is thus an essential sourcebook).

3 A. Miller, *Timebends* (London, Methuen, 1987), p. 359.

4 E. Kazan, *A Life* (London, Pan Books, 1989), p. 26.

5 See *Saturday Evening Post*, 27 August 1949.

6 D. Baglivo, *Hollywood Rebels: Montgomery Clift* (Ciak Studio video, 1982).

7 Bosworth, op. cit., p. 155.

8 Ibid., pp. 202, 214, 215.

9 W. Goldman, *Adventures in the Screentrade* (London, Futura, 1985), p. 14.

10 J. Kotsilibas-Davis, *Myrna Loy: Being and Becoming* (London, Bloomsbury, 1987), p. 286.

11 J. Huston, *An Open Book* (London, Columbus Books, 1988), p. 302.

12 J. M. Kass, *The Films of Montgomery Clift* (Secaucus, NJ, Citadel Press, 1979), p. 75.

13 J. Kobal, *People Will Talk* (London, Aurum Press, 1986), p. 405.

14 J. Goode, *The Making of* The Misfits (New York, Limelight Editions, 1986), pp. 93–4.

15 R. La Guardia, *Monty* (New York, Arbor House, 1977), p. 178.

16 Bosworth, op. cit., p. 155.

17 Ibid., passim.

18 Ibid., p. 74.

19 Kotsilibas-Davis, op. cit., p. 288.

20 Kazan, op. cit., p. 641.

21 The Transcendentalists were a group of New England thinkers who flourished during the early to mid-nineteenth century. They articulated the hitherto unexpressed ambition of young American intellectuals to escape from the narrow, formal teachings of the church and the materialistic attitudes of a provincial society into the more spacious fields of speculation and idealistic action.

22 R. W. Emerson, 'The Transcendentalist', *Selected Essays* (Harmondsworth, Penguin Books, 1985), p. 249.

23 L. Grobel, *The Hustons* (New York, Charles Scribner's Sons, 1989), p. 491.

24 La Guardia, op cit., p. 150.

25 Bosworth, op. cit., p. 301.

26 Kazan, op. cit., p. 642.

27 La Guardia, op. cit., p. 163.

28 W. J. Weatherby, *Conversations with Marilyn* (London, Robson Books, 1976), p. 75.

29 Bosworth, op. cit., p. 215.

30 E. Kazan, *An American Odyssey* (London, Bloomsbury, 1988), p. 220.

31 Interview with the author, London, 6 March 1990.

32 Grobel, op. cit., p. 496.

33 Kass, op. cit., pp. 7–8.

34 Miller, op. cit., p. 350.

35 Parker, op. cit., p. 169.

36 Kotsilibas-Davis, op. cit., p. 287.

37 Goldman, op. cit., p. 14.

38 Parker, op. cit., p. 63.

39 Weatherby, op. cit., p. 42.

40 Kass, op. cit., p. 7.

3 Marlon Brando

1 C. Higham, *Brando* (London, Sidgwick & Jackson, 1987), p. 311.

2 T. Capote, 'The Duke in His Domain', *A Capote Reader* (London, Hamish Hamilton, 1987), p. 543.

3 During this period he also met the writer James Baldwin, who became a significant influence on Brando. See W. J. Weatherby, *James Baldwin: Artist on Fire* (New York, Donald I. Fine Inc., 1989).

4 D. Shipman, *Marlon Brando* (London, Sphere, 1989), p. 9.

5 B. Thomas, *Brando* (London, W. H. Allen, 1973), p. 93.

6 Ibid.

7 An anecdote recounted in S. Callow, *Being an Actor* (Harmondsworth, Penguin Books, 1985), p. 173.

8 C. Rodley, 'Marlon, Madness and Me', *20/20*, April 1989.

9 A. Walker, *It's Only a Movie, Ingrid* (London, Headline, 1988), p. 162.

10 E. Kazan, *A Life* (London, Pan Books, 1989), p. 374.

11 S. Graham, *Scratch an Actor* (London, W. H. Allen, 1969), p. 76.

12 Rodley, op. cit.

13 *Sunday Mirror*, 3 September 1989, p. 24.

14 Thomas, op. cit.

15 Rodley, op. cit.

16 Kazan, op. cit., p. 459.

17 Capote, op. cit.

18 *Guardian*, 20 August 1990, p. 32.

19 Capote, op. cit., p. 539.

20 Ibid., p. 521.

21 E. Kazan, *An American Odyssey* (London, Bloomsbury, 1988), p. 80.

22 G. Melly, *Revolt into Style* (Oxford, Oxford University Press, 1989), p. 30.

23 P. Kael, 'Marlon Brando: An American Hero', *Kiss Kiss Bang Bang* (London, Arena, 1987), p. 190.

24 P. Bosworth, *Montgomery Clift: A Biography* (New York, Harcourt Brace Jovanovich, 1978), p. 312.

25 Ibid.

26 Capote, op. cit., p. 540.

27 Kazan, *A Life*, op. cit., p. 806.

28 Interview with the author, London, 6 March 1990.

29 Kael, op. cit., p. 194.

30 *Films Illustrated*, August 1976, p. 454.

31 Interview with the author, London, 6 March 1990.

32 Kazan, *A Life*, op. cit., p. 809.

33 *Guardian*, 30 September 1989, p. 18.

34 *Sunday Times*, 21 January 1990, p. E6. (It is interesting to compare Brando's attitude to that of Woody Allen: the same critical remarks, the same contradictions.)

35 Kazan, *A Life*, op. cit., p. 213.

36 Shipman, op. cit., p. 19.

4   James Dean

1 Bob Dylan, 'With God on Our Side', 1963, published by M. Witmark & Sons.

2 M. St Michael, *James Dean in His Own Words* (London, Omnibus, 1989), p. 10.

3 D. Dalton, *James Dean: The Mutant King* (London, Plexus, 1983) pp. 7–8.

4 E. Kazan, *A Life* (London, Pan Books, 1989), p. 46.

5 *Picturegoer*, 14 December 1957.

6 D. Dalton and R. Cayen, *James Dean: American Icon* (London, Sidgwick & Jackson, 1985), p. 44.

7 F. Truffaut, '*Feu de James Dean*', *Arts*, September 1956.

8 Kazan, op. cit., p. 578.

9 J. Morella and E. Epstein, *Brando: The Unauthorised Biography* (New York, Nelson, 1973), p. 58.

10 R. Schatt, *James Dean: A Portrait* (London, Sidgwick & Jackson, 1987), p. 36.

11 Kazan, op. cit.

12 E. Morin, *The Stars* (London, John Calder, 1960), p. 124.

13 Truffaut, op. cit.

14 Dalton and Cayen, op. cit., p. 53.

15 Kazan, op. cit., pp. 577–8.

16 St Michael, op. cit., p. 47.

17 Ibid.

18 P. Bosworth, *Montgomery Clift: A Biography* (New York, Harcourt Brace Jovanovich, 1978), p. 260.

19 Dalton, op. cit., p. 248.

20 Dalton and Cayen, op. cit., p. 7.

21 BBC Radio 4, 30 September 1985.

22 Ibid.

23 R. Lindner, *Rebel Without a Cause* (New York, Grove Press Inc., 1944).

24 B. Hadleigh, *Conversations With My Elders* (London, GMP Publishers Ltd, 1989), p. 12.

25 St Michael, op. cit., p. 62.

26 D. Hanna, *James Dean* (New York, Starlog Press, 1988), p. 8.

27 W. N. Beath, *The Death of James Dean* (London, New English Library, 1988), p. 22.

28 K. Anger, *Hollywood Babylon II* (London, Arrow Books, 1986).

29 Beath, op. cit.

30 J. Hyams, *Mislaid in Hollywood* (London, W. H. Allen, 1973), p. 42.

31 J. Parker, *Five for Hollywood* (London, Macmillan, 1979), p. 78.

32 BBC Radio 4, 30 September 1985.

33 *Picturegoer*, 21 December 1957.

34 A. Camus, *The Rebel* (Harmondsworth, Penguin Books, 1971), p. 47.

35 A. de Tocqueville, *Democracy in America*, Vol. II (New York, Vintage Books, 1945), p. 145.

36 Ibid., pp. 145–6.

37 Dalton, op. cit., p. 271.

38 M. Dawber, *Wish You Were Here, Jimmy Dean* (London, Columbus, 1988), p. 113.

39 Parker, op. cit., pp. 105–6.

40 Dawber, op. cit., p. 42.

41 St Michael, op. cit., p. 75.

42 Ibid.

43 The popularity continues. In 1989 the Dean estate netted more than 1 million dollars from 250 companies that license his name and image (see 'Rebel Within a Clause', *20/20*, March 1990, pp. 33–9).

44 BBC Radio 4, 30 September 1985.

5   The Legacy

1 P. Schrader, *Film Comment*, March/April 1976.

2 A. de Tocqueville, *Democracy in America*, Vol. II (New York, Vintage Books, 1945), p. 106.

3 As compared, for example, with another Scorsese movie, *The King of Comedy* (1982).

4 J. and J. Hinckley, *Breaking Points* (New York, Chosen Books, 1985), p. 341.

5 P. Cowie, *Coppola* (London, Faber and Faber, 1990), p. 165.

6 P. McKay, *Robert De Niro* (London, New English Library, 1988), p. 40.

7 Ibid., p. 63.

8 B. Mills, *Mickey Rourke* (London, Sidgwick & Jackson, 1988), p. 9.

9 *New Musical Express*, 8 April 1989, p. 6.

10 P. Kael, *Taking It All In* (London, Arena, 1987), p. 32.

11 Mills, op. cit., p. 33.

12 *Film Monthly*, September 1990, p. 37.

13 See R. Slotkin, *Regeneration through Violence* (Middletown, Wesleyan University Press, 1973).

14 J. Strummer and M. Jones, 'The Right Profile', 1979, published by Riva Music Limited/Nineden Limited.

15 *Sunday Mirror Magazine*, 29 January 1989, p. 13.

16 It is interesting to note that, of recent actors who continue this spirit of rebellion and self-analysis, two of the most distinctive are comics: Woody Allen and Robin Williams.

17 T. W. Adorno, *Minima Moralia* (London, New Left Books, 1974), p. 50.

18 D. Shipman, *Movie Talk* (London, Bloomsbury, 1988), p. 36.

19 *Independent on Sunday*, 8 July 1990, p. 18.

20 D. Dalton and R. Cayen, *James Dean: American Icon* (London, Sidgwick & Jackson, 1988), p. 7.

21 Shipman, op. cit., pp. 53–4.

22 A. Camus, *The Rebel* (Harmondsworth, Penguin Books, 1971), p. 9.

23 R. W. Emerson, 'The Trancendentalist', *Selected Essays* (Harmondsworth, Penguin Books, 1985), p. 249.

Bibliography

Montgomery Clift

Babuscio, J., 'Screen Gays: Montgomery Clift', *Gay News*, 104, 1974.

Baker, P., 'Suddenly Last Summer', *Films and Filming*, 21 June 1958.

Bosworth, P., *Montgomery Clift: A Biography* (New York, Harcourt Brace Jovanovich, 1978).

Bradley, L., 'Censored', *Empire*, October 1989, pp. 56–61.

Brown, J., *The Fabulous Lunts* (New York, Athenaeum, 1986).

French, P., *Westerns* (London, Secker & Warburg/BFI, 1973).

Goldman, W., *Adventures in the Screentrade* (London, Futura, 1985).

Goode, J., *The Making of* The Misfits (New York, Limelight Editions, 1986).

Kass, J. M., *The Films of Montgomery Clift* (Secaucus, NJ, Citadel Press, 1979).

La Guardia, R., *Monty: The Biography of Montgomery Clift* (New York, Arbor House, 1977).

McCambridge, M., *The Quality of Mercy* (New York, Times Books, 1981).

Maxford, H., 'Montgomery Clift and Elizabeth Taylor', *Idols*, Vol. 1, No. 12, February 1989, pp. 4–6.

Miller, A., *Timebends: A Life* (London, Methuen, 1987).

Morley, S., *Elizabeth Taylor* (London, Pavilion, 1989).

Pepitone, L. and Stadiem W., *Marilyn Monroe Confidential* (New York, Simon and Schuster, 1979).

Rosten, N., *Marilyn: A Very Personal Story* (London, Millington Ltd, 1980).

Sloman, T., 'Tarnished Angel', NFT programme, May 1990, pp. 8–12.

Taylor, E., *Elizabeth Taylor by Elizabeth Taylor* (New York, Harper & Row, 1984).

Thomson, D., *America in the Dark* (London, Hutchinson, 1978).

Viertel, S., *The Kindness of Strangers* (New York, Holt, Rinehart & Winston, 1969).

Weatherby, W. J., *Conversations with Marilyn* (London, Robson Books, 1976).

West, N., *Miss Lonelyhearts* (New York, New Directions, 1960).

Williams, T., *Suddenly Last Summer* (New York, Signet, 1960).

Wright, W., *Sixguns and Society* (Berkeley, University of California Press, 1975).

Marlon Brando

Alpert, H., 'Marlon Brando and the Ghost of Stanley Kowalski', *The Dreams and the Dreamers* (New York, Macmillan, 1962).

Brando, A. K., *Brando for Breakfast* (New York, Crown, 1979).

Brian, D., *Tallulah, Darling* (New York, Pyramid Publications, 1972).

Capote, T., *A Capote Reader* (London, Hamish Hamilton, 1987).

Carey, G., *Marlon Brando: The Only Contender* (London, Robson Books, 1985).

Downing, D., *Marlon Brando* (London, W. H. Allen, 1984).

Fiore, C., *Bud, the Brando I Knew* (New York, Delacorte Press, 1974).

Gelmis, J., 'The Beast in Brando', *Weekend Guardian*, 30 September 1989, pp. 17–18.

Gilliat, P., 'A Countess from Hong Kong on Screen', *Unholy Fools* (London, Secker & Warburg, 1973).

Higham, C., *Brando: The Unauthorised Biography* (London, Sidgwick & Jackson, 1987).

Morella, J. and E. Epstein, *Brando: The Unauthorised Biography* (New York, Nelson, 1973).

Offen, R., *Brando* (Chicago, Henry Regnery Co., 1973).

Rodley, C., 'Marlon, Madness and Me', *20/20*, April 1989, pp. 38–51.

Shipman, D., *Marlon Brando* (London, Sphere, 1989).

Siclier, J., 'L'ange et le primate', *Le Monde*, 10 August 1989, p. 22.

Thomas, B., *Brando* (London, W. H. Allen, 1973).

Thomas, T., *The Films of Marlon Brando* (Secausas, NJ, Citadel Press, 1973).

Vickers, H., *Vivien Leigh* (London, Hamish Hamilton, 1988).

Walker, A., *It's Only a Movie, Ingrid* (London, Headline, 1988).

Weatherby, W. J., *James Baldwin: Artist on Fire* (New York, Donald I. Fine Inc., 1989).

Williams, T., *Memoirs* (New York, Doubleday, 1975).

Winters, S., *Shelley: Also Known as Shirley* (New York, William Morrow, 1980).

James Dean

Adams, N., 'Jimmy's Happiest Moments', *Modern Screen*, 1956.

Archer, E., 'Generation Without a Cause', *Film Culture*, Vol. 2, No. 1, 1956.

Astrachan, S., 'New Lost Generation', *New Republic*, February 1957.

Babuscio, J., 'Screen Gays: James Dean', *Gay News*, 79, 1973.

Bast, B., *James Dean: A Biography* (New York, Ballantine Books, 1956).

Beath, W. N., *The Death of James Dean* (London, New English Library, 1988).

Breen, E., 'He Wasn't Perfect', *Chronicle-Tribune Magazine* (Manon, Indiana), 28 September 1975.

Capen, J. B., 'The Strange Revival of James Dean', *Indianapolis Star Magazine*, July 1956.

Cook, J., 'Jimmy Dean Is Not Dead', *Motion Picture*, May 1956.

Dalton, D., *James Dean: The Mutant King* (London, Plexus, 1983).

Dalton, D. and R. Cayen, *James Dean: American Icon* (London, Sidgwick & Jackson, 1985).

Dawber, M., *Wish You Were Here, Jimmy Dean* (London, Columbus Books, 1988).

Dean, E. W., 'The Boy I Loved', *Photoplay*, March 1956.

Devillers, M., *James Dean on Location* (London, Sidgwick & Jackson, 1987).

Dos Passos, J., *Mid-Century* (Boston, Houghton Mifflin Co., 1960).

Dudar, H. J., 'The Legend of Jimmy Dean', *New York Post*, 19 August 1956.

Fairmount News, Special Issue, October 1955.

Fuchs, W., *James Dean: Footsteps of a Giant* (Berlin, TACO Publishers, 1986).

Goodman, E., 'Delirium Over Dead Star', *Life*, 24 September 1956.

Guinness, A., *Blessings in Disguise* (London, Hamish Hamilton, 1985).

Hanna, D., *James Dean* (New York, Starlog Press, 1988).

Harry, B., 'James Dean and the Vampire Lady', *Idols*, Vol. 1, No. 2, March 1988, pp. 28–9.

— 'James Dean and Dusty Dreams', *Idols*, Vol. 1, No. 10, November 1988, p. 48.

— 'Marlon and Jimmy', *Idols*, Vol. 2, No. 1, March 1989, pp. 8–9.

— 'Dean: Scandals', *Idols*, Vol. 2, No. 2, April 1989, pp. 27–9.

Heffernan, H., 'The Cult That Won't Quit', *Detroit Free Press*, 31 August 1956.

Herndon, V., *James Dean: A Short Life* (New York, Doubleday & Co., 1974).

Hoskyns, B., *James Dean: Shooting Star* (London, Bloomsbury, 1989).

Howlett, J., *James Dean: A Biography* (New York, Simon & Schuster, 1975).

Hyams, J., 'James Dean', *Redbook*, September 1956.

'The James Dean Story', *Picturegoer*, 7, 14 and 21 December 1957.

Kreidl, J. F., *Nicholas Ray* (Boston, Twayne, 1977).

Lalonde, G., 'Perché James Dean E'Ancora Vivo', *Cinema Nuovo*, March 1957.

Lambert, G., 'Rebels and Causes', *Twentieth Century*, March 1956.

Lindner, R. M., *Rebel Without a Cause* (New York, Grove Press Inc., 1944).

McCarthy, J., 'It's Me, Jimmy', *Modern Screen*, December 1956.

Martinetti, R., *The James Dean Story* (New York, Pinnacle Books, 1975).

Mitgang, H., 'The Strange James Dean Death Cult', *Coronet*, November 1956.

O'Shea, A., 'How a Dead Actor Was Exploited', *Detroit Free Press*, 4 November 1956.

Ray, N., 'Portrait de l'acteur en jeune homme: James Dean', *Cahiers du Cinéma*, December 1956.

St Michael, M., *James Dean in His Own Words* (London, Omnibus Press, 1989).

Scullin, G., 'James Dean: The Legend and the Facts', *Look*, October 1956.

Steinbeck, J., *East of Eden* (New York, Viking Press Inc., 1952).

'Talk of the Town', *New Yorker*, 2 August 1969.

Thomas, T., *I, James Dean* (New York, Popular Library, 1957).

Truffaut, F., '*Feu de James Dean*', *Arts*, September 1956.

Wood, N., 'You Haven't Heard the Half About Jimmy Dean', *Photoplay*, October 1955.

Wutherich, R., 'The Last Story About Jimmy', *Modern Screen* October 1955.

— 'Death Drive', *Modern Screen*, October 1957.

General

Abosh, K., 'Al Pacino', *Empire*, April 1990.

Andrew, G., 'Building Bridges', *Time Out*, 28 February–7 March 1990.

Anger, K., *Hollywood Babylone* (Paris, J. F. Pauverte, 1959).

— *Hollywood Babylon II* (London, Arrow Books, 1986).

Atkins, T. R. (ed.), *Sexuality in the Movies* (New York, Da Capo Press, 1984).

Baudelaire, C., *The Painter of Modern Life and Other Essays* (trans. J. Mayne, New York, Da Capo Press, 1986).

Bloom, H., *The Anxiety of Influence* (Oxford, Oxford University Press, 1973).

Brode, D., *The Films of the Fifties* (Secaucus, NJ, Citadel Press, 1976).

Callow, S., *Being an Actor* (Harmondsworth, Penguin Books, 1985).

Camus, A., *The Rebel* (trans. A. Bower, Harmondsworth, Penguin Books, 1971).

Caplan, P. (ed.), *The Social Construction of Sexuality* (London, Tavistock, 1987).

Cohen, E. E., 'A Teen-Age Bill of Rights', *New York Times Magazine*, 7 January 1945, p. 54.

Cowie, P., *Coppola* (London, Faber and Faber, 1990).

Czarnowski, S., *Le cuite des héroes et les conditions sociales* (Paris, Alcan, 1919).

D'Aurevilly, J. A. B., *Of Dandyism and of George Brummell* (trans. D. Ainslie, London, Dent, 1897).

D'Emilio, J., *Sexual Politics, Sexual Communities. The Making of a Homosexual Minority in the United States 1940–76* (Chicago, University of Chicago Press, 1983).

De Tocqueville, A., *Democracy in America* (2 vols., New York, Vintage Books, 1945).

Dempsey, M., 'Taxi Driver', *Film Quarterly*, 29 (Summer), 1976.

Denby, D., 'Mean Streets', *Sight and Sound*, 43 (Winter), 1973–4.

Dowdy, A., *The Films of the Fifties* (New York, William Morrow, 1973).

Dunn, J., *Interpreting Political Responsibility* (Cambridge, Polity Press, 1990).

Durgnat, R., *Sexual Alienation in the Cinema* (London, Studio Vista, 1972).

Easty, E. D., *On Method Acting* (New York, HC Publishers, 1966).

Ehrenreich, B., *The Hearts of Men* (London, Pluto, 1983).

Emerson, R. W., *Selected Essays* (Harmondsworth, Penguin Books, 1985).

Field, A., *Picture Palace: A Social History of the Cinema* (London, Gentry Books, 1974).

French, B., *On the Verge of Revolt* (New York, Frederick Ungar Publishing Co., 1978).

Garcia, J., 'Harley Heaven', *New Musical Express*, 8 April 1989.

Garfield, D., *The Actors' Studio* (New York, Macmillan, 1984).

Gilbert, J., *A Cycle of Outrage: America's Reaction to the Juvenile Delinquent in the 1950s* (New York, Oxford University Press, 1986).

Gilliatt, P., *Unholy Fools: Wits, Comics, Disturbers of the Peace* (London, Secker & Warburg, 1973).

Goldberg, H., *The Hazards of Being Male* (New York, New American Library, 1977).

Goldman, W., *Adventures in the Screentrade* (London, Futura, 1985).

Goldstein, R. M. and E. Zornow, *The Screen Image of Youth: Movies About Children and Adolescents* (Metuchen, NJ, Scarecrow Press, 1980).

Goodman, J., 'Paul Newman', *20/20*, January 1990.

Graham, S., *Scratch an Actor: Confessions of a Hollywood Columnist* (London, W. H. Allen, 1969).

Grobel, L., *The Hustons* (New York, Charles Scribner's Sons, 1989).

Heyward, J., 'The Return of Al Pacino', *Films and Filming*, February 1990.

Hinckley, J. and J., *Breaking Points* (New York, Chosen Books, 1985).

Huston, J., *An Open Book* (London, Columbus Books, 1988).

James, C. L. R., *The Struggle for Happiness* (eds. A. Grimshaw and K. Hart, Oxford, Basil Blackwell, 1991).

Johnson, S., 'Fine Young Cannibals', *Independent*, 1 February 1990.

Jones, J., *From Here to Eternity* (New York, Avon Book, 1975).

Kael, P., *I Lost It at the Movies* (Boston, Little, Brown and Co., 1965).

— *Kiss Kiss Bang Bang* (London, Arena, 1987).

— *Taking It All In* (London, Arena, 1987).

Kanin, E., 'Male Aggression in Dating – Courtship Relations', *American Journal of Sociology*, 63, 1957, pp. 197–204.

Kanin, G., *Hollywood* (London, Granada, 1975).

Kauffman, S., *A World on Film* (New York, Delta, 1966).

Kazan, E., *An American Odyssey* (ed. Michel Ciment, London, Bloomsbury, 1988).

— *A Life* (London, Pan Books, 1989).

Klapp, O. E., 'The Folk Hero', *Journal of American Folklore*, LXII, 1949, pp. 17–25.

— 'Heroes, Villians and Fools, as Agents of Social Control', *American Sociological Review*, Vol. 19, No. 1, February 1954, pp. 56–62.

Kobal, J., *People Will Talk* (London, Aurum Press, 1986).

Kolker, R. P., *A Cinema of Loneliness* (New York, Oxford University Press, 1980).

Kotsilibas-Davis, J. and M. Loy, *Myrna Loy: Being and Becoming* (London, Bloomsbury, 1987).

Kurtz, R., 'Body Image – Male and Female', *Transaction*, 6 December 1968, pp. 25–7.

Landis, Paul, *Understanding Teenagers* (New York, Appleton-Century-Crofts, 1955).

Leaming, B., *Orson Welles: A Biography* (London, Weidenfeld & Nicolson, 1985).

Lynd, H. M. and R. S., *Middletown, a Study in Contemporary American Culture* (New York, Harcourt, Brace & Co., 1930).

McCann, G., *Marilyn Monroe: The Body in the Library* (Cambridge, Polity Press, 1988).

— *Woody Allen: New Yorker* (Cambridge, Polity Press, 1990).

McKay, P., *Robert De Niro: The Hero Behind the Masks* (London, New English Library, 1988).

McVicar, J., 'Inside Eye', *Independent*, 1 February 1990.

Maccoby, E. and C. Jacklin, *The Psychology of Sex Differences* (Stanford, Stanford University Press, 1975).

Madsen, A., *The New Hollywood* (New York, Crowell, 1975).

Melly, G., *Revolt into Style* (Oxford, Oxford University Press, 1989).

Metcalf, A. and M. Humphries (eds.), *The Sexuality of Men* (London, Pluto, 1985).

Mills, B., *Mickey Rourke* (London, Sidgwick & Jackson, 1988).

Morella, J. and E. Epstein, *Rebels – The Rebel Hero in Films* (Secaucus, NJ, Citadel, 1971).

Morin, E., *The Stars* (London, John Calder, 1960).

Murphy, E., 'Kiefer Sutherland', *Film Monthly*, May 1990, pp. 34–5.

Olivier, L., *Confessions of an Actor* (London, Weidenfeld & Nicolson, 1984).

Paris, B., 'Word Perfect: Robert De Niro', *20/20*, October 1989, pp. 53–65.

Parker, J., *Five for Hollywood* (London, Macmillan, 1989).

Peachment, C., 'An American Buffalo in London', *Time Out*, 6–12 September, 1984.

Peary, D., *Close-ups* (New York, Simon & Schuster, 1988).

Pleck, J. H. and J. Sawyer, *Men and Masculinity* (Englefield, NJ, Prentice Hall Press, 1987).

Plummer, K., *Sexual Stigma: An Interactive Account* (London, Routledge & Kegan Paul, 1975).

Pye, M. and L. Myles, *The Movie Brats* (New York, Holt, Rinehart & Winston, 1979).

Riley, W., 'De Niro: Melting the Ice', *Film Monthly*, May 1990, p. 42.

Rosenbaum, J., 'Circle of Pain: The Cinema of Nicholas Ray', *Sight and Sound*, Autumn 1973, p. 221.

Roszak, B. and T. (eds.), *Masculine/Feminine: Readings in Sexual Mythology and the Liberation of Women* (New York, Harper & Row, 1969).

Russo, V., *The Celluloid Closet* (rev. edn, New York, Harper & Row, 1987).

Shipman, D., *Movie Talk* (London, Bloomsbury, 1988).

Sinclair, M., *Those Who Died Young* (London, Plexus, 1979).

Slotkin, R., *Regeneration through Violence* (Middletown, Wesleyan University Press, 1973).

Stanislavsky, K., *An Actor Prepares* (New York, Theater Arts Books, 1936).

Stauth, C., 'Sylvester Stallone', *20/20*, April 1990.

Steinem, G., 'The Myth of Masculine Mystique', *International Education*, 1, 1972, pp. 30–35.

Steiner, G., *Real Presences* (London, Faber and Faber, 1989).

Strasberg, L., *A Dream of Passion* (London, Bloomsbury, 1988).

Stuart, F., *The Effects of Television on the Motion Picture and Radio Industries* (New York, Arno Press, 1976).

Thoreau, H. D., *Walden/Civil Disobedience* (Harmondsworth, Penguin Books, 1983).

Trilling, L., *Sincerity and Authenticity* (Cambridge, Mass., Harvard University Press, 1972).

Tyler, P., *A Pictorial History of Sex in Films* (Secaucus, NJ, Citadel Press, 1974).

Tynan, K., *Profiles* (London, Nick Hern Books, 1989).

Walker, A., *Superstars* (London, Phaidon Press, 1978).

Warshow, R., *The Immediate Experience: Movies, Comics, Theater, and Other Aspects of Popular Culture* (New York, Doubleday, 1962).

Wayne, J., 'The Male Artist as a Stereotypical Female', *Art Journal*, 32, Summer 1973, pp. 414–16.

Wentworth, H. and S. Berg Flexner (eds.), *Dictionary of American Slang* (2nd edn, New York, Thomas Y. Crowell, 1975).

White, E., *States of Desire* (New York, Dutton, 1980).

Zinman, D., *Fifty Films from the Fifties* (New York, Arlington House, 1979).

Zolotow, M., *Billy Wilder in Hollywood* (London, Pavilion, 1988).

Index